# Texas

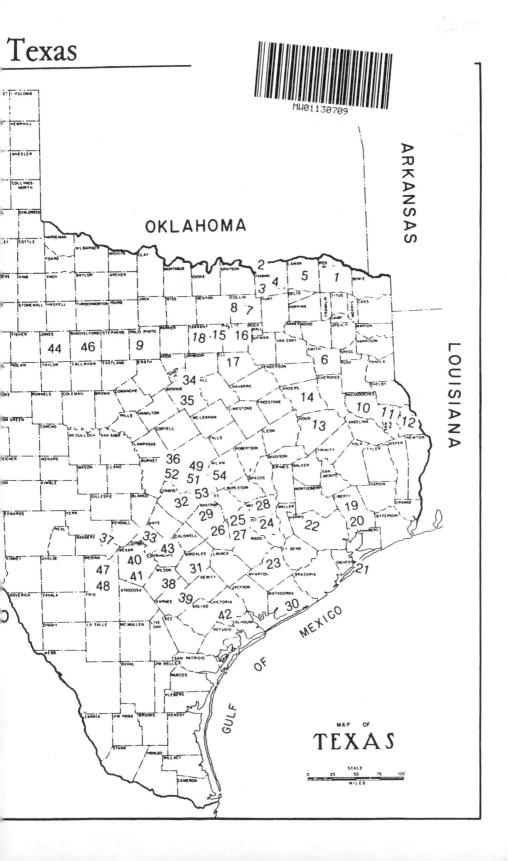

MAP OF

TEXAS

SCALE

0   25   50   75   100

MILES

# Historic Churches Of Texas

## The Land and The People

By
Frank A. Driskill   Noel Grisham

EAKIN PRESS ★ Austin, Texas

1994 REVISED EDITION



Published in the United States of America
By Eakin Press
An Imprint of Sunbelt Media, Inc.
P.O. Drawer 90159 ★ Austin, TX 78709-0159



ISBN 0-89015-267-5

*To the pioneers whose faith helped mold Texas*

# Contents

# Acknowledgments

The authors wish to extend their gratitude to the many people who have helped make this publication possible. Without their assistance the project could not have been completed.

Special credit is due historians and archivists who have given so freely of their time and knowledge. Included in this group are Ben Rogers, Baptist archivist in Fort Worth, Dr. Lawrence L. Brown, Episcopal historian in Austin, David L. Veal, Episcopal historian in San Antonio, Sister Delores Kasner, Catholic archivist in Austin, and Dr. W. Carrol Fancher, Methodist district superintendent in Nacogdoches.

Also Bill B. Hedges, Methodist historian in Galveston, Dr. Walter N. Vernon, Methodist historian in Nashville, Tennessee, Alfredo Nanez of Edinburg, and Bruno C. Schmidt, Methodist historian in Austin.

Other historians who have contributed on single churches and synagogues are Dr. William P. Boyd of Austin, T. H. Johnson of La Grange, Carvin Youngbloom of Round Rock, Mrs. Minerva M. Garza, Mrs. Perry Kallison, and Mrs. Sue Wiseman of San Antonio, Marcus Wells of Round Rock, John P. Caskey of Galveston, Mrs. Mae K. Maxwell of Crockett, Robert H. Robinson of Nacogdoches, Charles W. Fisher, Jr., of Liberty, Mrs. W. T. Baker of Dallas, William E. Leopold of Galveston, Joe Pinson of Clarksville, Monsignor Ralph J. Smith of Bandera, Monsignor Erwin A. Juraschek of Czestochowa, Father Benard Goebel of Panna

Maria, Gerald Hubertus of Castroville, Mrs. Exa Clark of San Augustine, Chester M. Patten of Seguin, Ardene A. Wuthrich of Fredericksburg, Paul W. Hartfield of Serbin, Jess Bigbee of Independence, and Mrs. Mellie Williams of Bastrop.

Arnold Peterson of Round Rock and William F. Driskill have contributed by helping with the photography. Others who helped assemble material are Mrs. Mary Farrell of Dallas, Mrs. Adelia K. Neu of Austin, Sam Malone of San Augustine, Richard L. Barton, Sr., of La Grange, Larry Jackson of Round Rock, James L. Lindsey of Cedar Park, Reuel Lemmons of Austin, Mrs. Pauline Morse of Dallas, Mrs. Joan Ellington of Houston, Mrs. Shirley Jackson of Round Rock, and Mrs. Doris M. Johnson of Austin.

# Introduction

It has frequently been said that the history of Texas is found in the history of her land. To understand this, it is necessary to know the background of the immigrants who occupied the land and to be familiar with the religious faiths and customs they brought with them.

Texas, considered one of the most cosmopolitan states in the Union, has provided a home for people from many nations. In many cases, the immigrants came directly to Texas, through Galveston. Immigrants from one nation usually brought a single religion, but this was not always true, as in the case of the Germans, who were both Catholic and Protestant.

Mixed groups, such as those with the Austin and DeWitt colonies, came with more than one religion. Significantly, however, religion was a vital element in the lives of many of those who came.

The religious picture during those early days is not always clear. One writer, J. C. Towns, is quoted as saying: "As far as the Republic of Texas is concerned, it is only by inference that we have any idea as to the prevailing religion or its influence upon the growth and the destiny of a people."

Little early recorded history deals with the part religion played in shaping the future of those who came to settle the land. However, a study of more than a hundred years shows that most immigrants were known as a dedicated people who were serious about religion. It has become evident that the family, the church, and the state were basic and viable institutions for the early settlers and furnished the foundation upon which their futures depended.

As long as Texas was a part of Mexico, the Catholic faith was the only religion the colonists could legally practice. This law was nominally observed, but there were frequent reports about circuit riders coming through and holding services in private homes. After Texas became an independent republic, other faiths began to organize churches. The development of these early houses of worship and the circumstances under which they were chartered form the basis for this publication.

Since it is not possible to cover all of the historic churches in the state, it has been necessary to select qualified examples from each religious group. Historians and archivists have been helpful in suggesting significant churches to include.

No attempt has been made to discuss religious philosophy; such is not the purpose of the book. Any effort to be "theological" would destroy the historical value of the work. It should be noted that no other publication has attempted to cover churches of all religious groups in a single volume.

Some of the selections are based not on age but on contributions they have made to the communities they serve. The listings have been placed in alphabetical order. To further simplify the presentation, the selections have been broken down into three basic categories: major historic churches, ethnic historic churches, and unusual historic churches.

The material available on churches, temples, and synagogues in Texas is scattered and difficult to find. By bringing the information together, the authors hope to provide an insight into religion, geography, and history, under one cover. Ultimately, the reader will gain a better perspective and a broader understanding of a diverse but essentially united people.

FRANK A. DRISKILL
NOEL GRISHAM

# I

## THE BAPTISTS

As far back as 1830, a few Baptist preachers had done sporadic work in Texas. Z. N. Morrell was active in making a mark on early Texas history as he assisted Mexican and Texas officials in maintaining law and order. Morrell, a Baptist minister, helped with establishing several early churches. In 1837 he organized, at Washington-on-the-Brazos, one of the first Baptist churches in Texas. One of the members of this church was Noah T. Byars, in whose blacksmith shop the Texas Declaration of Independence was adopted and signed.

The Union Baptist Association was formed in 1840 when messengers from Travis, Independence, and La-Grange met for this purpose. Many claim that this, the largest of the associations in the state, centered at Houston, is the mother of Texas Baptist work.

At the second session of the newly organized association, the messengers organized a Baptist education society. Thus was begun the primordial germ of the present Baylor University, with its separate colleges at Waco, Belton, Dallas, and Houston.

Texas Baptists have always concentrated on evangelism and missions. The early church at Washington appointed James R. Jenkins to appeal to the United States Baptist Convention for help in evangelizing Texas. Responding to this appeal, James Huckins, W. M. Tryon, and Rufus C. Burleson soon came into Texas with the thrust of a Texas tornado or West Texas dust storm. The following church histories will prove the dedication and effectiveness of these men. By 1848, largely under their leadership, fifty churches had been organized into the Baptist State Convention. Noah Hill was sent as a missionary among the slaves, and by 1945 there were 400,000 black Baptists in Texas.

Thomas J. Pilgrim organized the first Sunday school in Texas at San Felipe. Since the Mexican law forbade the establishment of any church other than Roman Catholic and since the Sunday school began taking on an appearance more of a church than a school, the Mexican authority dissuaded the continuance of the San Felipe Sunday school.

Under the Republic of Texas, which began in 1836, the Sunday schools — many of them Union Sunday schools operated for all religious groups — fared rather well. By 1945, there were 3,159 Baptist Sunday schools with an enrollment of 549,000.

Benevolent work was greatly enhanced with the establishment of Buckner Orphans' Home in Dallas. In 1942 an orphans' home for Mexican children was established in San Antonio.

Hospitals were established in Dallas and Houston in 1903 and 1907 respectively. Later, Hillcrest Memorial Sanitarium in Waco, Hendrix Memorial Hospital in Abilene, and Valley Baptist Hospital and Baptist Hospital in Beaumont were established. Baptists of all sects (there are several different Baptist groups) by 1950 numbered about one million, and since that time growth has been substantial.

The Woman's Missionary Union Auxiliary to the Texas Baptist Convention has been active and effective with both local work and foreign missions.

*The Baptist Standard,* which consolidated the several Baptist journal publications, has the largest circulation of Baptist literature in the United States.

Source: *The Handbook of Texas,* Vol. I.

# UNION BAPTIST CHURCH
## (OLD NORTH CHURCH)
### Nacogdoches — 1838

Elder Isaac Read began conducting gospel meetings under spreading oak trees four miles north of Nacogdoches about 1835–36. Soon after the Battle of San Jacinto and Texas independence from Mexico, the Liberty schoolhouse was built among the same oak trees where Elder Read preached. When the school was completed, Read moved indoors and continued his sermons.

Elder Robert G. Green met with Elder Read, and they set in motion the formal organization of the church. The church was constituted with the following members: John Eaton and wife, of Mount Moriah Church; Charles H. Whitaker, Mulberry Church; Sarah Tipps, Bethel Church, all of Lincoln County, Tennessee; Mary Crain and Emily Knight, Friendship Church, Bedford County, Tennessee; Ruth Anderson, Liberty Church, Cooper County, Missouri; and a black man and woman, the property of B. F. Whitaker.

Isaac Read became the first pastor. Other pastors to serve the Union Baptist Church (or Old North Church) include Reverends Askew, Lewis, Moses Damron, B. E. Lucas, Conner, G. W. Butler, J. M. Milstead, John Sparkman, James Power, W. Melton, Joseph Lambert, W. W. Albritton, and A. T. Garrard.

The Old North Church does not claim to be the first Baptist church organized in the state, but it does claim to be the oldest continuous Baptist church in the state in the same location.

The church was called Union Church because the house was used by both Baptists and Methodists as well as Primitive Baptists.

The Washington Baptist Church, an earlier church, was organized with eight members in 1837. Elder Z. N. Morrell was pastor and H. R. Cartmell, deacon. In the latter part of 1838, the Washington Church, the first missionary Baptist church in Texas, was dissolved as its members

*UNION BAPTIST CHURCH (Old North Church), Nacogdoches.*

*UNION BAPTIST CHURCH marker.*

*INDEPENDENCE BAPTIST CHURCH – Pump organ acquired in the 1870s and still in use.*

*INDEPENDENCE bell tower.*

5

moved elsewhere. The earlier migrant Pilgrim Baptist Church was organized near Nacogdoches in 1824.

Sources:
1. B. F. Fuller, *History of Texas Baptists*.
2. Don Norman, *The Oldest Baptist Church in Texas* (Baptist Archives, Fort Worth, Texas, Southwestern Baptist Theological Seminary).

## INDEPENDENCE BAPTIST CHURCH
### Independence – 1839

Organized in September 1839 by Elder Thomas Spraggins of Mississippi, the church was constituted with twelve members, seven of whom were from South Carolina. When Elder Spraggins returned to his home state, T. W. Cox was elected pastor. He served until 1841, when Elder William M. Tryon became joint pastor.

Deacon J. Claw administered baptism to L. P. Rucker. When the validity of the baptism came under question, a controversy developed between Tryon and Cox. A vote was taken over the matter, and Tryon and his group won by a majority of one, after T. J. Jackson and his wife united with the church. The minority were excluded. Elder Tryon became pastor and continued with Independence Church until 1845.

In 1847, Elder H. L. Graves, president of Baylor University, was chosen as pastor. Independence, the first home of Baylor University, was located in the same county with and near Washington-on-the-Brazos, where the Texas Declaration of Independence was formulated. Independence became the Texas crossroads for higher education, religion, and politics.

It was in the first church structure at Independence in 1854 that Sam Houston yielded to the preaching of Dr. Rufus C. Burleson. Later in the year, Dr. Burleson baptized Houston in Rocky Creek Pool. Houston had previously attended Concord Baptist Church with his wife, Margaret Lea, and his mother-in-law and sister-in-law.

Once Houston joined the Baptist church, he gave his

*BAPTIST CHURCH, Independence.*

7

active support to the cause as reflected by the following event. Rev. J. W. D. Creath, after having lost his horse, went to Houston's home for assistance. The former president of the Republic supplied the grounded pastor with another horse and said: "Take him; the King's business requires haste."

Among the many distinguished pastors to serve the church were Thomas Spraggins. T. W. Cox, William Tryon, H. L. Graves, George W. Barnes, Sr., S. G. O'Bryan, Rufus C. Burleson, H. C. Renfro, Michael Ross, William Carey Crane, and H. F. Buckner.

The bell which hung in the tower beside the church for 113 years fell on March 5, 1969, and is now in the Texas Baptist Historical Museum at Independence. Sam Houston's wife, Margaret Lea Houston, and her mother, Nancy Lea, and two servants lie buried in the fenced plot across the road from the bell tower. It was the desire of Mrs. Lea that she be buried within the sound of the church bell.

Sources:
1. Texas Baptist Historical Center–Museum, Independence, Texas.
2. Texas Baptist Archives, Southwestern Baptist Theological Seminary, Fort Worth, Texas.
3. Jess Bigbee, pastor and museum director at Independence.

## PLUM GROVE BAPTIST CHURCH
### La Grange – 1839

Organized on the west side of the Colorado River above La Grange, Plum Grove Church is only a few months older than the Baptist church at Independence. The Plum Grove Church was organized by R. G. Green and Eli Dancer and thirteen original members in March 1839. (The Independence Baptist Church was organized by Thomas Spraggins and Elder T. W. Cox in September 1839.) Some of the members of Providence Baptist Church near Bastrop assisted with the organization.

Although Plum Grove had three ordained ministers in

*PLUM GROVE BAPTIST CHURCH, La Grange.*

9

the church, no regular pastor was called until Z. N. Morrell was chosen in 1842.

Before the organization of the church, Morrell had held a protracted meeting in the home of Deacon William Scallorn near the place where the church was later built. At these home services, Mrs. Eli Dancer professed her faith but wanted to unite with a small Primitive Baptist Church twelve miles away. Because the pastor of the Primitive Baptist Church, Abner Smith, was then an invalid, the church requested Morrell to administer the rite of baptism. This baptism in the Colorado River, in March 1839, was Morrell's first baptism in Texas and the first west of the Trinity River, according to Baptist church historian B. F. Fuller. Other distinguished pastors to preach at Plum Grove include P. B. Chandler, William Carey Crane, Rufus C. Burleson, R. E. B. Baylor, and D. C. Routh.

A very successful revival at Plum Grove was held soon after the church's organization and attracted a large number of candidates for baptism. Word was spread about baptisms that would be administered at a given time and place in the Colorado River. The idea of baptism by immersion was so novel in the new land that people came from forty miles down the river at Columbus to witness the event.

After the baptisms, Judge Baylor presented a very fervent and inspiring sermon in the small house and brush arbor beside the Colorado. Then church members and ministers Morrell and Baylor gathered around the table in the little log cabin and partook of the Lord's Supper for the first time in Texas.

In the early part of 1840, the La Grange Baptist Church (Clear Creek Baptist Church) was organized by T. W. Cox and James Huckins, the first Baptist missionary to Texas. The Travis Church, ten or twelve miles south of Brenham, was constituted in the summer of 1839 by Thomas W. Cox and Judge Baylor. Cox became the first pastor. Thus the Independence Church, the Plum Grove Church, and the Travis Church were all organized in 1839.

T. W. Cox was considered a leader of the Baptist church, but because of some of his religious views gleaned from Alexander Campbell in Virginia, he and a number of the early Baptists in Texas were separated over doctrinal issues. The Plum Grove Church also had problems of its members dividing over the matter of missionary work and a strong Primitive Baptist element.

On August 29, 1869, members of the Plum Grove Church met with members of the Pleasant Retreat Church at the Pleasant Retreat School and voted unification and consolidation. The name of Plum Grove Baptist Church was retained. The first pastor of this, the second Plum Grove Church, was W. C. Boone; the church clerk was W. P. Karnes.

Early members of Plum Grove Baptist Church included the William F. Drisdales, the William Scallorns, the J. M. Kirks, the W. P. Darbys, the McClures, the W. L. Morgans, the McCollums, the Steelers, the Nelsons, the Wrights, the Millers, the J. L. Morgans, and the Pughs.

Sources:
1. B. F. Fuller, *History of Texas Baptists,* Travis Church, La Grange Church, Plum Grove Church (Baptist Archives, Southwestern Baptist Theological Seminary, Fort Worth, Texas).
2. Conference with T. H. "Coach" Johnson (who met and married Martha Morgan from Plum Grove while they attended school at Baylor University).
3. T. H. Johnson, *Plum Grove Baptist Church, 1839–1904.*
4. T. H. Johnson, *The La Grange Baptist Church of Christ and First Presbyterian Church, 1853–1884.*

# FIRST BAPTIST CHURCH
## Galveston – 1840

On January 30, 1840, Galveston's First Baptist Church was organized in the home of Thomas H. Borden by James Huckins, one of the first two Baptist missionaries sent by the American Baptist Home Mission Society. The charter members were George Fellows of New Hampshire, David R. Wright and Mrs. Abigail W. Bartlett of Massachusetts, and Mrs. Louisa R. Borden and Lewis Graves of New York. These charter members were joined on promise of letter

*FIRST BAPTIST CHURCH, Galveston, second sanctuary.*

from Barnabas Haskell and Mrs. Abigail Haskell of Connecticut and Mrs. Sarah A. Burnet of Louisiana. By a gift of $2,500, Elder Jesse Mercer of Georgia had assisted the Mission Board in sending the missionaries to Texas.

The niece of Elder Mercer, Penelope, and her husband, Gail Borden, Jr., were the first persons to be baptized in the Gulf of Mexico. The ordinance was administered on the south side of the island. With the background sound of the rolling billows, the service, witnessed by a crowd of spectators, began with a prayer which was followed by the song "Jesus and Shall It Ever Be, a Mortal Man Ashamed of Thee?"

Emotions were much in evidence as the baptized came out of the water to receive the praises of the small congregation which now numbered thirteen.

Gail Borden, Jr., the first to be baptized in the Gulf waters, was one of the state's most distinguished citizens. An inventor, and co-editor of one of the first three newspapers in Texas (all in San Felipe), he developed a meat biscuit which sold from Texas to New York and was the first to invent and develop the process for condensed milk.

Black members were received into the church for the first time on February 9, 1840. A Sunday school was organized in 1846, and the first house of worship was dedicated in September 1847.

During the Civil War, the church was closed for a short time because of the blockade of Galveston Harbor by the U.S. gunboat *South Carolina* on July 4, 1861. The new house of worship, which was dedicated on June 10, 1883, was destroyed by the great storm in Galveston in September of 1900.

A new house of worship was dedicated January 6, 1905, and a new Sunday school building was dedicated on May 14, 1933.

Early pastors of the church included James Huckins, John Freeman Hillyer, Robert H. Taliaferro, Jacob Beverly Stiteler, James H. Stribling, William Howard, William Overton Bailey, Albert Theodore Spalding, Abner Whatley Lamar, William Mercer Harris, Luther Little, Edward

Stubblefield, Julian Harrison Pace, Edwin Frank Adams, Thomas Harvey, and Harold Lord Fickett.

Sources:
1. *The Herald of First Baptist Church, Galveston,* January 28, 1940.
2. *Handbook of Texas,* Vol. I.

## FIRST BAPTIST CHURCH
### Houston — 1841

In 1837, after a few houses had been built and while some people were living in tents, Z. N. Morrell, a veteran Baptist missionary, preached a sermon to a small group in Houston. Later, on April 10, 1841, the First Baptist Church was organized in the home of Mrs. Piety Hadley with sixteen members, four of whom were black. The organization was perfected by James Huckins, who became the first pastor. S. P. Andrews and I. B. Bigalow were elected deacons. On the first Sunday in May, a few weeks after the church's organization, the Lord's Supper was observed. Church records, meager for the first three years, reveal that in 1844 services were held in the home of L. B. T. Haldey. At this time, William M. Tryon was invited to be resident pastor of the church. Tryon was succeeded by Dr. Rufus C. Burleson, who saw the church grow to 140 members. Dr. Burleson guided the church through struggles and difficult times until 1851, when he resigned the pastorate to become president of Baylor University.

With some financial assistance from Southern states, the first church building was erected on the site later occupied by the *Houston Chronicle*. It was dedicated on the fifth Sunday in May of 1847, with the address being given by H. L. Graves, president of Baylor University.

The church was not without problems because of a difference of opinions held by the people who had converged on the church from so many different states of the east, north, and south. Founders of the church were seriously concerned when some wanted to advocate alien immersion. Of almost equal concern were the matters of dancing, dram-drinking, theater-going, pew rentals, and the

14

*FIRST BAPTIST CHURCH, Houston.*

choir. Introduction of the organ as an aid to worship caused displeasure and discord, but this problem was solved by the mysterious disappearance of the organ, which was later found beneath the waters of Buffalo Bayou.

Prior to the Civil War, the church was served by Pastors Gilbert T. Morgan and George W. Tucker. During the war, the church was helped through difficult times by N. T. Moore, T. A. Massey, and Dr. William Carey Crane, the last of whom was induced to accept the presidency of Baylor University at Independence.

A Swedenborgian Methodist, J. E. Carnes, indicated a desire to become a Baptist and serve the church as pastor at the close of the Civil War. As supply pastor for only a short time, Carnes left the church abruptly without any known cause.

Dr. J. B. Link, editor of the *Texas Baptist Herald*, became supply pastor and F. M. Law came to the church as a self-supporting missionary. These two men helped to improve the condition of the church building and to inspire the members to greater dedication. B. A. Shepherd, a banker and non-member, helped the church financially.

Other pastors were T. B. Pitman, R. M. Humphrey, Dr. W. O. Bailey, Dr. L. D. Lampkin, Dr. B. F. Riley (who helped revive a somewhat demoralized church which was further beset by the loss of the church building during the 1900 Galveston storm), Dr. J. L. Gross (who helped organize Memorial Hospital), Dr. J. B. Tidwell, Dr. J. B. Leavell, and Dr. E. D. Head.

A later pastor was Dr. W. Douglas Hudgins, who came to the church when Dr. Head became president of Southwestern Baptist Theological Seminary in Fort Worth. After four years in Houston, Dr. Hudgins was called to the famed First Baptist Church of Jackson, Mississippi.

Dr. K. Owen White was pastor from July 1953 to June 1, 1965. Dr. White saw the church membership greatly increase, yet his work was not confined to the sixth largest city in the United States. He visited Baptists in England, Hawaii, and Japan. He had the honor of serving as president of both the Texas Baptist Convention and the Southern Baptist

16

Convention. In 1965, Dr. White became coordinator of missions for the Greater Los Angeles area.

John Bisagno (Brother John, as he prefers to be called), was pastor of this historic church as of 1980 and was the first native-born Texan (reared in San Antonio) to serve the church. He moved to Houston from First Baptist, Pine Bluff, Arkansas.

By 1980, First Baptist Church of Houston had grown to 14,000 members. With a majestic building resembling a great music hall, Gerald Ray, with a staff of six people, directed one of the most elaborate church music programs in the world. This is an interesting aspect of the church when one recalls the fate of the organ in earlier days of the church.

Much of the success and growth of Houston's First Baptist Church has occurred in recent years. One historian, observing that congregations tend to select opposites in successive pastors, made the following analysis of the pastors of Houston's historic church:*

Dr. Leavell in 1917 was a very firm, strong-minded, perhaps authoritarian minister.

Dr. Head was a kind, steady, gentlemanly Christian statesman.

Dr. Hudgins was a precise man with a flair for the unusual in his preaching.

Dr. Hunt was youthful, vigorous, steady, progressive. (He seems to receive more accolades than any other minister except perhaps for "Brother John.")

Dr. White was dedicated, older and conservative.

Dr. Smith was progressive, positive, perhaps even brash.

John Bisagno has succeeded where Dr. Smith "failed."

Sources:

1. *Centennial History*, Union Baptist Association; *125th Anniversary, First Baptist Church*, Houston, Texas.

2. Baptist Archives, Fort Worth, Texas.

3. Conference with Gerald Ray, minister of music and church historian.

*4. *An Analysis of Christian Ministry Seminar Pastoral Ministry in Historical Perspective From 1917 to 1974* (by Steve M. Lyon, led by Dr. Gerald March) Southwestern Baptist Theological Seminary, March 22, 1974.

# FIRST CONCORD BAPTIST CHURCH
## Rye – 1845

In 1979 First Concord Baptist Church celebrated its 134th birthday and claimed to be the oldest continuously existing rural church in Texas. The church numbered among its charter members the wife of Sam Houston, his mother-in-law, and his sister-in-law.

The church meets in its third building, which was erected in the late 1930s. Although the church has a long history, it has never had as many as one hundred members and has never had a full-time pastor. Sam Houston never joined this church, but he would attend with his family when at home. (He later joined the Independence Baptist Church.)

B. F. Brown founded the church with the assistance of Margaret Lea Houston, Nancy Lea, Mrs. Antoinette Bledsoe, Joseph and Benjamin Ellis, and Judge Archer B. Worsham.

In 1857 the church was reported to have "ten male members, sixteen female and five colored" for a total of thirty-one members. In Texas, prior to the Civil War, it was not unusual for blacks to have membership in predominantly white churches. Under Mexican law, before 1836 and Texas independence, it was not compatible with government statutes to have slaves, although this law was not rigidly followed.

A little discord existed in the Concord Church because of a split in the church by the presence of some missionary Baptists (MBA). The MBAs left the church, accusing the others of preaching and teaching evolution. At this time of disharmony the MBAs tore some of the pages out of the church records book and scattered them all over the community.

An interesting incident occurred while Sam Houston Cain was the pastor at Concord. Residents had built a platform in front of the church for a Fourth of July dance. When it began to rain they assumed they could move inside the church building. But Brother Cain and two other men, with

18

*FIRST CONCORD BAPTIST CHURCH, Rye.*

19

the aid of their shotguns, kept the revelry outside and "watered down."

In 1980, Royce Vaughn, in the old American tradition of schoolteacher-preacher, was serving the old church with pride and effectiveness as he held forth in the historic pulpit every Sunday morning and evening and conducted Wednesday evening prayer meetings. When he was not teaching Texas history at Tarkington Prairie Junior High School, he was at the church.

Sources:
1. *The Baptist Standard,* December 5, 1979.
2. *134th Anniversary First Concord Baptist Church,* Rye, Texas (1979).
3. Archives, Southwestern Baptist Theological Seminary, Fort Worth, Texas.
4. Ben Rogers, archivist.

## FIRST BAPTIST CHURCH
## Gonzales — 1847

The city of Gonzales was laid out by Spanish colonists. The plan featured wide streets and large plazas, but the city never developed to be the large metropolis of utmost beauty it was ambitiously hoped to become.

Z. N. Morrell preached the first Baptist sermons in Gonzales in 1840. By the close of 1841, ten members were gathered together constituting the church, adopting at that time the articles of faith held by the United Baptists of West Tennessee. Morrell assisted the little church with regular monthly meetings and weekly prayer meetings until the time of the Mexican invasion of the Republic of Texas. As Indian problems and the Mexican conflict impeded its growth, this church was dissolved.

The present Baptist church in Gonzales was organized on July 31, 1847, with four men and five women. Officers in the church were Richard B. Ellis and P. B. Chandler, with Ellis serving as pastor. T. J. Pilgrim, who had earlier founded the first Sunday school in Texas at San Felipe, was elected clerk. Other members were Benjamin Weeks, Mary

20

*FIRST BAPTIST CHURCH, Gonzales.*

Weeks, Sarah J. Pilgrim, Joseph Bennett, Mary Bennett, John L. Johnson, Sophia James, and Mary Boykin.

Early pastors serving the church following Ellis were Elder J. T. Powell, Elder J. H. Stribling, Elder J. H. Thurman, R. M. Stell, R. A. Massey, J. N. Russell, J. S. Abbott, H. M. Burroughs, J. V. E. Covey, G. W. Smith, J. L. Lloyd, and B. W. N. Simms.

In 1854 the church erected a building of which it could boast as being "among the best in the state." The church house, measuring forty by sixty feet, was a well-framed building that was plastered on the inside. The church contributed liberally to missions, both home and foreign, and also engaged in numerous benevolent enterprises.

The most distinctive feature of this church was its Sunday school, under the superintendency of Professor Pilgrim. Like the first Sunday school at San Felipe, the Sunday school was operated on the union principle. Regular school studies, together with Bible studies, were conducted for any denomination that wanted to participate.

Only after Pilgrim died did the Sunday school come entirely under the direction of the church. Under the pas-

21

torate of G. W. Smith, much interest in Bible study developed and competitive examinations were introduced.

The church claimed to have the model deacon in the dedicated and generous M. Eastland. For the assistance of state and foreign missions the church provided annually $25 from the Sunday school, $25 from the church, and $25 from Eastland.

Source:
1. Baptist Archives (Southwestern Baptist Theological Seminary, Fort Worth, Texas).


## FIRST BAPTIST CHURCH
### Bonham — 1852

In early November 1852, J. R. Briscoe, a pioneer Baptist preacher, gave leadership for organization of Bonham's First Baptist Church. Originating in the Masonic Hall, the church had six charter members: S. D. Rainey, Mrs. Mary Rainey, Mrs. Martha Gilbert, Miss Lizzie Russell, David Coward, and B. F. Fuller.

Briscoe became the church's first pastor at an annual salary of $125. The first church home after meeting in the Masonic Hall was a log cabin located in the same place where all succeeding buildings have been erected.

A wooden structure, complete with a small steeple, was erected in 1855 and served the church until 1882. That year the growing church erected a large and beautiful building, which served the congregation until 1919.

During the church's work and worship in this building, there was much growth and progress. In 1901 the pastor, Dr. D. G. Whittinghill, resigned in order to go to Rome, Italy, as a missionary. Later in the same year, Miss Mary D. Willeford, a Bonham schoolteacher, was sent by the church to China, where she labored for thirty-five years.

Capable evangelists such as George W. Truett, F. M. McConnell, M. E. Dodd, and Sid Williams presented inspiring and motivating sermons at Bonham's First Baptist Church.

22

*FIRST BAPTIST CHURCH, Bonham.*

Dr. George W. Truett gave the dedicatory address for the opening of a new church building in 1921. This facility was to serve until a modern building was erected for the 1960s and beyond.

In this modern facility one of the most historic funerals in the United States was conducted for Sam Rayburn, Bonham's favorite son who served as Speaker of the United States House of Representatives longer than any other person. Four presidents of the United States sat on the front pew at First Baptist Church in Bonham. Presidents Harry S. Truman, Dwight D. Eisenhower, John F. Kennedy, and Lyndon B. Johnson joined a host of people to listen attentively to the funeral address by Elder H. G. Ball. Ball was pastor of Sam Rayburn's home church, the Primitive Baptist Church of Tioga, a small community near Bonham.

The Primitive Baptist preacher, considered by many as being less educated, did not embarrass his city brethren, as

*THE FOUR PRESIDENTS who attended the Rayburn funeral.*

*FIRST BAPTIST CHURCH – pew where four U.S. presidents sat.*

24

some had suspected he would. The text of his address is presented in full. The reader may judge on the qualifications of the country preacher "under pressure" of a new environment and an awesome responsibility.

We are paying loving tribute of respect and honor to one who has been a friend to us all. Words are found inadequate, and yet they have a meaning. Flowing words of men and platitudes and pens have described some of the greatness of our good friend who has been drawn from the walks of this life; and yet, we feel in our hearts, as individuals, there is something we, ourselves, would like to say in the passing of God's child from the walks of this life in this world. Death inevitably brings a depth of sorrow to the hearts of loved ones and to the extent that their lives have reached out to the multitude of people, such as our good friend's life has. It makes us realize that not only are we sorrowful in our hearts, but that the world — most of it — is weeping with us. There are few people in the world whose lives have touched the lives of so many. There are few people who have been fortunate enough with health and training to give the compassionate loving kindness to those who were less fortunate than themselves. Such was the life of our good friend. Speaker of the House of our United States.

The poor, the lowly, the less fortunate of life were objects of his consideration and compassion, and many a time have they felt the touch of his kindness, his kindly words, and the realization of a faithful and devoted life. Such men are not born; they are made.

So, we realize, as the apostle has told us, "Him that is great among you, let him become your servant." In the field, on the farm not far from this place, the inspiration in the life of this man began. He climbed into the realms of higher things in life until he attained the place that he loved to live and labor. He lived and served in the capacity that he served so many years. He was a servant to so many people in the world. It is not a dreadful and fearful thing to be a servant. He served those whom he loved in the cause of freedom that our hearts seek after.

I think of the expression of the Apostle Paul, "I am now all things to all men." Paul was able to meet the great of the earth or the poor, the noble or the agnostic,

25

and he was able to bring himself in harmony with them and their life so that they might be of service to the classes of men in the world. And so, our good friend made himself a servant, not of the classes but of all the men and women and the boys and the girls and the children who have fought for and loved the freedom that our great country affords us. He maintained this out of his energy. Now he can say, in the language of the Apostle Paul in his letter, "I have fought a good fight." Of the people who knew our good friend, they know he has fought a good fight. In the liberties and freedom of our country he has fought a good fight. For the friends in this community and all those he represented, he has fought a good fight. He has been a fair and loyal man. He has kept faith, not only with the people of Fannin County, but the adjoining counties. He has kept faith with the democracy of our country. I think it can be truthfully and nobly said, "He has finished his course."

I am sure that had it been the Lord's will to lengthen his life, even for another 10 years, he would have been happy to fight our battles and fight for the rights that he so nobly stood for. He was ready for his going. The time of his departure was at hand. He has met it nobly, not fearing the consequences of death nor of the hereafter. He not only met the national community obligations, but he met it as a faithful servant of God. I think no man could have been able to have faithfully served so well without the love of God in his heart to administer and to lead to righteous conclusions.

The achievements of his life have been rehearsed by some of our hearers. Some of the great, noble things that he has done has been commemorated time and again, but it has been said that the most noble thing that he has done was to align himself with the church and the Father that he so much loved. He accomplished many objectives and achievements, but I am sure there is no achievement or honor that has come to us in life as great as following the Lord Jesus Christ. He has been an example of faithful devotion because of his conviction in faith and in the reality of the training of his early years. In this, we realize that God's child has a bright future, which is eternal.

I am reminded in my thinking of the Lord when he

led the children of Egypt. The Lord, I am sure, was the light that lighted the path, but it was the Lord himself who darkened the way to prevent the children of Egypt from being taken into bondage. So, death brings to us a deep penitence of grief and the realization that our loved ones are separated from us for a time. It may seem that darkness is over us in that respect, but to our good friend, the sunshine of God's everlasting love has lighted his path into eternal glory where there will be no strife, nor war or destructions, but where all will be eternal peace. There are promises that the Lord has made for us, "when our earthly tabernacle is gone, we have a place in heaven." This is God's promise to his children. Though the soul has taken its last flight, the mortal soul that made him the loving man that he was, has gone back to God to bask in the everlasting sunshine until the morning of the resurrection.

In the 15th chapter of I Corinthinas, He tells us that our bodies are natural, but they will be raised spiritual; that they are corruptible, but they shall be raised incorruptible. This is God's promise. The fulfilling of the promise of God by your good friend and mine has lived and died. I would like to leave with his very devoted family these words. He said: "Let not your heart be troubled. You believe in god, believe also in Me. In My Father's house are many mansions. If it were not so, I would have told you. I go to prepare a place for you, and if I go and prepare a place for you, I will come again and receive you unto Myself that where I am, there ye may be also."

I would like to emphasize one thought. Jesus said: "I go to prepare a place for you." To some, we think He was talking to our friend. Suppose that when he was a boy the Lord had said: "Sam, I go to prepare a place for you, and if I go and prepare a place for you, I will come and receive you unto Myself." So, when you come to think of your loved one, try to think of the glories that the Lord has prepared for him into which we all hope, by the goodness of God, to enter.

In the abiding faith that we have in God, and in His unerring spirit, we continue to live and trust in Him.

Pastors to serve the Bonham church other than J. R. Briscoe, the founding minister, include A. E. Clemens, J. A.

Fuller, S. J. Wright. Rev. Portman, Rev. Mitchell, J. W. Connelly, J. T. Miller, S. A. Beachamp, T. S. Potts, J. F. Duncan, A. B. Miller, Luther Little, D. G. Whittinghill, W. S. Splawn, J. E. Hughes, T. G. Davis, S. A. Cowan, Ernest Quick, F. M. McConnell, W. H. Horton, R. M. Jennings, S. R. Smith, J. I. Gregory, J. W. Salzman, Donald H. Morgan, James W. Hatley, Jack Carson, Mac Hargrove, and W. C. Beasley.

Miss Audra Wakefield, a 1922 graduate of the University of Texas, served this church as a dedicated and capable secretary for many years.

Sources:
   1. *First Baptist Church Centennial Celebration 1852–1952.*
   2. Conference with the pastor, W. C. Beasley.
   3. Conference with Sam Rayburn Library curator and director, H. G. Dulaney.


## FIRST BAPTIST CHURCH (MBA)
### Italy, Texas – 1869

Organized in 1869, the church first met in the Houston Creek schoolhouse and was called the Houston Creek Baptist Church of Christ. When the name of the town was changed to Italy in 1881, the church adopted the name First Baptist Church of Italy.

With twelve charter members and a continuous existence, the congregation moved from the schoolhouse in 1881 to a church building made available by the Presbyterians when not used for themselves. About 1885 the congregation built their own structure somewhere on North Ward Street.

Their second building was erected in 1893 and was dedicated with a sermon by Rufus C. Burleson of Waco. Burleson was president of Baylor University when it was located at Independence. While there on November 19, 1854, he baptized Sam Houston, Texas' famous patriot. Burleson became president of Baylor University in Waco when it merged with Waco University in 1886.

*FIRST BAPTIST CHURCH, Italy.*

The following men have served First Baptist Church as pastors since 1869:

| | |
|---|---|
| D. D. Swindall, 1869–73 | C. C. Lee, 1873–75 |
| Josiah Leake, 1875–79 | C. Clark Leake, 1879–85 |
| D. D. Swindall, 1885–87 | R. W. Thompson, 1887–88 |
| E. R. Freeman, 1888–91 | A. D. Brooks, 1891–94 |
| W. R. Selvidge, 1894–97 | M. A. McKinney, 1897–99 |
| J. F. McClung, 1899–1905 | J. S. Elliott, 1905–07 |
| C. H. Bell, 1907–08 | J. Y. Fincher, 1909–10 |
| W. M. Daily, 1910–12 | S. A. Hayden, 1912–13 |
| F. L. Tomlinson, 1913–17 | C. R. Meadows, 1917–23 |
| L. B. Jenkins, 1923–25 | M. A. Roberts, 1925–27 |
| W. T. Bratton, 1927–29 | H. D. Parnell, 1929–36 |
| W. O. McClung, 1936–38 | E. D. Keller, 1938–44 |
| W. P. Murchison, 1944–45 | H. L. McNish, 1945–48 |
| H. M. Dry, 1948–50 | Craig Branham, 1950–53 |
| B. C. Wilkins, Sr., 1953–55 | Dale Leggett, 1955–59 |
| Clyde Coleman, 1959–62 | Edwin Crank, 1962–64 |
| W. F. Smith, 1964–67 | Charles Burdett, 1967–70 |
| Tony M. Cleaver, 1970– | |

Two other Missionary Baptist churches of historical

significance near Italy are First Baptist Church of Ennis (1873) and the Bristol Baptist Church of Ennis (1858).

Sources:
1. R. C. Vance, *A History of M.B.A. of Texas 1900–1953*.
2. Ellis-Hill (Counties) Baptist Association, *100 Years of Service for the Master*.
3. Conference with Freddie Leggett.

# FIRST BAPTIST CHURCH
## Dallas – 1868

First Baptist Church of Dallas is not one of the state's oldest churches, but it is the largest Baptist Church in Texas and in the world. It did not enjoy early beginnings under the leadership of such early stalwart Baptist missionaries as Rufus C. Burleson, James Huckins, Z. N. Morrell and William Tryon, who thirty years earlier had much influence around La Grange, Independence, Houston, and Galveston. Such was also true of other great but smaller Baptist churches in Waco, Lubbock, Amarillo, and Abilene.

At the time First Baptist Church was being organized, noted outlaw Sam Bass was operating in the area, and the saloons on Elm Street were attractive to many of Dallas' first citizens.

Gen. Richard M. Gano, a Disciple of Church of Christ minister, had already gained a large audience from the few religiously inclined people of the area, as had the Methodists and Presbyterians.

Although late to begin in Dallas, First Baptist was the only one of the first four Baptist churches to survive.

The congregation was organized in the same lower room of the Masonic Lodge where sixteen years earlier the Christian Church (later the Pearl and Bryan Church and the Garland Road Church of Christ) had organized. Old records of the church indicate that "Brothers and sisters in and around the City of Dallas who held letters of dismission from Sister Baptist Churches . . . assembled in the Masonic Hall for the purpose of being organized into a regular Bap-

30

*FIRST BAPTIST CHURCH, Dallas.*

31

tist Church of Jesus Christ. Eleven persons, three men and eight women, presented themselves for membership that first day. They were Enoch G. Mays, William L. Williams, Mrs. William L. Williams, John Hanna, Mrs. M. L. Bowen, Mrs. C. E. Mays, Mrs. A. C. Mays, Mrs. N. E. Collins, Mrs. Martha Seegar, Mrs. S. C. Akard and Mrs. M. E. Kerfoot . . . The group then read the familiar covenant still in common use in Baptist Churches, and Harris read selections from the New Hampshire Baptist confession of faith, which the group affirmed . . . The group was then pronounced a 'regular organized Church of Christ.' " (McBeth, *Centennial History First Baptist Church of Dallas,* 29).

From the first eleven people who met for worship on July 30, 1868, and named the congregation First Baptist Church of Dallas, the church had grown to approximately 21,000 members by 1980.

The history of First Baptist Church of Dallas is very much the history of two world-famous pastors. From 1897 until 1980 — a period of eighty-three years — Dr. George W. Truett and Dr. W. A. Criswell served the congregation as pastors. Dr. Criswell continued his ministry in 1980.

As of 1980, the church complex encompassed four city blocks in downtown Dallas. Its sanctuary choir of 320 voices and a 75-member orchestra performed at the Sunday worship service and the evening service.

Pastors who preceded Dr. Truett at First Baptist Church were W. W. Harris, C. A. Stanton, W. Abram Weaver, G. W. Rogers, J. H. Curry, R. T. Hanks, A. M. Simms, and C. L. Seasholes.

Among the well-known personalities and ministers to speak at First Baptist are noted evangelist Billy Graham (long-time member of this congregation), President Woodrow Wilson, "Gipsy" Smith of England, Dr. B. H. Carroll, Dr. E. Y. Mullins, Dr. J. M. Frost, Arthur Flake, Dr. T. Townley Lord, Toyahiko Kagawa of Japan, Dr. C. Oscar Johnson, Dr. R. G. Lee, Miss Alma Hunt, and Dr. Rushbrooke of London.

When First Baptist Church of Dallas is mentioned, many middle-aged and older people, both Baptist and non-

Baptist, think of the inimitable Dr. George W. Truett. People of all religious beliefs have been named "George T." with the "T." being for Truett in honor of the great preacher, World War I chaplain, world traveler, and humanitarian.

Dr. W. A. Criswell, his successor, received his Ph.D. degree from Southern Baptist Theological Seminary in Louisville, Kentucky, at the age of twenty-seven. He preached without notes and made use of his mastery of Hebrew and Greek in his well-prepared sermons. Dr. Leon McBeth, in his *Centennial History,* described Dr. Criswell's pulpit manner in this way: "He begins quietly, but as he enters the main burden of his message his magnificent voice may rise to a shout or fall to a dramatic whisper. His voice is one of Criswell's most valuable assets. With unique ease, he can express pathos, courage, indignation, love — the entire range of emotions."

Dedicated to local and international missions and benevolences, First Baptist Church of Dallas organized First Baptist Academy to serve schoolchildren from kindergarten through the twelfth grade. Criswell Center for Biblical Studies, organized in 1970, grants both undergraduate and graduate degrees.

Dallas is regarded as a religious community of dedicated men and strong churches. Dr. Nolan Estes, a deacon of First Baptist, was superintendent of Dallas Public Schools for many years. He was succeeded by his good friend, Dr. Linus Wright, an elder at Garland Road Church of Christ, which was organized on the same location as was First Baptist. Many persons of substance and valor are to be found in all of Dallas' many churches, synagogues, and religious orders. First Baptist of Dallas has been a formidable pacesetter.

Sources:

1. Carr M. Suter, Jr., *O Zion, Haste* (The Story of Dallas Baptist Association).

2. *First Baptist Church of Dallas* (Centennial History, 1868–1968).

# II

## THE CATHOLICS

The history of the Catholic church in Texas prior to the separation of Mexico from Spain in 1820–21 is that of Spanish exploration and conquest and of the missions in Texas. The work of Franciscans was hampered by revolutionary movements in Mexico and by a lack of priests to minister to people over such a broad expanse of land. A few priests worked in the Spanish settlements at San Antonio and Goliad, and in the Irish colonies at Refugio and San Patricio.

John Timon was appointed prefect-apostolic of Texas in 1840, soon after Texas independence, and in 1841 John M. Odin was appointed vicar-apostolic. Texas was raised to the status of a diocese in 1847, and Odin became the first bishop of Galveston.

An estimated 10,000 Catholics lived in the Republic of Texas in 1841. By 1847, this number doubled as people came to the new republic from the United States and from Europe. First congregations were established at Galveston, San Antonio, Houston, Victoria, Castroville, Brazoria, and Nacogdoches. Smaller groups attended the old missions at San Antonio, Refugio, and Goliad. Catholic families were dispersed across the state in Austin, Laredo, San Patricio, Cuero, Gonzales, Seguin, Velasco, and Richmond. Twelve priests, most of them of the Vicentian Congregation, assisted Bishop Odin with organization and supervision of new parishes.

The Ursuline Academy was founded at Galveston in 1847, and the Oblates of Mary Immaculate began their work in Brownsville in 1849. Other schools and academies were established in Brownsville, San Antonio, and Galveston. By 1860, there were forty-two priests, forty-four chapels and churches, four churches under construction, five schools for boys, four academies for girls, and a college in Galveston.

In 1861, Bishop Claude-Marie Dubuis succeeded Bishop Odlin in Galveston. Succeeding Dubuis was Nicholas A. Gallagher, who died in 1918 and was followed by Christopher E. Byrne.

The diocese was divided in 1874 with the creation of a second diocese in San Antonio and the vicarate apostolic of Brownsville. When San Antonio was ranked as an archdiocese in 1926, Arthur J. Drossaerts became the first archbishop of the See and Province. In 1941, Robert E. Lucey succeeded Drossaerts as archbishop. A new diocese was created in 1911 at Corpus Christi and earlier, in 1890, the Diocese of Dallas had been created under Thomas F. Brennan.

In extreme western Texas at El Paso, the bishop of Durango was in charge until the area was placed under the bishop at Tucson. From 1890 to 1914, El Paso was assigned to the Diocese of Dallas. In 1926 the Diocese of Amarillo was established.

When the Diocese of Austin was created in 1948, it absorbed portions of the Dioceses of Galveston, San Antonio and Dallas, with Louis J. Reicher as bishop.

By 1949, the Catholic population of Texas was estimated to be in excess of one million.

Sources:
1. *Handbook of Texas,* Vol. II.

# MISSION NUESTRA SEÑORA DEL CÁRMEN
## Ysleta – 1682

Fourteen miles east of El Paso on Highway 80, Broadway of America, is the oldest town both in Texas and in the United States—older than St. Augustine, Florida, and Santa Fe, New Mexico, and fifty years older than George Washington. Franciscan fathers lived there from 1539 to 1541 before they left to establish a mission in Ciudad Juárez, Mexico.

In 1680, Governor Otermin, a Spaniard, led a group of 400 refugees from Ysleta, New Mexico, to Ysleta, Texas, following a revolt of native Indians against the Spanish rule. These refugees included a few Spaniards and almost 400 Tigua Indians.

The old mission has burned twice and the sanctuary is the only part of the old structure still standing. When the refugees went to Ysleta in 1680, they went there for their protection and also for the protection of the settlement of Indians already there.

No known missionaries had been at Ysleta until May 15, 1692, when Fray Joaquin de Hinojosa was commissioned by the king of Spain to take charge of the mission. The king, grateful to the loyal and prosperous inhabitants, granted them a tax-free tract of land of fifteen square miles.

Ysleta's people were doing rather well until 1831, when Comanche and Apache warriors swept down across Texas on the Comanche "war trail" and raided and ravaged the town and mission. It took eight years for the community of aboriginal Americans, Spanish *conquistadors,* and Anglo settlers to recover from the raid.

In 1842 the town experienced another disaster when the Rio Grande brought prolonged flooding that destroyed crops and adobe houses. After the Mexican War, the peace treaty set the Rio Grande as the boundary line between Mexico and the United States. However, Ysleta, which was first in Mexico, came to be in the United States when the fickle river changed its course.

Ysleta is a good example of the metamorphosis of the United States, as the Anglo-American takes his distinctive place beside the Indian, the Mexican, and the Spaniard. Here people live in peace and harmony as each group retains its own customs, manners, and habits — therefore preserving its own identity.

Coordinated with their religious beliefs and practices, the Tigua Indians, living in the eastern part of town near the railroad station, today maintain their tribal organization with a chief as their leader. The chief summons his followers by beating on a tom-tom as the tribal chief did more than 300 years ago. The Indians still celebrate the same feast days and dance the same dances as practiced by their forefathers. Chief Mariano Comonero, a loyal United States citizen, sent two of his sons to fight in World War II; they served in France.

The western part of Ysleta is the residence of Spanish and Mexican families. In the center of town is the residence of Anglo, Mexican, and Spanish families.

The land around Ysleta is fertile and very productive with the aid of ample irrigation. Egyptian (long staple) cotton is produced in abundance, as is alfalfa. Peaches, plums, and melons are plentiful. And fittingly, as Ysleta is the Indian word for pear, many carloads of pears are exported annually.

The mission, which was designed to remind the Indians that "man does not live by bread alone," is still serving the people and proclaiming that material essentials will be added for those "seeking first the kingdom of God . . ." The Tiguas have not fared badly.

Sources:
1. *Ageless Ysleta Patriarch of New West in Old America,* Catholic Archives of Texas, Austin, Texas.
2. Conference with Sister Delores Kasner, O. P., archivist.
3. Connie Sherley, "El Paso Gaining Renown as Center for Conventions." *Austin American-Statesman.* January 7, 1973.

*MISSION NUESTRA SEÑORA DEL CÁRMEN, Ysleta.*

# SAN FERNANDO CATHEDRAL PARISH
## San Antonio — 1731

Founded on July 2, 1731, San Fernando Parish was located in San Fernando de Bexar (present-day San Antonio). It was established by a few families from the Canary Islands under a type of parish and municipal government—the first of this type in Texas.

Before the people of the *villa* began worship in this church, they had assembled in a temporary chapel in the *presidio* of the Mission San Antonio de Valero (the Alamo) for a short time. On May 13, 1734, the cornerstone for the new church was laid but the actual construction began four years later. The church was financed by donations of $5,000 from the royal treasury and $12,000 from the viceroy of New Spain. The gift from the viceroy, made ten years after the $5,000 contribution, was for completion of the construction. On November 6, 1749, under the title of San Fernando, the church was blessed and opened for services.

The church has existed under four different dioceses: Guadalajara, Linares (including the provinces of Texas, Nuevo Leon, Coahuila, and Nuevo Santander), Galveston, and finally the Diocese of San Antonio in 1874.

During its years of service, the church has been under the governments of Spain, Mexico, the Republic of Texas, the Confederacy, and the United States. It was atop this church that Col. William B. Travis posted lookouts to sound the alarm at the approach of the Mexican army. From the steeple of this church, Santa Anna flew the scarlet "flag of no quarter" during the several days' siege of the Alamo. It is believed that the burnt remains of some of the defenders of the Alamo were buried beneath the sanctuary of San Fernando by Col. Juan N. Seguin. At the northeast entrance of the church is a marble sarcophagus in which these disinterred bodies were placed in 1936.

The grand old structure has suffered much from fires, floods and wars, but periodic repairs have kept the church a major center of tourist attraction as well as for serving the religious concerns of the people as in its beginning. Addi-

39

*SAN FERNANDO Catholic Church, San Antonio.*

tions have been made together with massive remodeling, but the main structure is essentially the same as it was many years ago.

The Claretian fathers came to San Antonio in 1902 and assumed responsibility for the spiritual care of about 8,000 Mexican-Americans living in San Antonio. These fathers also attended other missions around the city and recorded 65,985 baptisms, 8,080 marriages, and 12,430 funerals in this multi-century-old church.

The archives of the church include priceless records and documents of the Franciscan missions of San Antonio including those of the Alamo and San José Mission.

The parish in 1980 numbered 600 families. Priests

40

serving the parish were the Claretian fathers Joseph Nuevo, pastor, and Vincent Andres and Martin Sanz, associate pastors assisted by Brother Francis Blackman C.M.F.

Sources:
1. *San Fernando Cathedral Parish,* Catholic Archives of Texas (Austin).
2. Conference with Sister Delores Kasner O.P., archivist.

## ST. MARY'S PARISH
## Victoria – 1824

Although not known by their present names, Victoria and St. Mary's began at the same time. Don Martín de Leon founded the colony of Nuestra Señora de Guadalupe de Jesus Victoria by locating forty-one "deserving Mexican families" at a point on the lower Guadalupe River. One of the first things that Don Martín did was to order the erection of a Catholic church on the main square. East of Victoria's present city hall and across the street from present-day St. Mary's, a crude hand-hewn log building was completed in 1830 and dedicated, as was the town, to the Virgin of Guadalupe. Since there was no resident priest at Victoria in her early days, Mass was offered occasionally by the priests from La Bahía Mission.

When Santa Anna was defeated by the Texans at San Jacinto in 1836, the church suffered disaster when the original families felt constrained to abandon their homes and flee to Mexico for safety. During the next four years, the log chapel served in brief succession as a barracks, a courthouse, and a Presbyterian church.

The original name of the church, Our Lady of Guadalupe, gradually came into disuse and in time the church came to be known simply as St. Mary's. Father John Odin and three Vicentian companions from New Orleans landed on July 12, 1840, at Linnville on Lavaca Bay. Their first stop was at Victoria and their mission was to reorganize the church there, making it the first Catholic parish canonically erected in the Republic of Texas.

*ST. MARY'S Catholic Church, Victoria.*

The first resident pastor was Eudaldus Estony, C.M., who officiated his first wedding on July 29, 1840, and first baptism on July 30, 1840, in the newly resurrected parish of Our Lady of Guadalupe.

Father Augustine Gardet, one of St. Mary's most dynamic pastors, went to Victoria in 1856 to begin a thirty-five-year tenure. In 1863 the pastor motivated the parish to build a new brick church at the corner of Bridge and Church streets. Land for the new building was donated by the widow of Don Martín de Leon. Giving them his own house for a convent and girls' school, Father Gardet brought the Sisters of the Incarnate Word and Blessed Sacrament from Brownsville to Victoria in 1866. In 1868 he founded St. Joseph's school for boys and expanded it in 1880 to include a seminary. For several years many Texas priests received their education in this seminary.

The present near-Gothic structure was begun in 1902 and was dedicated in 1904. The Texas State Historical Survey Committee designated this most impressive structure as a Texas Historical Landmark.

Written large in the history of St. Mary's Parish is the name of Monsignor F. O. Beck, who served the church from 1941 until 1967. During his tenure, St. Mary's Hall was built, the church was completely remodeled, and in 1959 the present parish rectory was built.

The parish in 1980, served by Fathers Ray Rihn and John Orr, numbered more than 800 families in its membership.

Sources:
1. *St. Mary's Parish, Victoria.*
2. Catholic Archives of Texas (Austin).
3. Conference with Sister Delores Kasner, O.P., archivist.

## ST. MARY'S CATHEDRAL BASILICA
### Texas' Oldest Cathedral and
### Galveston's Oldest Existing Church Building
### 1842

In 1836, when Texas won her independence from Mexico, religious groups other than those which were Catholic came into the new Republic. To some extent Catholicism began to wane for a few years.

John Timon, C.M. (Congregation of the Mission), traveled to Texas to investigate religious conditions. Finding only two priests in the new country, Father Timon could understand that his Catholic brethren suffered more from religious neglect than from persecution.

Father Timon surveyed the many miles along the Gulf of Mexico and reported on the needs of the people. Rome, in 1840, declared the Republic of Texas a prefecture Apostolic and named Father Timon its first prefect and the Very Rev. John Odin, C.M., its vice-prefect.

43

For seven years, Father Timon and his associate worked tirelessly to establish Catholicism in Texas. Ten new churches were erected and four more were started. They established a school at Brown's settlement in Lavaca County and another at Brazoria. Eight Ursuline Sisters arrived in 1847 from New Orleans and opened a school in Galveston.

In this same year, Pope Pius IX signed and sealed the pontifical bulls in Rome on May 4, erecting Texas into a bishopric and establishing the Diocese of Galveston. Most Rev. John Odin, C.M., was its first bishop, with Galveston as the See City, or center of authority.

Principal cities in the Galveston Diocese of a hundred and forty years ago were: Galveston, Houston, Nacogdoches, Austin, Eagle Lake, San Antonio, Castroville, Victoria, Goliad, Refugio, Brazoria, Corpus Christi, Laredo, and Ysleta.

St. Mary's Church, seat of the bishop of the Diocese of Galveston, had humble beginnings. Fathers Timon and Odin and other prominent Galvestonians, N. D. Labadic and Col. Michael Menard, founder of the city of Galveston, were able to raise enough money to construct a wooden-frame house. This building, twenty-two by fifty-five feet, was dedicated on February 6, 1842, to the Blessed Virgin Mary.

During the hurricane season in September 1842, a storm toppled the small and fragile church. Determined that a church should be housed in a more durable structure, Father Odin welcomed two Vincentian priests to Galveston, Fathers J. M. Paquin and John Brands. In 1844, the same year of the priests' arrival, Galveston suffered a costly epidemic of yellow fever. Father Paquin was one of the 400 citizens to die.

During the next year, relatives of Father Paquin sent, by means of the ship's ballast, 500,000 bricks from Belgium for the construction of the larger, more permanent church.

Work on the new St. Mary's Church was begun by laying the cornerstone on March 14, 1847. Father Louis Chambodut, rector of the cathedral, made entry on the baptismal register. It read in part:

*ST. MARY'S CATHEDRAL BASILICA, Galveston.*

In the year of our Lord, 1847, on the 14th of March, in the first year of the Pontificate of His Holiness, Pius IX; in the 71st year of the Independence of America; James K. Polk being president of the United States of America; Pickney J. [J. Pinckney] Henderson, Governor of the State of Texas; John P. Sydnor, Mayor of the City of Galveston; the Most Reverend John Odin, Bishop of Claudiopolis and Vicar Apostilic of Texas; assisted by the Very Rev. John Timon, visitor of the Congregation of the Mission in America . . .

On November 26, 1848, the cathedral was dedicated, with Father Timon as principal speaker.

The Civil War touched Galveston and St. Mary's with a blazing, ravaging week during the Battle of Galveston, which began on December 25, 1862. Shore batteries of Confederate artillery fired upon five Union gunboats anchored in Galveston Harbor. The federal gunboat *Owasca* made her way down the channel and severely assaulted the streets of the city. By the end of several days, U.S. forces of the 42nd Massachusetts Regiment had control of Galveston. However, on New Year's Day, Gen. John B. Magruder, bringing up ships "armored" with bales of cotton, retook the island for the Confederacy.

For some time, St. Mary's was damaged to the extent that Bishop Claude Dubuis was forced to inform church members that he could say Mass in the church only on dry days.

In 1884 the famous architect Nicholas J. Clayton directed the raising of the two front towers to bring them into proper proportion to the central tower. What Sir Christopher Wren did for London in building St. Paul's Cathedral and other buildings after the great fire, Clayton did for Galveston. Grace Episcopal Church, the Ashbel Smith Building (University of Texas Medical Branch), and Col. Walter Gresham's residence, later known as "Bishop's Palace," were designed by this same renowned architect who had designed St. Mary's central tower in 1876.

Bishop Nicholas Gallagher was consecrated in St. Mary's Cathedral in 1882 and became the Diocese of

46

Galveston's third bishop. After extending the services of the diocese by bringing in the Jesuits, Basilians, Josephites and Paulists, the bishop introduced the Sisters of Charity of St. Vincent de Paul, Good Shepherd Sisters, Sisters of the Holy Family, and the Dominican Sisters, who in early years conducted the Cathedral Parochial School in their own convent.

In 1896, Father James M. Kirwin succeeded Bishop Gallagher as rector of St. Mary's. He served until his death thirty years later. During his tenure in Galveston, Father Kirwin witnessed that infamous storm on a weekend in September.

Of the half-dozen churches in Galveston, the cathedral suffered the least damage in the 1900 hurricane. Both Bishop Gallagher and Father Kirwin survived the storm, which left 6,000 dead and 3,600 demolished buildings, and they assisted the stricken city in all possible ways.

In 1918 the Most Rev. Christopher Byrne was consecrated bishop and in the same year became fourth bishop of the Diocese of Galveston. It was because of this bishop that the Gresham residence came to be known as "Bishop's Palace" (Bishop Byrne's Palace in the Sky).

Source:
1. John Cannady, comp., *St. Mary's Cathedral Basilica.*


## SAINTS PETER AND PAUL CHURCH
### New Braunfels – 1846

In 1844, Prince Carl of Solms Braunfels, Germany, and Jakob Lindheimar (considered by some as the father of Texas botany) rode into the lands of the Tonkawa, Karankawa, Lipan, and Waco Indians. The area where they eventually settled was named New Braunfels because the prince's castle in Germany was located at Braunfels on the Lahn River. Prince Carl was appointed commissioner-general for the colony which the *Adelsverein* (Association of Noblemen) in Germany proposed to establish there.

During the last two months in 1844, German immigra-

47

nts began arriving on the coastal area as the first of 6,000 to come to Texas, landing at Indianola and moving inland as opportunities permitted.

From the Texas lands, these sturdy Teutonic people would emulate the industry of those left in their homeland as they "wrested from the land all it was meant to give," as stated by Father Flannagan.

The devout Catholic farmers endured a plague of grasshoppers in 1877, which was described as an almost total blacking of the land as the crops were almost completely consumed. The next year a drought and famine killed many of the cattle and work horses.

The German immigrants who came first to New Braunfels in 1845 were both Catholic and Protestant (Lutheran), with the Protestants outnumbering the Catholics about two-to-one. Each group was promised land on which to build a church. There was to be independence and equality in this new land of liberty, the people were assured.

The Catholics erected a small log cabin which was served when possible by Bishop Odin and Father Emmanuel Domineck. This first church was replaced by a building made of black walnut and dedicated to St. Peter in September 1849. In this second church building, Father Claude Dubuis celebrated the first Mass on September 10, 1849. (First Mass is said to have been celebrated under an oak tree with either Father Leinhart or Father John Gregory Pfanner coming from Castroville for the occasion.)

The first resident pastor for Saints Peter and Paul was Father Gottfried Menzel, who served from 1849 until 1851. The following year, seventy-six families were on the parish list as the church was led by Father Leopoldus Moczygemba.

In 1859 a Community of Benedictine Fathers arrived at the parish and continued their services until 1868. Plans had been made for a new and larger church, but the conditions of the Civil War caused a few years' delay.

With the laying of the cornerstone on July 25, 1871, by Bishop Dubuis, the new building (the same one currently used) was erected under the guidance of Father Peter Benr and was dedicated to Saints Peter and Paul.

It is said that the new church was built around and over the old black walnut church. In this way, there was a continuous meeting place for the members. Built upon a high place, overlooking the beautiful panorama of the Comal Valley, the floor of the church is built of the same pure limestone of the surrounding area. With pride in their magnificent edifice, parishioners today call attention to the fact that the flooring is of similar material to the ground upon which Solomon built the great temple and also similar to the ground of the Mount of Olives on which Jesus once prayed.

Father J. M. J. Wack, most celebrated of the church's priests, served the church for twenty-five years with distinction from 1889 until 1927. It was in 1918, during Father Wack's tenure, that an epidemic of influenza struck the city, claiming the lives of forty-five members of Saints Peter and

*SAINTS PETER AND PAUL Cathedral Parish, New Braunfels.*

49

Paul. Father Wack and the people, on this occasion of grief, made a vow to build a grotto, a replica of the one at Lourdes. Members of the church—farmers, ranchers, men young and old—worked diligently in gathering materials for the grotto. Much pageantry and celebration has centered around the grotto for many years, including such events as the Palm Sunday blessing of the palms before the grotto and the following procession to the church.

Saints Peter and Paul Church has extended its services to provide excellent educational facilities and programs for many years. Through the benevolence of Hippolyt Dittlinger, owner of Dittlinger Lime Company, a house was built for the Sisters of Divine Providence, who came to teach in the school which Dittlinger had built for Mexican-American children. Archbishop Droassarts appealed to the Holy Family Fathers of the Netherlands for missionaries to work among the Spanish-speaking people. Father Elsing responded to the appeal by bringing a group of four to New Braunfels in March 1926. The small church was blessed by Archbishop Lucey in 1944, thus extending services to the Spanish-speaking people. The Fathers of the Congregation of the Holy Family serve the two parishes, which are actually part of the history of Saints Peter and Paul.

St. Thomas Chapel, a mission of the church, serves the area around Canyon Dam. Msgr. Drozd was assigned pastor of St. Thomas Open Air Chapel at Canyon Lake on June 3, 1970. The church began to function as a "drive-in church." Enclosed in a glassed-in area, the priest administered Mass to people as they stayed in their cars in inclement weather. Attendance reached as high as 900 by 1980.

The chronology of priests to serve the church follows:

| | |
|---|---|
| 1852–1854 | Rev. Leopold Moczygemba OMC |
| 1854–1857 | Rev. Dominicus Mesens OMC |
| 1857–1859 | Rev. Alphonse Zoeller OMC |
| 1859–1861 | Rev. Aemilion Wendl OSB |
| 1861–1866 | Rev. Theodor Grundner OSB |
| 1866–1868 | Rev. Columban Schmidtbauer OSB |
| 1868–1870 | Rev. L. J. Fleury |
| 1870–1877 | Rev. Peter Behr |
| 1877–1879 | Rev. Anton Kullman |

| 1879–1884 | Rev. George Lagleder |
| 1884–1889 | Rev. John Kirch |
| 1889–1923 | Rev. J. M. J. Wack |
| 1923–1927 | Rev. F. O. Beck |
| 1927–1948 | Rev. J. J. Robling |
| 1948–1954 | Rev. Armand Weber |
| 1954–1964 | Rev. Henry Herbst |
| 1964–1970 | Rev. Anthony Drozd |
| 1970– | Rev. Patrick Flannagan |

Source:
1. Monica Fuhrmann, Geneviene Moeller, Emma Wille, Elvera Zengler, *The History of Saints Peter and Paul Church and Parish.*
2. Conference with Rev. Patrick Flannagan.

## ST. MARY'S CHURCH
Fredericksburg – 1846

Several Catholic families were among the first Germans to settle in the area now known as Fredericksburg. The Catholic group first met regularly either in the home of John Leyendecker, a schoolteacher, or in the so-called *Vereins Kirche.*

Two missionaries arrived at Fredericksburg in 1847 and remained for two weeks. Before leaving, they urged the people to build a small church and promised them a resident priest.

In the fall of 1849, a lot was purchased for $18 and a small wood-and-stone church was built. Across the street, two more lots and a small one-room house to serve as a rectory were acquired. Before the people could complete their plans to have the facilities and the resident priest, a deadly cholera epidemic left several entire families dead and the survivors in pitiful condition. After the people then endured a crop failure and famine, their persistence finally

51

*ST. MARY'S Catholic Church, Fredericksburg.*

rewarded them in the summer of 1849 with the resident priest.

In February of 1861 a new stone church was begun, a jewel of antique architecture which the builders designed as they built and built as they designed. This old church *(marienkirch)* at W. San Antonio and S. Orange streets underwent repairs and restoration in 1980. Next door is the new church, which was constructed in 1908 at a cost of $40,000. The new building is one of the most outstanding examples of Gothic architecture in the Southwest. Sisters of Divine Providence have operated St. Mary's School, as part of the church's services, for more than one hundred years.

Father Tom Palmer, his associate Father Francis Kalina, and their secretary, Maxine Jordan, graciously "show and tell" the past and present of Fredericksburg's historic St. Mary's.

Sources:
1. *A Capsule History of St. Mary's* (1969).
2. Conference with Maxine Jordan, secretary.

## ST. MARY'S CHURCH
## Austin — 1852

First known as St. Patrick's, the name of the church was changed in 1866 by the pastor, Rev. Nicholas Feltin, to St. Mary's of the Immaculate Conception.

The first priests to serve the needs of the Catholic people of Austin came as missionaries from Bastrop. The first Catholic baptism recorded in Austin was for a baby girl, Lucy Catherine, the daughter of James and Mary Ann Brady. The baptism was administered by Rev. Michael Sheehan on October 17, 1852. The first Catholic marriage ceremony in Austin joined William H. Carr and Catherine Finning. Father Sheehan solemnized the ceremony on April 7, 1853.

It was early in 1853 that Father Sheehan took up residence in Austin and began construction of a church at the northeast corner of East Ninth and Brazos streets. He remained in Austin five years, completing the church's construction in 1855. Beginning in 1857, and for the following seven years, Rev. G. Mackin, Rev. Michael Prendergast, Rev. T. M. Fouse, Father Gury, John T. McGee, and John Mayer served the new church.

Father Feltin, who changed the original name of the church to its present name, was a man of skill and industry. He performed manual labor, as in building the rock schoolhouse on East Tenth Street, and walked many miles in order to assist the sick and distressed. When he died in San Antonio five years after his retirement in Austin, it is said that more people attended his funeral than had attended any other such service in San Antonio prior to that time.

Rev. Daniel J. Spillard, C.S.C., took charge of St. Mary's on May 4, 1874, and laid the foundation for the present St. Mary's Church. The famed Nicholas J. Clayton of Galveston was the architect who supplied the building design. The lot

53

on which the new church was to be built was under litigation, and although the successful lawyer's fee was a donation the lot cost the church more than expected. Father Spillard was constrained to verbalize his feelings as he said: "May the Lord preserve us from such donations."

A small school was built in 1878, about one mile east of the present administration building on land later known as St. Edward's University Farm. Later, demand for a boarding-school led to the erection of another building. In 1881 the first students enrolled in St. Edward's Academy. A charter was granted by the State of Texas in 1885, by which St. Edward's College had its beginning. Rev. P. J. Franciscus, C.S.C., became St. Edward's first president.

Sisters of the Holy Cross arrived in Austin in 1874 and did much for education of the people in St. Mary's community. The sisters, who had begun teaching in a rock schoolhouse on East Tenth Street, moved to a new location on East Seventh and Eighth streets on the site which formerly served as the residence for the president of the Republic of Texas. The girls of the parochial school were transferred to the new St. Mary's Academy, and the Brothers of Holy Cross took over the direction of the boys in the parochial school. Many of Austin's businessmen (both Catholic and non-Catholic) attended the school and gleaned much learning from the brothers who taught there.

Among other distinguished leaders of St. Mary's are Reverends John O'Keefe, Michael A. Quinlan, J. J. O'Rourke, James H. Gallagan, William Lennartz, and James J. O'Brien.

Michael Butler, among the many benefactors of St. Mary's, donated a 2,000-pound bell in 1866. Outreach of St. Mary's included much charity and good services to the people of Austin. These included the establishment of a new hospital, called Seton Infirmary after Mother Elizabeth Seton, the American foundress of the Sisters of Charity of St. Vincent de Paul.

One significant event, as a part of the history of St. Mary's, was the investiture of Dr. Carlos E. Castañeda as a Knight of the Holy Sepulchre. On Sunday, October 12, 1941, in Gregory Gymnasium on the University of Texas

*ST. MARY'S OF THE IMMACULATE CONCEPTION, Austin.*

campus, the Most Rev. Christopher E. Byrne, bishop of Galveston, celebrated the Solemn Pontifical Mass. The Most Rev. Francis C. Kelley, bishop of Oklahoma City–Tulsa, conferred the honor and delivered the sermon.

In 1980 this grand, historic church in the state capital was served by Father William Donahue, C.S.C.

Sources:
1. *The Official Catholic Directory of the St. Mary's Parish,* March 19, 1943, Austin.
2. Conference with Sister Delores Kasner, O.P., archivist, Austin, Texas.

55

# CHURCH OF THE ANNUNCIATION
## Houston – 1869

Houston is no longer the struggling village it was when A. C. and John Allen founded it in March 1836. The Bayou City, a relocated Harrisburg, had for several years received supplies from New Orleans and transported them to the merchants at San Felipe for "The Old Three Hundred" who came into the Mexican state of Texas-Coahuila.

Stephen F. Austin's colonizers were required to be believers of the Catholic religion or "persons of character and integrity" recommended by Catholics. As Austin had witnessed the transition from Spanish to Mexican rule, he also understood that both patron nations were Catholic. Aside from the earlier French and Spanish missions' survival in a wilderness among Indians, some of whom had been forced off their eastern lands, settlers did not give a high priority to religious activity. Neither the official Catholic religion nor Protestants put forth more than minimal efforts at formal religion.

When the war for independence brought forth a new nation, the Republic of Texas, in 1836, religious freedom, although not completely suppressed in prior years, was afforded to all. Early to arrive on the religious scene in Houston was Father Timon. Through his tireless efforts, he revived the faltering faith of the new pioneers and also obtained land for Saint Vincent's Church on the corner of Franklin Avenue and Caroline Street. Bishop John Odin, the first bishop of Galveston, according to available records of the church, moved to Houston and baptized William Paschal on January 11, 1841.

Among the most noteworthy of the priests serving this first Catholic church in Houston during her war-torn years was Father Augustine d'Asti (1859–1866).

Two outstanding citizens and Texas heroes served by Saint Vincent's parish were Dick Dowling, of the Sabine Pass encounter, and John Kennedy, whose trading post was a refuge for the poor, regardless of race or creed.

As the number of Catholics increased, so did the need

for a larger church. In 1869, Father Querat, pastor of Saint Vincent's, purchased bricks from the old courthouse that was being demolished. The bricks would be used for a new church, Annunciation, to be built on the corner of Crawford Street and Texas Avenue.

Until 1878, old Saint Vincent's served a good purpose as it became a religious center for the many in-migrating Germans who had visions of establishing a little "New Germany" in Texas. After 1878, the German congregation became integrated into Annunciation Parish.

The architecture of the church is symbolic of the confluence of Texas cultures as it combines Romanesque features, Norman and Gothic styles in its exterior, a Spanish or German spiral, provincial pinnacles, Italian arched windows, German twin towers, and English buttresses. The interior is neoclassical.

The Annunciation church was dedicated on September 10, 1871. The first recorded baptism was of Emma Duvernoy, whose father, Gustav Duvernoy, served both this church and the Jewish synagogue as organist for twenty-five years. The first couple to be married in the church was John T. Browne and Mollie Bergin. Browne later served with distinction as mayor of the city of Houston for two terms.

Father Thomas Hennessy, an English-speaking pastor, served the church and added three new parishes to Houston. Rev. George T. Walsh began service with the church in 1914. An innovator, Father Walsh added a heating system to the church, a coeducational parish school, Catholic Women's Club, and a Mexican clinic, forerunner of San José Clinic.

In 1925, Father Walsh was made a domestic prelate, becoming Houston's first monsignor. Father Thomas Hogan succeeded Father Walsh and on October 7, 1943, Father Forank was installed as pastor. In its first one hundred years of existence, Annunciation Church had only five pastors.

James Cardinal McIntyre, the first cardinal to officiate in Houston, celebrated the Pontifical Mass in this church. Other well-known personalities to be honored in Annuncia-

CHURCH OF THE ANNUNCIATION, Houston.

tion Church were Dennis Day, Irene Dunn, and Blanche Foley, the church's greatest benefactor and granddaughter of the John Kennedy who owned a trading post.

Sources:
    1. Sister Mary Brendan O'Connell, V.I., Incarnate Word Convent, Bellaire, Texas.
    2. Msgrs. Theodore de la Torre and Anton J. Frank, *Centennial Annunciation Church, 1869-1969.*

# SACRED HEART CHURCH
## Muenster — 1889

The beautiful and massive facilities at Sacred Heart Church in Muenster, Texas, are most impressive. One might expect to find such facilities in a large city, but not in a town with hardly more than 1,000 residents.

The parish buildings include the large sanctuary, a rectory, a two-story parish hall and cafeteria, St. Joseph Club building, music hall, grade school building, high school building, and a twenty-one-bedroom convent.

On December 8, 1889, in the Flusche Land Office, the first Mass in Muenster was said. This marked the official opening of the colony that three brothers — Emil, Anton, and August Flusche — had come to found. The town was named for the capital of the brothers' native province of Westphalia in Germany.

The Mass was no longer celebrated in the land office when the second story of the store was completed and used for services until a school was built in 1890.

In 1891 construction was begun for a small frame church, but a storm demolished the building before it was completed. The people then began work on another church building which was completed and dedicated April 24, 1892, by Bishop Thomas Brennan. A year later, this church suffered the same fate of the other building as it, too, was destroyed by a storm. The northern part of Texas along Red River has long been known as the land of storms.

Undaunted by past disasters, the parish decided in 1898 to build a large and sturdy edifice of brick to serve the combined purposes of church, school, and convent. The building was completed and dedicated by Bishop Edward Dunne.

Originally the parish had been dedicated as St. Mary's. The name was changed to Sacred Heart in 1893, due perhaps to the abundance of parishes in other places which were named St. Mary's.

The Benedictine Fathers began service with the parish

59

*THE SACRED HEART Parish, Muenster.*

in 1893, and two years later the Olivetan Benedictine Sisters arrived to teach in the parish school.

The old church was razed in 1949 to make way for the new church, which was completed and dedicated along with the high school on October 7, 1954. Bishop Augustine Danglmayr, titular bishop of Olba and a native son of the parish, officiated.

A large relief statue of Christ, made of Cordova cream limestone, marks the front of Sacred Heart Church. This building, the church's fourth, was built in a modified Gothic style.

The first child baptized was Anne Hesse, who later married August Walterscheid. Rev. H. Brickley of Gainesville officiated.

The first couple to be married was Stephen Grewing and Margaret Knauf. The wedding was conducted by Hugo Fessler in the new frame church on April 21, 1901.

The first confirmation was administered by the bishop of the new Diocese of Dallas in Muenster on April 4, 1892.

60

The first burial was that of Frances Wilde, a child, with Rev. P. Hugo, O.S.F., officiating on April 10, 1890.

Muenster, Texas, is a long way from Muenster, Germany. As the people thought enough of the city of their homeland to name their new abode in honor of their prior Teutonic dwelling place, their forebears could only be impressed and proud of their Texas relatives on the new frontier.

Sources:
1. Catholic Archives of Texas, Austin.
2. Conference with Sister Delores Kasner, O.P., archivist.

# III

## THE DISCIPLES OF CHRIST

The Disciples of Christ (Christian Church) is part of the Restoration movement which began in Kentucky in 1804. Led by Barton W. Stone and later joined by Thomas and Alexander Campbell and Walter Scott in Virginia, Pennsylvania, and Ohio between 1809 and 1823, these men and others sought to unite the different religious groups.

This religious order, well united and using the title Christian Church and Church of Christ interchangeably, moved westward with the tide of migration to Texas. The earliest group coming to Texas was led by Collin McKinney, for whom Collin County and the county seat of McKinney are named. With the group finally established in Grayson and Collin counties, they organized Old Liberty or Mantua Church, which eventually became First Christian Church of Van Alstyne. This is the oldest Christian or Disciples Church in Texas, which in 1980 was still strong and active.

In January 1836, Lynn D'Spain and Mansil Matthews led an entire congregation through Texarkana into the area of Clarksville in Red River County. From this group, churches were later begun in Rockwall and Nacogdoches. In Nacogdoches, Hettie D'Spain married Joseph Addison Clark, later to be the father of Addison and Randolph Clark, founders of Add-Ran College (the forerunner of Texas Christian University).

In 1833, Dr. William Defee, a medical doctor, began

preaching in Sabine, San Augustine, and Shelby counties. He organized Antioch Church four miles from San Augustine. This church, organized in the home of Rhoddy Anthony in 1836, was continuous from its founding and was still active and strong in 1980. It never experienced the division from the original pattern and remained with the more conservative Church of Christ. Churches in early years were established at Rio Navidad, San Patricio, Live Oak Well in Fayette County, and in Washington and Lamar counties.

Frontier individualism made this group wary of overorganization and ecclesiastical control. They felt, too, that liberalism was "divisive and should be avoided."

However, the matter of organization did emerge at a statewide meeting of ministers held at Thorp Spring as early as 1879. That conference was followed by annual meetings at Waxahachie, Bonham, Ennis, Bryan, Sherman, and Austin.

At Austin, in 1886, the Texas Missionary Society was organized. This, together with introduction of instrumental music in the worship, led to a division between conservative and liberal elements in the Restoration movement. *The Firm Foundation,* published in Austin, began spreading the word of the conservatives, and the *Christian Courier* spoke for the liberal or progressive group.

By 1906, a separation of the two groups had occurred—the Church of Christ as the conservative group and the Disciples of Christ (Christian Church) as the progressive or liberal group.

In its early years, the Disciples organized several small colleges but only two survived—Jarvis Christian College for Negroes and Texas Christian University. The Disciples also operate Juliette Fowler Homes for Orphans and Aged.

In 1946 the Disciples of Christ (Christian Church) had 86,414 members who were served by 544 ministers.

Sources:
1. Dr. Carter E. Boren, *Religion on the Texas Frontier.*
2. *Handbook of Texas,* Vol. I.

# FIRST CHRISTIAN CHURCH
## Van Alstyne – 1846 (1841–42)

The predecessor of First Christian Church of Van Alstyne, the first Disciples of Christ congregation in Texas, was founded during the winter of 1841–42 at McKinney's Landing in Bowie County near the Texas-Arkansas border. Collin McKinney, pioneer settler and signer of the Texas Declaration of Independence, was the leader of the Bowie County congregation which had worshiped informally since 1831. Between 1844 and 1846, the group moved to Liberty (later called Mantua), three miles southwest of Van Alstyne. In 1846, under McKinney and J. B. Wilmeth, the congregation was reorganized as the Liberty Church, with eighteen members.

In 1854 the First Mantua Christian Church was built. In this early structure, a rail in the center aisle separated men from women. No offering plate was passed, as donations were placed on the communion table. Members con-

*FIRST CHRISTIAN CHURCH, Van Alstyne.*

64

structed their own hymn books, which doubled as souvenir and recipe books. Founders of churches in many cities including Galveston, Sherman, and Glen Rose were members of Mantua Church.

In 1887 the Mantua group organized in the new town of Van Alstyne. The Mantua and Van Alstyne churches joined memberships in 1891.

A question has arisen about this church's longevity as compared with the First Christian Church at Lancaster, organized July 5, 1846. However, Van Alsyne has a definite unbroken lineage to Old Liberty and Hichman's Prairie at McKinney's Landing. Lancaster moved fewer miles from its beginning place, but its predecessor congregation did not begin as early as the winter of 1841–42.

One cannot recall the beginning of Van Alstyne's First Christian Church without recalling the life of a very interesting man, Collin McKinney, for whom both the county and county seat are named. Ministers for the church have included William McKinney, C. M. Wilmeth, A Cartwright, J. H. O. Polly, R. C. Horn, and B. F. Hall. Minister in 1980 was Hugh W. Moody.

Sources:
1. Texas State Historical Marker.
2. Dr. Carter E. Boren, *Religion on the Texas Frontier.*
3. *Handbook of Texas,* Vol. I.


# FIRST CHRISTIAN CHURCH
Lancaster – 1846

On Sunday, July 5, 1846, the First Christian Church of Lancaster had its beginning. At Ten Mile Creek, below the present site of Lancaster and near the home of Roderick A. Rawlins, eleven men and three women organized the church. As a group separate from the Cold Springs congregation, the Lancaster church was begun prior to 1870.

The charter members, most of them relatives of Rawlins, were Roderick Rawlins, Millie (Parks) Rawlins, who was second wife of Roderick Rawlins and half sister of Curtis

Parks, William Rawlins, Jr., William Rawlins, Sr., who was a nephew of Roderick Rawlins, H. M. Rawlins, J. M. Rawlins, Lucinda Keller, Malinda Rawlins, Zebedee Heath, who later married Nancy A. Rawlins, Joseph P. Rose, W. H. Newton, Peter Hall, and A. Bledsoe.

Roderick Rawlins, William Rawlins, Sr., and John M. Rawlins were all ministers of the gospel. All three, according to tradition, had been influenced and baptized by Barton W. Stone.

The church had no known formal records prior to 1880, but consultations, letters, newspapers, magazines, and church publications offer much information about this period.

Brother E. Elgin preached often for the Lancaster church since his home was there. As late as 1879, the congregation was still without a church building, as F. R. Burnett stated that he preached to the group in the "Methodist house."

In the 1880s, the church experienced growth under the leadership of W. B. Carnes. The congregation built a new house of worship in 1888. Wiley B. Anderson conducted a Sunday school, and Carnes reported that members of the congregation "were not dividing over the organ or other innovations." But before the much-loved Carnes finished his tenure in Lancaster, a trend began that was to divide the North Central Texas "captives of the word" in years to come.

Brother Rosecrans, from the Central Christian Church in Dallas, which had been organized in 1863, held a Sunday School Institute at Lancaster. Rosecrans advocated both the Missionary Society and instrumental music in worship. Rosecrans had assistance with advancing some innovations, as his views were later shared by W. H. Wright, a former minister of Dallas' oldest Church of Christ, which was located at Pearl and Bryan streets and which dated its organization to 1855.

In the fall of 1893, Sister Cole at the Lancaster church asked the women of Central Christian Church in Dallas to assist in forming a society. In 1898, Randolph Clark estab-

lished Randolph College in Lancaster and was influential in helping the local Christian Church.

Some distinguished ministers to serve the church in Lancaster include the following: Reverends Trimble and Henry Panghorn, Wiley B. Carnes (first resident minister in 1888–92), J. B. Cole, Randolph Clark, Addison Clark, W. B. Parks, John O'Keefe, B. B. Sanders, and Dr. L. N. D. Wells, who conducted a union meeting.

On October 2, 1960, the church dedicated a new building on spacious acreage on the West Belt Line Road.

The First Christian Church of Lancaster is considered by many as the second oldest Disciples church in Texas — second only to Van Alystyne Christian Church, which dates to McKinney's Landing in Bowie County in 1841–42.

Sources:
1. Carter E. Boren, *Religion on the Texas Frontier.*
2. *Handbook of Texas*, Vol. II.

## CENTRAL CHRISTIAN CHURCH
Austin – 1847

Beginning in 1847, Central Christian Church of Austin grew slowly for several decades. The congregation, after the Civil War, was meeting in a log house on Congress Avenue between Fourth and Fifth streets. In 1867 a frame building was erected at Eighth and Calhoun streets and was used as a meeting place for the next five years. A two-story house with a basement for a Sunday school replaced the other building in 1872 as church membership increased.

A stone building that was later erected on Eighth and Calhoun was sold to the Eastern Orthodox Church, St. Elias, which used the stone in the old building to erect a new structure on Eleventh Street.

Elder W. H. D. Carrington preached each Sunday morning to approximately one hundred worshipers. During Carrington's later ministry in the 1870s, the congregation divided into two "imbittered factions." Carrington rebuked the two groups as having about as much love for the other as "the Jews had for the Samaritans in older times." Within a short time, church attendance declined to a very small number.

In 1879, W. E. Hall, a very capable and personable minister, began a five-year ministry. He constrained the people to live good, righteous lives — to refrain from drinking, gambling, dancing, and theater attendance. His evening sermons had much appeal for the young people. Youth from other Austin churches were attracted to his popular and eloquently delivered sermons.

Although the minister was relatively progressive, he did remove a "divisive organ" from the church which had been placed in the Sunday school while he was on vacation in 1882. Minister Hall did attend "Cinderella," a fund-raising social, for which he received criticism from some of the older, more conservative members of the church.

A few members had complained that Hall's $2,500 yearly salary was excessive. Addison Clark, while conducting a twelve-day meeting in July 1883, was unable to reconcile Hall and dissatisfied members of the congregation, after which Hall left the Austin ministry.

Although membership declined during the next two or three years, a significant event took place in this church as delegates from across the state met and formed the Texas Christian Missionary Society. The formation of this society and introduction of the organ into church worship caused the separation of the church into two groups. One of the older women who objected to worshiping with instrumental music remarked: "Now that you have the organ, where are you going to get a monkey to dance to the music?" The group which withdrew eventually became the University Avenue Church of Christ; the old church became Central Christian Church.

In 1929 Central Christian Church erected a new building on Guadalupe Street. The building, an example of fourth-century Italian architecture, was designed by Robert Leon White, chairman of the Department of Architecture at the University of Texas and also a member of the church.

Central Christian Church in 1980 was one of about sixty churches which comprised the Bluebonnet Area of the Disciples of Christ, with headquarters in San Antonio. The euphonious name was given to the area by almost unanimous vote. The dissenting vote was cast, according to the executive director of Inman Christian Center in San Antonio, Daniel H. Sauceda, when his young son suggested the title "Yellow Rose." The Texas Bible Chair at the University of Texas is supported by the Bluebonnet Area of Churches. Central Christian Church has had much interest in the

*CENTRAL CHRISTIAN CHURCH, Austin.*

69

chair, which was begun by a remarkable scholar, Dr. Frank Jewett.

Among the church's pastors since the turn of the century were Doctors Lowber, Kerns, Garrison and E. M. Sadler, who became president of Texas Christian University. Dr. John Barclay served the church masterfully for twenty-eight years, beginning in 1941. He was followed by Mark Randall and Dr. James L. Stoner. In 1980 the congregation was being served by an interim pastor, Dr. Edward L. Kirtley.

The church in 1980 had a membership of about 600. Earlier, before the University Christian Church was begun, the church had as many as 1,200 members.

The church in 1980 was served by the following leaders: Elders Douglas Barkley, William P. Boyd, Oscar Cullen, J. Loyd Detlefs, Noble Doss, Abe E. Geiman, Emmett Harris, W. K. Jennings, Jr., Ben McDonald, C. J. Menn, Burt Montgomery, Harold Page, Leslie Phares, Dr. Emmette Redford, Robert Rheiner, John Sullivan, Burnell Waldrep, and Gen. Frank Wood; Deacons Jim Anderson, W. C. Aten, Jimmy Gaines, Lamar Gordon, Bill Heard, Floyd Herring, J. C. Reese, Brian White, Geoffrey L. Stoner, James D. Stoner, Albert Wilson, John Rice, Judson Wise, Ken Allen, George C. Holland, J. W. Johnson, Taylor Gaines, Vance Naumann, James Swearingen, John Doyle, Howard Bounds, M. E. Bounds, Thomas White, and Walter White; Deaconesses Blanche McClanahan, Mary Beth Page, Mary Lee Philippi, Louise Wood, Casey Allen, Georgia Turner, Betty Alexander, Lucille Pribble, Pansy Wilson, Cherry Waldrep, Margaret Hayes, Laverne Phares, Inez Gaines, Norma Naumann, JoAnn Gray, Sharon McGraw, Joyce White, Dora Thompson, Helen Penick, Pearl Acres, Sharon Anderson, Betty Doyle, Mattie Mae Cullen, Nancy Gaines, Mayme Harris, Nadene Noren, Mable Reed, Ruhama Reese, Beth Roberson, Wanda Rich, Gertrude Clark, Opal Cullen, Helen Geiman, Nell Littrell, and Martha Lockhart.

Deaconesses Emerita include Mrs. C. A. Armacost, Mrs. J. O. Baggett, Mrs. Bryant Collins, Mrs. P. G. Crum, Mrs. Charles Koch, Mrs. G. H. Lewis, Mrs. A. H. Neighbors,

*TEXAS BIBLE CHAIR – University Christian Church, Austin.*

Mrs. Jessie Nunnelle, Mrs. J. Lee Stambaugh, Mrs. J. B. Swearingen, Mrs. T. M. Trimble, Mrs. E. H. Weber, and Mrs. Lee Wilcoxon.

Sources:
1. *Central Christian Church* (Golden Jubilee Edition, 1979).
2. Carter E. Boren, *Religion on the Texas Frontier.*
3. Stephen D. Eckstein, Jr., *History of the Churches of Christ in Texas.*
4. Conference with William P. Boyd.

## FIRST CHRISTIAN CHURCH
### Palo Pinto – 1857

Like many of the state's churches, both great and small, Palo Pinto's First Christian Church began rather informally in a home.

Dr. Stephen Slade Taylor, in whose home the congregation was organized, was the first preacher, and his wife, Eleanor, was the song leader. The early settlers, as organizing members, were Johnny Lynn, James A. Jiwell, D. B.

71

Cleveland (the first county clerk of Palo Pinto County), I. W. Price (the first county tax assessor and collector), George and Cal Hazelwood, and C. W. Massie. Other pioneer members to join the religious group were William Veale, George Bevers, C. C. Corbin, J. C. Son, and David Barton Warren.

In 1882 the first regular church house was built; in 1980, this original building was still serving the congregation as it had for the past ninety-eight years. Although the building has been repaired and remodeled, it still contains the original marble-top communion table, the pulpit, and the pastor's chair.

The old church building was once used also by the Presbyterians. The noted Baptist preacher, rancher, and Indian fighter, G. W. Slaughter, preached to the Baptists in this building.

Addison and Randolph Clark, co-founders of Add-Ran College, Lee Clark, and Granville Jones are noted ministers who preached for this congregation. In its long history, the church has had only one resident minister other than Dr.

*FIRST CHRISTIAN CHURCH, Palo Pinto.*

Taylor. Baxter Golightly served the church as local minister in 1903–04.

In the same way that nearby Graford Church of Christ received young ministers and professors from Abilene, Palo Pinto received supply ministers from Texas Christian University in Fort Worth. Coming from Fort Worth have been Homer T. Wilson, John W. Marshall, S. A. Thomas, R. A. Highsmith, Dr. Clinton Lockhart, and Doctors McKissick, Cockrell, Lord and S. W. Hutton. Dick Wells has commuted from Mineral Wells to serve the church as a part-time minister.

In its early years, the church had annual fish frys and ice cream socials at a favorite campsite at the "Maddox Hole" on Eagle Creek, a few miles north of Palo Pinto. People converged on the campsite, riding horses or in wagons and buggies for the full day of fishing, cooking, eating, and sharing.

Six generations of Dr. Taylor's family have attended the Palo Pinto Church, and the same is true of the I. W. Price family. Descendants of the Cleveland and Bevers families are members, as were their freedom-loving and truth-seeking pioneer forebears.

Source:
1. *History of Palo Pinto County.*


## BASTROP CHRISTIAN CHURCH
### Bastrop – 1857

The Bastrop Christian Church was established sometime prior to 1877, with the first services being held in the courthouse. A small rock church building on the same location of the church in 1980 first served the congregation.

H. K. McDonald, on September 25, 1867, purchased the site for the church and delivered the deed to James H. Wilkins, A. A. Erhard, and J. M. Beavers, elders of the Bastrop Christian Church. In 1895 the building was constructed by John White. It is of New England Victorian architectural style with stained-glass windows and a very tall

73

*BASTROP CHRISTIAN CHURCH, Bastrop.*

spire, which has been a Bastrop landmark for many years. When the church building was completed in 1895, the dedicatory address was given by B. B. Sanders, the pastor, and Homer T. Wilson.

The three trustees who signed a new charter in 1895 were A. A. Erhard, A. C. Erhard, and T. W. Caine, owner and publisher of the Bastrop advertiser for many years. Among the charter members were Dr. and Mrs. Caton Erhard, Mr. and Mrs. Adolph A. Erhard, Mrs. Dalia Grimes Kennedy, Mrs. Jones Trigg, Mrs. Lula Hood, and Mr. and Mrs. N. A. Morris.

The bell in the new church building was taken from the earlier rock structure, but had first served a steamboat that had plied the Colorado River.

In 1970 Bastrop Christian Church gave a lasting memo-

74

rial to the city of Bastrop's hospital by sponsoring the "Roberta Terry Memorial Chapel" as a part of the hospital.

For some periods of time, the Bastrop Christian Church was inactive, but the congregation has been continuous and the building has served the needs of Lutherans and Baptists (two groups) as they were in process of building their structures.

Herman Holt helped revitalize the congregation in 1978. At that time the church purchased property north of the church building. The congregation has since been led by Deacons Cecil Long, president of Bastrop's First National Bank, Claude Sharp, Jerry Woehl, and David Smith.

The pastor in 1980, Robert K. Long, was a direct descendant, through his mother's side of the family, of the Thorps on whose land Add-Ran College was established as a forerunner, to some extent, of both Texas Christian University and Abilene Christian University.

Sources:
1. Texas State Historical Marker.
2. *The Bastrop Christian Church Building.*
3. Conferences with Cecil Long and Mrs. Effie Sharp.
4. Telephone conversation with Mrs. Cecil Long (descendant of the Thorps of Thorp Spring College).


## FIRST CHRISTIAN CHURCH
Bonham – 1868

The Disciples of Christ, or Christian Church, was one of the first religious groups to organize in Fannin County. Its early history is very much the history of one remarkable man.

On May 31, 1868, Elder Charles Carlton, a graduate of Bethany College (of which the distinguished Alexander Campbell was founder and president), together with twenty-seven charter members organized First Christian Church of Bonham. Carlton was born in England and as a young man spent many hours on the high seas, where he devoted much time to reading and independent study.

*FIRST CHRISTIAN CHURCH of Bonham.*

Carlton went to Bonham in 1867 to serve as head of Bonham Female College, which was sponsored by the Masonic Lodge and supported by the citizens of Bonham. Although chiefly the administrator for the college for thirty-five years, Carlton served as minister for the Bonham church he had organized. For his service to the church he received no regular salary. Carlton continued preaching until his death in 1902.

The first frame building was erected in 1878; in 1912, the church's present classical revival structure was built. Charles M. Schoonover was minister at its dedication.

Sources:
1. Carter E. Boren, *Religion on the Texas Frontier.*
2. Juanita C. Spencer, *Bonham and the Town of Bailey Inglish.*

76

# FIRST CHRISTIAN CHURCH
## Taylor – 1877

In June 1876 a townsite called Taylorsville was laid out when the I.G.N. Railroad extended its westernmost terminal to Round Rock. The next year, in April of 1877, John Allen Gano, Jr., organized a Union Sunday school. The Sunday school was conducted in a small, box-like schoolhouse located on the corner of Sixth and Vance streets.

In December of 1877, Gen. Richard M. Gano of Dallas, brother of John Allen Gano, Jr., was invited to preach for a gospel meeting in Taylor. The meeting, conducted in the Odd Fellows Hall located at Main and Fifth streets, was a great success as General Gano was a remarkable scholar and speaker.

These two Gano brothers were the sons of John Allen Gano, Sr., a noted gospel preacher in Kentucky, who had been closely associated with Barton W. Stone and Alexander Campbell. The senior Gano was the grandson of John Gano, the Baptist preacher and colonial chaplain who baptized George Washington in 1783. General Gano organized

*FIRST CHRISTIAN CHURCH, Taylor.*

77

the second oldest Church of Christ in Dallas (still in continuous existence in 1980). Howard Hughes, the famous billionaire recluse, was a great-grandson of John Allen Gano, Sr.

The First Christian Church of Taylor was organized on December 9, 1877, with twenty-two members. As Brother Gano's meeting closed, there were forty-two members on the roll. Elders elected were Judge G. R. Scott and G. W. Hamilton; deacons were C. P. Vance, James Hamilton, J. A. Gano, and C. Mendel.

For $1,003, the congregation built its first meeting place — a plain frame building. A. P. Aten, the first regular minister for the church in 1879, was followed the next year by J. A. Abney. Among the early ministers were E. B. Challenner, John Ferguson, and J. B. Sweeney (1877–86), during whose eventful pastorate the Young People's Society of Christian Endeavor was organized with A. J. McCarty as president. It was also during Rev. Sweeney's tenure that the new church building was erected and dedicated by F. M. Raines.

In nearby Circleville, a Christian Church assembled in a schoolhouse. John Allen Gano, Jr., spoke to the Circleville congregation on August 16, 1891, and Addison Clark of Add-Ran College began a protracted meeting on the San Gabriel River on August 20, 1892.

Among the names of early members of the Taylor church were Bullock, Vance, Simons, Dr. Brown, Mrs. Lillian Gray, Mendel, Challenner, McCarty, Glendenning, Barton, Noble, Scruggs, Dozier, Tally, Bland, Marse, Miss Law and Mr. Buck Wills, Nunn, Dabney, Stearns, Bush, Council, Tarkington, Easley, Turner, Mrs. Mae Ake, Pendleton, Howard Dodd, the Minor Browns, and Dr. Bledsoe and family.

Ministers of later years were George L. Bush, Walter P. Jennings, S. D. Perkinson, J. H. Hughes, W. H. Bagby, Philip Fall King, Presley F. Herndon, John F. Bradbury (a student of the illustrious scholar Dr. J. W. McGarvey), W. O. Dallas, T. J. Ogle, C. C. Klingman (a brilliant man and former Church of Christ minister), and A. G. Abbott. It was during

Abbott's tenure that Texas Governor W. Lee O'Daniel, a member of the Christian Church, visited the Taylor congregation. Abbott's salary was considered quite adequate for this time as it was $140 per month plus parsonage. (The Texas governor's annual salary was then about $6,000.)

Charles Ferguson was selected as the new minister in 1941. Frederick Ross began his ministry in Taylor in 1943 and served in the National Guard as chaplain. Fred Ross, who was minister at the close of World War II, was succeeded by Bruce Banks. C. B. Irahood was a minister with outstanding musical ability who served the Taylor church.

During Irahood's ministry, some discord arose in the church which led to withdrawal of some members and organization of a second and "independent" Christian church in Taylor. Claude Pearce, the next pastor to serve the church, sought reconciliation between those who had recently become divided. Travis Pugh, a TCU graduate, came from Arkansas in 1955 and was succeeded by the following pastors: John Horber, Jerry Mallory, and Clyde D. Foltz.

Among the members of the Taylor church, other than those already listed, have been the Harkins, Campbells, J. Frank Smith, Dr. and Mrs. Eric Stromberg, Gillespies, Outlaws, Kogers, Coxes, Joneses, Hopkinses, Fred R. Parks, Johnsons, Hamblens, Browns, Brazils, Landrums, Codges, Dolsens, Haskins, Mae Pipkin, Brymers, and Harrises.

Sources:
1. Clara Jones, *History of First Christian Church, Taylor Texas.*
2. Carter E. Boren, *Religion on the Texas Frontier.*

EAST DALLAS CHRISTIAN CHURCH
Dallas – 1903

Growing out of the oldest Christian Church in Dallas, East Dallas Christian Church was actually begun by eight women of Central Christian Church. These women, very active in Central Church, wanted a congregation nearer to their homes.

First these women began a Sunday school and Ladies

79

*EAST DALLAS CHRISTIAN CHURCH, Dallas.*

Aid Society at the home of Mike H. Thomas, Sr. A Cottage Prayer Meeting group was later formed by the women at the Arthur A. Everts home.

It was not long before the men were encouraged by their wives to build a modest building, "a tabernacle," which cost about $300 for lumber, nails, and paint. The men completed the building in thirty days due to the fervent supervision of the women. It was Mrs. F. S. Roberts who suggested the name for the church, first located on the southeast corner of Peak and Victor streets.

At the opening of the Bible school session on November 15, 1903, more than one hundred people were present; of those, more than sixty-five individuals signed the book of charter members.

The Christian Women's Board of Missions was formed on January 11, 1904, and met on Mondays for worship and for study of worldwide missions. For the 1904 year, the group collected a total of $111.95 for missions. The women also started a circulating library of thirty-two books dealing with missionary work.

Very soon after organization, the church started Christian Endeavor Societies, a forerunner of Christian Youth Fellowship.

In 1907 the church moved to Junius and Peak streets and occupied a frame building which was supplanted by the church's first brick building in 1912. In this building, the membership increased from 300 in 1912 to 1,800 in 1922.

The cornerstone for a new sanctuary was laid on June 15, 1924, in order to supply the demands of a fast-growing congregation. The time capsule in the cornerstone contained the scripture ". . . that they all might be one . . . that the world may believe" (Jno. 17:21).

In April 1925 a new church with auditorium and five-story educational building was dedicated. It was not long before a faltering economy made it almost impossible for the church to meet its financial obligations. A floating debt of $90,000 was eased as members bought second-lien bonds in the amount of $50,000 and raised an additonal $40,000 in cash. As the days of the depression waned, the church during more affluent times made additions and renovations to the building as needed.

The following ministers have served the church: Reverends John A. Stevens, W. A. Fite, H. R. Ford, Cephas Shelburne, Dr. John Slayter, Dean Colby D. Hall, Dr. L. N. D. Wells, Dr. Thompson L. Shannon, Dr. W. A. Welch, Dr. Sloan Gentry, Dr. Beauford Norris, and Dr. James K. Hempstead.

Some other older Christian churches in the Dallas area in chronological order are:

First Christian Church, Lancaster — 1846
First Christian Church, Rockwall — 1850
Central Christian Church, Dallas — 1863
First Christian Church, Dallas — 1868
First Christian Church, Mesquite — 1870
First Christian Church, Richardson — 1873
First Christian Church, Garland — 1875

81

North of Dallas is the First Christian Church of Van Alstyne, regarded as the oldest Christian Church in Texas.

Sources:
1. "East Dallas Christian Church People Caring and Sharing for 75 Years," *Dallas Times Herald,* November 12, 1978.

# IV

## THE CHURCH OF CHRIST
## MOVEMENT IN TEXAS

European traditions were rapidly replaced by fresh philosophies of free and democratic men after the American Declaration of Independence was promulgated.

Throughout the latter part of the nineteenth century, the Churches of Christ, identified also as Disciples of Christ and Christian Churches, comprised the largest religious group in the United States indigenous to American soil.

Free-thinking men, bent on independence and individualism, were willing to abandon all ties with religion which had become divided and divisive. The Christian Association of Washington, Pennsylvania, brought together a group of men and women from different denominations who wanted to seek peace and unity by bringing all the people together in one church. They did not want to bind anything on one's faith and practice unless such was expressly taught by direct command or necessary inference.

Thomas and Alexander Campbell, Barton W. Stone, and Walter Scott were among the educated and capable leaders of the "Restoration Movement," as it was called. They sought the restored unity and purity of the church and a reasonable (not emotional) and practical religion as well as the enrichment of life. James A. Garfield, president of the United States, was a minister in this group.

As early as 1824, members of Churches of Christ began migrating to Texas from the eastern states. Collin McKinney, for whom Collin County and the county seat of

McKinney were named, was the first member of the Church of Christ to go to Texas, arriving September 15, 1824, near the place which came to be Texarkana. McKinney was a member of the committee which drafted the Texas Declaration of Independence and helped frame the Constitution prepared by that convention. McKinney, born in New Jersey in 1776, served under eight different governments during his lifetime.

The first Church of Christ was established in 1836 four miles from San Augustine. Antioch Church of Christ was organized in the home of Rhoddy Anthony by a medical doctor and former Baptist preacher, Dr. William P. Defee. An earlier congregation had been established by Mansil W. Matthews, a physician, teacher, and preacher. Matthews had led a group of adventurers from Alabama to the "promised land." On the first Sunday after their arrival on January 17, 1837, at Fort Clark (later Clarksville), a group of Alabamans, most of them members of the Church of Christ, met for worship. This church, unlike Antioch, organized later in the year, was not continuous. After the Civil War, Gen. R. M. Gano established Western Heights Church of Christ in Dallas and was very active as a minister. At one time he held a successful gospel meeting for First Christian Church in Taylor. During the war, the general, also a medical doctor, led his men into battle, bound up their wounds, and preached to them on Sundays.

When the Texas Missionary Society was organized in Austin in 1886, this, together with the introduction of instrumental music in the worship, led to the separation of the Church of Christ and the Christian Church. By 1906, the division into two distinct groups was completed.

Conservative elements in Add-Ran College took over the remnants of the college in 1910 and established Thorp Spring Christian College. (The liberal elements of Add-Ran College had moved to Waco and then to Fort Worth, establishing Texas Christian University.) Later, Thorp Spring College was moved to Cleburne and then to Terrell, where Churches of Christ operated as late as 1980 a college for African-Americans.

84

Churches of Christ operated many colleges during the early years of Texas. Two major colleges to continue with much success have been Abilene Christian University and Lubbock Christian College. Several orphans' homes have been operated by the churches, the most successful of which have been Boles Orphans' Home, Sunny Glen Home, Medina Valley Home, and Lubbock Children's Home.

*The Firm Foundation,* a weekly journal, was begun in 1884 by Austin McGary. McGary was succeeded by G. H. P. Showalter as editor-publisher. Showalter was succeeded by Reuel Lemmons, who was still editor of the journal in 1980. In 1949 Churches of Christ in Texas listed 1,036 ministers (sixty-two black and ten Mexican-American) for 1,884 congregations.

Extensive missionary work is supported by Texas churches in Germany, Italy, South America, and throughout the world.

Sources:
1. *Handbook of Texas,* Vol. I.
2. Dr. Carter E. Boren, *Religion on the Texas Frontier.*
3. Dr. Stephen D. Eckstein, Jr., *History of Churches of Christ in Texas.*

## ANTIOCH CHURCH OF CHRIST
### San Augustine – 1836

The Church of Christ at Antioch was organized in 1836 in the home of Rhoddy Anthony about four miles north of San Augustine. The name "Antioch" was used because "the disciples were first called Christians at Antioch" (Acts 11:26). Anthony was selected as an elder and served in this capacity about fifty years.

The minister who organized the church was a distinguished and capable man, Dr. William Defee. Although Defee was a medical doctor, he never neglected his preaching whenever and wherever an opportunity arose.

Dr. Defee lived on the Milani-San Augustine road

twelve miles from "Milani" and seven miles from San Augustine.

On July 18, 1847, Dr. Defee immersed eighty people into the Christian Church, or Church of Christ, in Shelby County and welcomed two Baptist ministers in Sabine County, Peter Eldridge and G. W. Slaughter, into the Reformation or Restoration movement. The constitution of the church in Shelby County, like the Church of Christ in Antioch, stated that, "All agree to take the Bible as the only infallible rule of faith and practice."

There is good evidence that the Antioch Church of Christ actually began in 1833. In Barton W. Stone's *Christian Messenger* of 1833 (Vol. III: 281 f.) Dr. W. P. Defee wrote from the region of Sabine, San Augustine and Shelby counties, "I have started a society on the Christian Doctrine."

The Antioch Church of Christ met in a log building on Rhoddy Antony's property until about 1870, when a new structure was erected. This building served the congregation for the next seventy-five years.

Dr. J. W. O'Banion, a former assistant superintendent of Dallas schools, was born in the Antioch community in 1875. He remembered the aged Anthony as a small, stooped man with snow-white hair and a long beard. Anthony would come to the building each Sunday with a basket containing the communion ware on one arm and Mrs. Anthony on the other. After arranging the communion table properly, Anthony would then sit down in his pew and await the beginning of the service.

The old log church at Antioch, which served also as a schoolhouse, was made available to other church groups as needed by them — Methodists, Baptists, Presbyterians, and others.

The site of the Antioch Church was a Spanish land grant deeded to the church by Stephen Passmoore. Land was also provided for a cemetery in which nine Confederate soldiers and almost all early members of Antioch Church were buried. First graves in the cemetery were marked by a cedar tree at the head of each grave. When the church in use

ANTIOCH CHURCH OF CHRIST, near San Augustine.

in 1980 was erected in 1938, cedar from the trees was used in the construction.

Among the early preachers for the Antioch Church were the following: Dr. William Defee, William Eaves, Brother Floyd, Nimrod Ware, B. M. Doggett, J. W. Strode, Dan Leak, Brother Bonnam, Brother Maskisik, B. F. Southers, Counsil Billingsley, John F. Brill, A. D. King, and P. F. Sullivan. Two of these ministers, Dan Leak and Brother Bonnam, were professors at Patroon College.

Mrs. Exa Clark, historian for Antioch Church and the large Church of Christ in San Augustine, is related to three of Antioch's past ministers — A. D. King, her grandfather; B. M. Doggett, her father; and J. W. Strode, an uncle.

The Antioch Church is and has been from its early beginning an active and community-serving church. Membership in 1980 was sixty-five and its peak enrollment in past years was about 125.

Sources:
    1. Dr. Carter E. Boren, *Religion on the Texas Frontier.*
    2. Dr. Stephen Eckstein, Jr., *History of the Churches of Christ in Texas.*
    3. Correspondence and conference with Mrs. Exa Clark.

# CHURCH OF CHRIST
## Gober – 1840

First known as Angel Chapel on Bear Creek, the church began meeting in a log schoolhouse south of the present city of Bonham. The school was known as Jackson School. O. I. Jackson and eight members constituted the congregation.

Located in the Red River Valley, this early church held services mainly for relatives of the Jackson family, who had come to the valley from Kansas City, Missouri. Other disciples who had been meeting at Moore's Chapel, sometimes called Harrison schoolhouse, merged with the Jacksons and others. Later they agreed to meet two Sundays each month at Jackson School and two Sundays at Bois d'Arc schoolhouse.

Elders in the early church were D. B. Austin, R. F. Henderson, and O. I. Jackson. Deacons were L. Grant and Levi Tittsworth.

In 1877 the old congregation held a meeting at Bethany near the Biggerstaff Cemetery. With the same elders and deacons, this group at Bethany went to Gober, to which

*GOBER CHURCH OF CHRIST, Gober.*

place the old Jackson school group had gone in 1855, with the founding of the town of Gober.

There is some interesting historical significance for this area of Texas: While Sam Rayburn from Bonham was Speaker of the United States House of Representatives, James Thurman of Gober was Speaker of the Texas House. Their homes were slightly more than ten miles apart. Some of Thurman's relatives were members of the Gober church.

Ministers have been R. C. Lee, Sam Swearingen, John Dodd, Jack King, R. G. Cook, Elmer Ray, J. F. Brashear (the church's first full-time minister), Grady Langford, Norman Doan, Carl McGovern, Pete Stone, Ray Foster, Dan Spears, and Connie Hollis. The minister in 1980 was Ron Henson from Denison. One church member, Mrs. Euell Deary (whose husband Emmett was an elder prior to his death), is a great-granddaughter of O. I. Jackson. Hulen Jackson, minister of the Duncanville Church of Christ, is a direct descendant.

Sources:
1. Dr. Stephen D. Eckstein, Jr., *History of the Churches of Christ in Texas.*
2. Conference with Una Broils, Mrs. Euell Deary, Elder Tom Green, and Sister Woodson.

## COLD SPRINGS CHURCH OF CHRIST
### Lancaster—1846

The oldest continuous congregation in Dallas County is Cold Springs Church of Christ. It had its beginning on December 22, 1846.

John Rawlins had come to Texas from Indiana during the prior year. Soon after his arrival, he was joined by his father, William Rawlins, and the rest of the family at Ten Mile Creek near Lancaster. The church first met at the Roderick Rawlins farm and also on the M. M. Miller farm in Lancaster.

Soon after the church began meeting, Anthony Bledsoe came from Kentucky with the assignment of surveying and

89

laying out the town of Lancaster. Bledsoe and his wife, a piano teacher, were members of the Cold Springs Church.

Mrs. Bledsoe had offered the church the use of her piano in order to enhance, in her opinion, the quality of music for the assembly. The members rejected the offer. However, one day when the members assembled in their church house, the piano was in one corner of the building hidden beneath a black cloth. (This event reverses the occasion in Houston's First Baptist Church, when some of its members made the organ disappear from the church. It was found later beneath the waters of Buffalo Bayou.) In 1847, when the piano was brought into the church, those who strongly opposed its presence walked out, led by John Rawlins, William Fleming, the Bandys, and the Heaths. Cold Springs Church was the first, but not the last, to divide over the matter of using instrumental music in worship.

After the division of the small group, those opposed to the innovation met at the John Rawlins home for several months until they could build on a site donated by Rawlins on Ten Mile Creek. Later, this group began attending the Pleasant Run Church. William Rawlins reported that Brother McVey preached for a meeting in which there were fifteen additions, ten of which were by immersion. By September of 1848, the church had gained twenty-six additions.

The first elders for this group were John Rawlins, Henry Atterberry, Charles Barnard, and William Fleming. The Pleasant Run group, who had first comprised the Cold Springs Church, continued its growth through the 1850s. William Rawlins and Jesse L. Thorpe, who moved from Iowa for his wife's health, were good promoters for the church, seeking the aid of such evangelists as Brother L. J. Sweet, who held meetings in 1854 and 1855 at the "quite large church." There were thirty additions during the 1854 meeting.

In the early 1870s the building burned and was rebuilt on the same site where the Cold Springs Church was still meeting in 1980. The 1870 building featured seats made of logs hewn by Henry Clay Rawlins.

Meetings were very successful and the church grew as

90

*COLD SPRINGS CHURCH OF CHRIST, Lancaster.*

C. L. Cole and C. Floyd preached at "Rawlins Schoolhouse" in 1886. John T. Poe, writer for *The Firm Foundation,* N. O. H. Polley, and G. I. Grasy preached at Cold Springs as one of their regular circuits. Grasy was of much influence at Ten Mile during his four years of evangelistic work, which terminated with a meeting in 1895 when he baptized twenty-one "confessing, repenting believers."

Cold Springs Church survived and flourished with stalwart men of the faith leading the way — such men as S. C. Fleming, Charles Barnard, H. C. Rawlins, J. T. Cheshier, G. C. Rawlins, J. A. Neal, G. B. Nash, and G. W. Reeves. In 1980, it was a large, strong, and uncompromising group of disciples.

Both the Cold Springs Church of Christ and the First Christian Church in Lancaster claim their foundation date from the same group of disciples — same charter members, elders, preachers. Before division over use of instrumental music in worship, church organization for missions and

91

other innovations, the names Christian Church and Church of Christ were interchangeable.

The Clarks who were the founders of Add-Ran College at Thorp Spring, forerunner of Texas Christian University, and their associates later also influenced the beginning of Abilene Christian University. Don Morris, longtime president of Abilene Christian College and a descendant of Zebedee Heath and relative of the Rawlins family, was reared at nearby DeSoto. The people who motivated the growth and development of both TCU and ACU were descendants of people who had been baptized by Barton W. Stone, an associate and fellow laborer with Alexander Campbell.

Sources:
1. Dr. Stephen D. Eckstein, Jr., *History of Churches of Christ.*
2. Dr. Carter E. Boren, *Religion on the Texas Frontier.*
3. Steve Ridgell, "History of Churches of Christ" (master's thesis, Abilene Christian University).
4. Ellen Bain, *History of Lancaster* (Lancaster Historical Society).
5. Conference with Ellen Bain of Town Square Realty of Lancaster.

## CHURCH OF CHRIST
### Graford — Ca. 1850

By 1900, the Graford Church of Christ had become one of the strongest Churches of Christ between Fort Worth and Abilene. Although the first regular church building was not erected until 1908, the congregation had met and prospered in homes of the members, in camp meetings, and under brush arbors. The land for the building was deeded to the elders for one dollar by the townsite committee.

In this beautiful country of rolling hills and almost mountainous terrain, there were many deer and buffalo on the grassy plains and in the valleys. The Brazos River and its tributaries always contained a good supply of fish for the pioneers. Most of the members of the Graford Church were farmers and ranchers.

In West Texas from 1850 until 1900, when pioneers

*GRAFORD CHURCH OF CHRIST, Graford.*

were moving west, religious ferver was in good supply as Methodists, Baptists, and members of the Church of Christ sought to establish themselves in the new frontier. This was a time of religious debate. People wanted their creeds to be supported by the teachings of the Bible. Determining what those teachings were was not always easy, and emotions were not always restrained as verbal combatants took to the debate platform.

Scholars from the eastern states who presented long and well-documented discourse in Graford included such men as Batsell Baxter, C. R. Nichols, Joe Warlick, Horace Busby, Jesse Sewell, A. R. Holton, and J. K. Bentley.

First elders, as recalled by older members, were N. J. McConnell, Jess Rogle, E. H. Walker, D. H. Ward, Johnny Walker, and Ira Scudder.

In earlier years, some migrating occurred between the Christian Churches and Churches of Christ. During a revival led by John M. Rice, the Johnson, Luce, and McClure families changed their membership from the Christian Church to the Graford Church of Christ.

The Graford Church was much older than Abilene Christian University, but when the Abilene school was established many of the ministerial students used this church as

93

their "proving ground." Preachers, other than those mentioned, to serve the church were Foy Wallace, Jr., Trine Starnes, Logan Buchanan, Luther Blackmon, J. C. Malone, Orville Filbeck, Jack Scott, Harold Vanderpool, Bill Jones, and George Bryant. A *cappella* singing has been led by capable song leaders Clemon Blackwell, Choice Bryant, Johnny Walker, Gene Martin, Ira Scudder, Sheridan Ragle, John D. Garland, and J. C. and Joey Shewmake.

In September 1950, Loyd Frederick became the first local, full-time minister. By the close of 1977, a large, new church house was completed west of Graford on Highway 254 to serve the old and still-growing church. The building and finance committee included John David Garland, Wiley D. Green, Bobby McAvoy, and Thomas Eubank.

Sources:
1. *History of Palo Pinto County.*
2. Grace Mann.


## UNIVERSITY AVENUE CHURCH OF CHRIST
### Austin – 1853

The Church of Christ began in Austin in 1853, when twenty-two members met for worship in the members' homes. This small group has had a continuous history and now assembles at University Avenue and MLK, Jr. Blvd. as University Avenue Church of Christ.

The Central Christian Church in Austin stated in its centennial memorial publication that after the Civil War, the Church of Christ built a log house in which to worship on Congress Avenue at East 4th Street. The church acquired a lot for a new home at 8th and Colorado streets in 1867. In 1894 the congregation was given a lot by Mrs. Hansbrough at 14th and San Bernard streets in East Austin, on which was built a frame house of worship. This served as a place for worship for about twenty-one years. Some of the members who attended church at this location were still members in 1980 and attending University Avenue Church. These members were Preston Showalter, Mrs. E. S. Blackburn, O. P. Schoolfield, Mrs. W. A. Holland, and Mrs. Edna Wallace.

In 1915 church members decided that it would be ideal to locate near the University of Texas, where many young members from across Texas were pursuing undergraduate and graduate studies. This location would also be near the state capital, where people visited when they came to Austin for business or pleasure. The beautiful new structure was erected between the state capitol building and the university campus, and on Sunday, September 25, 1949, the first service was held in the new facility.

Early elders to serve the church were E. Hansbrough and J. W. Jackson. These men were followed by E. L. SoRelle, M. B. King, and G. J. Steck (of the Steck-Vaughn Publishers family). Deacons were O. E. Nitschke, Bent Harris, J. W. Richardson, J. M. Hall, F. Hueber, G. J. Gatlin, G. H. P. Showalter, J. B. Rhodes, Carlos D. Speck, C. O. Rice, Dr. Russel A. Lewis (former superintendent of Austin public schools), and Fred D. Pinkston.

Among the early evangelists were A. J. McCarty, C. E. Holt. J. W. Jackson, Austin McGary, E. Hansbrough, E. L. SoRelle, Price Billingsley, and Foy Wallace, Sr. Local ministers have included G. H. P. Showalter, N. O. Ray, A. Ellmore, Foy Wallace, Sr., G. C. Brewer, Charles Heber Roberson, W. D. Bills, T. H. Etheridge, R. B. Sweet, F. L. Cox, Basil Shilling, J. D. Moss, John B. White, Eldridge B. Linn, Cecil Hill, Harrison Matthews, Dick Daughtry, and Larry Henninger, the minister in 1980.

Elders serving the church in 1980 were Ernest Cabe (longtime director of personnel for Austin public schools), Clayson Fuller, A. L. Horstman, Jake Isaac, Don Langford, Luke Robinson, and W. A. Sloan (a high school principal in Austin and navy reserve captain). Prior elders have been George Carlson, Otis Garner, Oliver Jackson (Olympic coach), O. P. Schoolfield, John Reynolds (executive vice-president of Nash-Phillips-Copus), and Roy Thomas.

Deacons included Jim Heath, Luke Robinson, Billy Ramsey, Urban Awbrey, Robert Upchurch, Robert Lewis, Warren Willhoite, Dr. Rodney Lloyd, Don Baker, Jerry

*UNIVERSITY AVENUE CHURCH OF CHRIST, Austin.*

Norwood, Dan Tillman, Norman Horn, G. E. Schmitt, A. E. Worley, Mike Boligia, Virgil Bernard, Johnny Buck, Henry Ramsey, Dr. Jack Turman, John White, and Dr. William Shive (one of the nation's foremost chemists).

University Church of Christ maintains a Bible Chair. From its beginning, it has had well-educated and outstanding scholars. The first Bible Chair director was Charles Heber Roberson. The church also maintains an Institute for Biblical Studies, which is staffed with young members who hold the highest graduate degrees, as well as a Student Ministry and a Christian Services Center.

Sources:
1. *Directory, University Avenue Church of Christ.*
2. *History of the University Avenue Church of Christ.*
3. Conference with Mrs. Luke Robinson, Jr. (assisting Frieda Cummings, secretary).

# GARLAND ROAD CHURCH OF CHRIST
## Dallas – 1855

The Garland Road Church is the oldest church of Christ in Dallas with a continuous existence. In 1855 the original group began meeting in the courthouse and Masonic Lodge (in the same room of the old Masonic building where sixteen years later the First Baptist Church of Dallas was organized). In 1861 a small building was erected on Carondelet Street (later known as Ross Avenue) when Dallas had a population of 3,000.

In 1881 the congregation moved to the corner of Pearl and Bryan streets. A second and larger church building was erected in 1902. Twenty-one years later, another, and larger, building was erected on this same location.

In 1955, when the church began meeting at Garland Road, there were 200 members. Twenty-four years later, the congregation had increased to 2,000. In 1972 a fifty-room medical building located next door to the church was purchased to serve as offices and as facilities for the Sharing Center.

*GARLAND ROAD CHURCH OF CHRIST, Dallas.*

97

Among the ministers to serve the church are the following: G. A. Dunn, Jesse P. Sewell, L. S. White, A. O. Colley, J. B. Nelson, C. M. Pullias, Coleman Overby, Boyd D. Fanning, Adair P. Chapman, Virgil Bentley, and Bob Barnhill. Gary Beauchamp began his service with the church in 1977.

From this church have come many elders, deacons, and ministers who have served in the Dallas area and throughout the world. The church has been strong in benevolent work and missions.

Sources:
1. *History of Garland Road* (a church publication, 1979).
2. Conference with Nell Rudd, church secretary.
3. Conference and correspondence with John and Grace "Mitt" Mann and secretary, Mrs. Rudd.

## WESTERN HEIGHTS CHURCH OF CHRIST
Dallas — 1872

Western Heights Church of Christ is the oldest Church of Christ in the city of Dallas that has worshiped continuously in one place (1912 North Winnetka).

The church was established in 1872 by Gen. Richard M. Gano, assisted by Maj. B. J. Johnson, one of his Civil War friends. They conducted their first meeting in the old Mount Airy schoolhouse. Heralds on horseback rode about the city advertising the revival to citizens of Dallas.

Other than Dallas citizens, families from De Soto, Jimtown, Eagle Ford, Lisbon, and Wheatland attended. Baptismal services were held in nearby Coombs Creek. Shortly after 1872, the membership of the church was augmented by the arrival of "Weeping" Joe Harding's congregation from Tennessee.

General Gano was a remarkable man. He was the son of John Allen Gano, a student of Barton W. Stone. Whenever Alexander Campbell was visiting in Kentucky, he usually stayed in the beautiful Bellevue, which was the home of the general's parents. General Gano's great-gra-

*WESTERN HEIGHTS*
*CHURCH OF CHRIST, Dallas*

*GEN. RICHARD M. GANO.*

ndfather was the Baptist preacher, John Gano, who baptized George Washington in 1783.

General Gano moved to Texas in 1856 and worked as a physician and farmer. He settled in northeast Tarrant County and in 1859 was elected to the Texas legislature. When the Civil War broke out, Gano became an officer in the Confederate army and rose to the rank of brigadier general. He is said to have fought in seventy-two Civil War battles. One of his men later remarked, "During the war, he led his men into battle, doctored them when they were wounded, and preached to them on Sunday."

General Gano was an active minister for Churches of Christ for forty years. His activities were not confined to the Dallas area. As a great speaker and learned Bible scholar, he traveled to churches for revival meetings throughout the state. Once he held a meeting for the First Christian Church in Taylor in which there was "very good community interest and acceptance."

Other members of the Confederate army who were very influential in the work of Churches of Christ and Christian Churches were John T. Poe, Austin McGary, and Addison and Randolph Clark, whose work led to the establishment of both Texas Christian University and Abilene Christian University.

Early ministers for the Dallas church before the turn of the century were Joe Harding, C. M. Wilmeth, L. A. Sweet, W. H. Walker, W. T. Barcus, C. J. Gastry, and T. R. Burnett.

More recent ministers have included A. L. Deveny, James L. Germany, J. L. Pummil, Earch C. Smith, E. M. Tackett, R. B. Sweet, G. W. McCollum, Tillit S. Teddlie, Brooks Terry, W. R. Craig, R. H. Beeman, Horace Teddlie, R. V. Hamilton, Robert O. Howard, Eugene Lowry, and John French.

An interesting footnote might be the story of Mrs. Mattie Hoard Crawford, who solicited funds for erecting the building in 1889. When Mrs. Crawford asked one man for a donation, replied that he was a saloonkeeper. She responded that this was all the more reason he should put his money to good use. He donated $100 to erect this building,

100

which in 1980 was still in use by the Western Heights Church of Christ as a Sunday school for the deaf.

Sources:
1. *The Firm Foundation,* Austin, January 4, 1972, March 27, 1973.
2. Carter E. Boren, *Religion on the Texas Frontier.*
3. Stephen D. Eckstein, Jr., *History of Churches of Christ in Texas.*
4. Correspondence and conference with John and "Mitt" Mann and secretary, Mrs. Rudd.

## CHURCH OF CHRIST
### Leonard – 1880

In the early 1880s, Ely Macon moved from Tennessee and began farming east of Leonard in Fannin County. Macon's Chapel was later built and served as a meeting place for the Church of Christ with the following members: R. H. Owens, Ben Mead, Frank Davis, W. C. Kuhn, T. F. Macon, D. W. Macon, C. C. Buchanan, and Mrs. Joe Gentry and their families.

Preaching for the members of the church of Macon's

*LEONARD CHURCH OF CHRIST, Leonard.*

101

Chapel, mostly blackland farmers, were the following visiting ministers: Thomas E. Millholland, Warren Starnes, Brother Freed (for whom Freed-Hardeman College in Tennessee was named), D. S. Ligon, J. P. Nall, John Sanders, and John Denton.

In 1919, when Macon's Chapel was damaged by a storm, the building was torn down and the church was relocated in Leonard. Some of the wood from Macon's Chapel was used in the construction of the church building in Leonard. A medical doctor in the nearby town of Bailey, Dr. C. C. Adair, was one of the wealthiest men of the area as well as one of the most devout members of Churches of Christ. Dr. Adair made a loan of $1,500 to the people at Leonard for the construction of their building.

Regular ministers of the Leonard church, in succession, were C. D. Record, H. B. Cash, Ray Waldrum, Lee Reynolds, E. C. McKenzie, Roy Howell, Otis Proffitt, Bill Baker, Brother Bankhead, and L. R. Fullerton. C. C. Buchanan, a well-informed local businessman, served the church as supply minister at different times.

L. R. Fullerton began serving the church as minister in 1957. He was very active in all civic affairs. In addition to serving the congregation well, he, like E. C. McKenzie before him, related well to people of other churches and was named "Most Outstanding Citizen" by the community.

For a short time, both the Church of Christ and the Christian Church existed in Leonard. Among the Christian Church members were Johnny Davis, the Griders, the Arnolds, and several of Leonard's most distinguished citizens. The co-existence was short-lived as the Christian Church dissolved, with some of its members going to the Church of Christ and others to the Presbyterian Church. Mrs. Vivian Cline, nearly ninety years of age in 1980, was the member with longest service. Ministers and church workers growing up in the Leonard church include Connie Hollis, Hugh Matthews, and Noel Grisham.

In 1980 the following elders served the church: Joe Sudderth, Cornell Griffith, and Chester Jackson. Deacons included Jerry Scoggins and Billy Watson. Earlier elders were R. W. Macon, J. R. Davis, and W. C. Burns.

Source:
1. Conference with Noel Owens, longtime member of the Leonard church.

# V

## THE EPISCOPALIANS

John Wurts Cloud was the first Episcopal priest in Texas. Popularly known as a clergyman, Cloud directed a school in Brazoria.

On September 25, 1838, the Foreign Committee of the General Convention of the Episcopal Church in the United States sent Caleb Semper Ives as a missionary to Texas. Arriving in Matagorda on December 12, the Episcopal missionary organized the first Episcopal church, Christ Church of Matagorda, on January 27, 1839. The second oldest Episcopal parish in Texas was organized in Houston on April 1, 1839, just one day after the Presbyterian Church in Houston was begun. Trinity Church in Galveston was next established, on February 6, 1841.

The Episcopal church in Texas wanted independence and requested that the House of Bishops grant Texas the three bishops which would be the canonical number required for independence from the mother church. The House of Bishops elected only Nicholas Hamner Cobb, missionary bishop for Texas. The Texans objected to this, claiming that the American church had no way of making the Texas brethren amenable to its canons.

The Diocese of Texas was organized at Matagorda on January 1, 1849, and on October 4, 1850, was admitted into Union with the General Convention. Alexander Gregg became the first resident bishop in 1859.

Missionary districts were established as Northern and Western Texas. Later, Northern Texas became the Diocese of Dallas in 1895 and Western Texas became the Diocese of West Texas in 1904. The Trans-Pecos area became a part of the Missionary District of New Mexico and Southwest Texas in 1895, and the Missionary District of North Texas was established in 1910.

After the Civil War, Anglo-Catholicism was introduced, with Stephen Maylan Bird, Sr., rector of Trinity Church, Galveston, as leader of the movement for many years. The Diocese of Dallas, the most Anglo-Catholic part of Texas, was not alone with Galveston in the Anglo-Catholic movement as there were other churches of this tradition which were established and survived at St. Peter's in Brenham, St. Bartholomew's in Hempstead, and St. Andrew's in Houston.

In 1873 a few Texas churchmen left the Protestant Episcopal Church to become a part of the Reformed Episcopal Church. This Reformed church existed only for a short time in Houston.

The Episcopal church in Texas, unlike the Methodist and Baptist churches and Churches of Christ, is eminently one of cities and industrial towns. Bishops other than Alexander Gregg have included George Washington Freeman, George Herbert Kinsolving, and Clinton Simon Quin.

By 1944, the church had grown to 196 parishes and missions, 104 clergy, and 50,396 baptized members.

Source:
1. *Handbook of Texas*, Vol. II.


## CHRIST CHURCH
Matagorda — 1839

The initial efforts of the Episcopal movement in Texas were centered in the area around Houston and Galveston, which extended south toward Victoria. The "mother church" of the Diocese of Texas, Christ Church at Mata-

CHRIST CHURCH, Matagorda.
*First Episcopal Church in Texas, organized January 27, 1939. Church building purchased pre-cut in New York state and shipped to Texas; erected 1840. Rebuilt after hurricanes several times. (Registrar's collection)*

gorda, was organized January 27, 1839, and became the first such church in the Republic.

The first rector of Christ Church was the Reverend Caleb S. Ives, who arrived on December 12, 1838, as a missionary in the Foreign Mission Service. He reported to the Foreign Committee in February that he was "officiating every Sunday, conducting a Sunday school, and teaching five days a week."

Like many others who had settled in the area, Ives had high hopes for Matagorda Bay, where produce from the Colorado River Valley would be transferred to ocean-going ships. His report to the mission reflects his thoughts. He wrote:

"This town is growing rapidly, and must, it is thought by many, eventually become the most important place in this Republic. That this, or some other one on Matagorda Bay,

106

must become a place of great commercial importance, no one can doubt who is acquainted with this country."

When Christ Church was organized the following January, he reported his expectations:

"It will, no doubt, be pleasing to the Missionary Society to learn that almost all the respectable families and individuals here are interested in, and gratified with, this step. I believe this is the first and only Church yet organized in the Republic."

His reference to the "only Church" obviously means the Episcopal church. In this he was correct, because the Christ Church in Matagorda was the first in Texas. Christ Church in Houston followed only a few months later.

The first church building in Matagorda was a prefabricated structure that arrived in Matagorda harbor in July of 1840, but its use was delayed because there was no money available to pay for the unloading of the materials and the erection of the building. Ives sent out a plea for funds to friends outside of the state to help with the final construction. Several donations came in, and the building was opened for service on Easter Sunday, 1841.

In March of 1845, a new era for the church in Texas developed with the appointment of George Washington Freeman as the new bishop. Although he was fifty-five years of age when he assumed this new post, the experience he had received in taking the Episcopal church into new frontiers, especially in Mississippi and Tennessee, served him well in Texas. He had been a devoted pastor in his earlier life, and he gave the infant church the same attention and energy.

In the summer of 1849, the diocese mourned the death of its first clergyman and missionary, Caleb S. Ives. The highly respected leader had been in poor health for several years and finally he requested a leave of absence to spend the summer in his native Vermont, where he hoped to escape the intense heat he had been encountering in Texas. He died in his hometown of Timmouth, Vermont, on July 27. Reverend Ives was mourned not only by those in Matagorda and the surrounding area, which he had served

107

directly, but by the entire diocese, which also had taken advantage of his wise counseling and steady leadership.

Until January of 1850, the Matagorda Church was kept open by its lay reader, W. L. Sartwell. Then S. D. Dennison from Massachusetts, in an attempt to escape some of the problems of his parish, came south by boat and eventually was appointed a missionary to help serve at Christ Church. Still more relief came from Chaplain J. F. Fish from New York, who was stationed in San Antonio with the army. He later organized Trinity Church there.

Prior to the Civil War, it was difficult to keep Christ Church alive with an active congregation. Without funds from the mission, services frequently were conducted by lay readers. Bishop Freeman was generous with his time and managed to fill in enough to give the work of the church added motivation.

It is the early history of the mother church at Matagorda that commands the most attention. There the Episcopal movement in Texas got the foundation necessary to carry forward a meaningful development in areas that were destined to develop and support a growing church.

By 1846, both Houston and Galveston had become self-supporting and were able to release funds from the domestic treasury to be used elsewhere.

Christ Church needed these funds. The town of Matagorda had not grown the way the early settlers had expected it to. The shallow harbor that obstructed navigation was the primary reason. Even today, the little town has a declining population of 600 in a county with a growing population of more than 35,000. About all that is left are a few historical sites — and a lot of memories of what might have been. The town was built on hope that did not materialize.

One of the historical attractions is Christ Church. It remains as a landmark in the little community and the hallmark of the Episcopal movement in Texas. Without the initial effort by Caleb Ives in those years immediately after the Republic was formed, the history of the church might have been entirely different.

Sources:
1. Morgan, "Christ Church — Matagorda, Texas 1839."
2. Lawrence L. Brown, *The Episcopal Church in Texas 1838-1874.*
3. *The Texas Almanac,* 1980.
4. Conference with Dr. Lawrence L. Brown.

## CHRIST CHURCH
Houston — 1839

Christ Church, founded on March 16, 1839, is one of the oldest churches in Houston. It may even be the oldest, but a conflict in some of the records raises a question that may not be answered without further evidence.

Houston was scarcely two years old when Christ Church was organized. At the time, the Episcopal church was just beginning to recover from the destructive forces of the American Revolution. It must be remembered that the Episcopal movement in America began in the original colonies long before it moved west. Many of the bishops and rectors who were responsible for the early parishes in Texas were called from Virginia and the Carolinas.

Christ Church in Houston was one of three which worked together to establish the Episcopal Church of Texas. The other two were Christ Church at Matagorda and Trinity Church in Galveston.

Many of the early Episcopalians in Houston were active in the government of the new Republic of Texas, and they held their first services in the Senate chamber of the Capitol. Under the leadership of Col. William F. Gray, who had recently come from Virginia, those who were interested in organizing a parish met on March 16, 1839, and agreed to organize a Protestant Episcopal Church in Houston. Members and friends agreed to furnish the land and the material for a new building.

Gen. Sam Houston had been elected president of the Republic of Texas, and the new government was in a position to give away large tracts of land. This brought people from the United States, England, France, Germany, and many of the smaller European countries. Many of these

109

*CHRIST CHURCH CATHEDRAL, Houston.*
*Second Episcopal Congregation in Texas. Third church, 1898.*
*(Registrar's collection)*

*ALTAR – CHRIST CHURCH CATHEDRAL, Houston.*

110

people were looking for freedom — freedom from want and fear, as well as the right to worship as they pleased.

With Houston growing at a rapid rate, it surprised many civic leaders when the capital of the Republic was moved to Austin. This move, and the depression that followed, brought a delay in the building of a new church. To have a place to meet, the Reverend Charles Gillette purchased a two-story frame schoolhouse and moved into it. Then in 1845, the first brick church was begun. It faced on Fannin Street and was consecrated by the Right Reverend George Washington Freeman in 1847.

Within a year, the first church was outgrown. To help ease the situation, a comfortable rectory was built on the San Jacinto corner of the church property. Then in 1859, the second church was started. Caleb Ives of Christ Church in Matagorda and Benjamin Eaton of Trinity Church in Galveston had come to Houston for the consecration of the first church. They remained close to the rectors and parishioners who were involved.

Charles Gillette, who is mentioned earlier in the account of the development of Christ Church, was born in Connecticut but attended the Virginia Theological Seminary. He came to Texas from a teaching post in Alexandria, Virginia, to become the first voluntary missionary to face the dangers of frontier life in Texas. After his initial efforts in helping with the Episcopal movement in Houston, he was called to Austin. His first effort to establish a parish was a failure because there was no permanent rector, so he returned to Houston. Then in 1856, he was called back when the parishioners in the Church of the Epiphany became divided over the question of slavery. This time he built a thriving parish in Austin, also called Christ Church.

The coming of J. J. Clemens to Houston's Christ Church in 1874 meant having the right man in the right place at the right time. A decade of postwar difficulties had passed, and Houston was ready to boom. It was a rapidly expanding industrial area and offered the young English-born rector a chance to develop his many talents. Clemens had been educated in America, in Pennsylvania and Vir-

111

ginia, so relocation to the Southwest was not as big a step as it might have seemed.

Clemens was twenty-nine years of age when he moved to Houston, and he gave Christ Church the finest and the only full decade of his ministerial life. He succeeded T. R. B. Trader, who had resigned because of differences of the size of the church that could not be enlarged because of the lack of funds, and because the vestry was unable to pay the $2,000 annual salary to which they had committed themselves. This was due largely to the inability to collect pew rents.

The first years at Christ Church for Clemens were not good. The city was thriving, but Christ Church was not. The church was so run down that the chancel and altar were stained from rain. The church yard between the rectory and the church was a black mud puddle.

The conditions he found did not slow down the young rector, and he started his work with enthusiasm and determination. Under his demanding leadership, the church was enlarged in 1877. A pipe organ was acquired, and a vested choir was added.

Clemens was a frail man and his health continued to deteriorate. He had acquired a cough that he was unable to shake, and the big downtown church became too much for him. At the suggestion of a close friend, Hugh Miller Thompson, who wrote him from Oxford, Mississippi, he accepted a post there as a missionary at large. After a year he went to Rhode Island because the colder climate was supposed to help his lungs. However, at the age of forty-two, Clemens died of tuberculosis.

William C. Dawson arrived at Christ Church in the spring of 1885 and established residence by bringing his family. One year later, he died. The post of rector of Christ Church was then filled by Charles Beckworth, who was of English ancestry. He has been described as a lean, bald, forthright young man with a strong will. Still, there is no record in the archives of Christ Church of his five years in Houston. The minutes and parish records dating back to 1843 apparently were destroyed by the storm of 1900.

In 1893, after the construction of a new parish hall, an attempt was made to enlarge the existing church, but it was revealed that the building, which had been constructed in 1859, was no longer safe. It was torn down, and the present church was built. Then in 1902, since Christ Church was still in a residential neighborhood, a distinctive new rectory was built to replace the old frame building.

The present church has survived yellow fever and cholera, epidemics, hurricanes, wars, and the rumor of wars. It was damaged by the hurricane of 1900 and again by the one in 1915. In 1938 the chancel, the organ, and the chapel were destroyed by fire.

Christ Church became the Cathedral Church of the Diocese in 1949. The first annual convention of the diocese was held in 1950.

In the so-called "modern era" there have been many outstanding leaders associated with the church. Through the years, the parish has figured prominently in shaping Episcopal history. One of the outstanding contributions has been to provide five bishops who have served in far-reaching areas.

Charles M. Beckworth, a former rector, was the consecrated bishop of the Diocese of Alabama in 1902. He died in 1928.

Henry D. Aves was a former rector of Christ Church and the first bishop to be consecrated in Texas. He was consecrated in 1904 and served as a missionary bishop of Mexico. He died in 1936.

James P. DeWolfe, a former rector of Christ Church, became the fourth bishop of the Diocese of Long Island. He was consecrated in 1942.

John E. Hinds, rector of Christ Church from 1940 to 1945, was consecrated in 1945 as bishop coadjutor of Texas. He became the fourth bishop of the Diocese of Texas in 1955.

H. Kellogg was dean and rector of the Christ Church Cathedral until 1952 and became the fifth bishop of that diocese in 1956.

Kellogg had been a colonel and a chaplain in the army

and he accepted the position as rector of Christ Church in 1946, the same year that Bishop Quin asked the diocesan council to designate a cathedral church for the diocese. Because Christ Church was the mother church in the largest city in the diocese, Kellogg appointed a vestry committee to look into all the possible problems cathedral status might bring.

In January 1947, the council's cathedral committee recommended that Christ Church in Houston be designated as a cathedral. Although it seemed to be a logical move, another year of negotiations was needed to reach an agreement. There were pros and cons to be considered, but in the end, Christ Church retained its parish identity and independence. Kellogg then became dean of the Cathedral Church but retained his position as rector of the parish.

Under the leadership of Dean Kellogg, Christ Church, as well as the entire diocese, made great strides. It would be correct to say that under his leadership the Episcopal movement in the Houston area came of age. He was a man of many talents, and his ability to put people at ease was a key to his success.

All year he seemed to gather jokes he would tell at the annual parish dinner to make the evening enjoyable. He never missed an opportunity to project the human traits that he possessed.

When the Petroleum Club in Houston was first organized and new quarters atop the Rice Hotel were being planned, Dean Kellogg became interested. The Christ Church rector always had a membership in the River Oaks Country Club, but he felt it would be pleasant for visiting ministers and bishops, who frequently lodged at the Rice Hotel during a week of missions, to be able to use the club for any brief periods of relaxation they might have. He asked one of his friends about a membership.

"It's only for the oil industry," the friend regretfully told him.

Dean Kellogg was not to be outdone. "Well," he said, "ministers spread oil on troubled waters." On the basis of this unchallenged logic, the friend presented the matter to

114

the admissions board, and special memberships were made available to the clergy of the city.

On June 3, 1951, Bishop Quin and Dean Kellogg laid the cornerstone for the combined Latham and Diocesan buildings. With their completion, the large downtown Episcopal complex, as it exists today, was rapidly taking shape.

As far back as 1943, Christ Church members had started a building fund but were still some $40,000 in debt. The church needed more room in Sunday school, in the guild hall and office building, but it seemed wasteful to spend a sizable amount of money for a makeshift addition to the already existing property.

On April 13, 1943, a solution to the problem was offered. The Cleveland brothers, Will and Sess, proposed that a $100,000 Latham bequest be made available to Christ Church for a building of general civic use. They were executors, along with the Houston Land and Trust Co., of the estates of Lucy Latham Bowles and her sister, Lennie Grosbeck Latham. Each sister had left $50,000 to be used for civic purposes as a memorial to their father, Capt. L. J. Latham. The exact nature of the civic purposes was left to the executors and the Cleveland brothers, as grandsons of Captain Latham who thought a building on the site of the old rectory could serve community and parish needs in a way that would meet the provisions of the two wills. This was confirmed in a friendly suit before a sympathetic judge.

J. Milton Richardson of St. Luke's Church in Atlanta, Georgia, was called to take the post of dean and rector of the Christ Church Cathedral when Dean Kellogg resigned in 1952 to go to Minnesota. He had been well received when he spoke at the 112th annual parish meeting, which marked Dean Kellogg's fifth anniversary at the Houston church.

Between the time Dean Kellogg left in June and Dean Richardson came in September, members had left the Christ Church Cathedral in alarming numbers. This was due in part to population shifts where members looked with interest at the new and more convenient neighborhood churches. Also, almost two years of disrupted Sunday

115

school had caused many young couples to take their children to churches nearer home. Now, when there was to be a change in leadership at Christ Church, they felt that it would be simpler to join their children in the neighborhood rather than transfer them back to Christ Church, which had a new building but an unknown academic future.

Christ Church Cathedral lost 448 members that year, the largest in history and the largest in the diocese that year. The reduction accounted for almost half of the total loss reported from all of the diocese churches.

Fortunately, Dean Richardson had a strong vestry who backed every move he made. It was also fortunate that he had a strong conviction that neighborhood churches could not survive unless there was a strong and virile downtown church to rally around. His philosophy was: "If we do our work well in the cathedral, every Episcopal Church in the area will be stronger."

His prediction came true. Christ Church weathered the danger period and entered an era which should establish it forever as the pivotal church for Houston and the diocese — no longer a mother church for missions, but a cathedral church for all Episcopalians.

Dean Richardson, as Fifth Bishop of Texas, continued his interest in Christ Church Cathedral until his death in March 1980.

Sources:
1. Marguerite Barnes [Marguerite Johnson], "A Happy Worldly Abode — Christ Church Cathedral, 1839/1964," *Houston Post.*
2. [Marguerite Johnson], "125 Years with the Episcopal Church in Texas."

## TRINITY EPISCOPAL CHURCH
Galveston — 1841

When Benjamin Eaton stood on the deck of the *Neptune* on January 13, 1841, the driving rain in his face did not prevent him from seeing the stretch of mud-flats and shallow water that lay between the steamboat and the wharf at

116

the foot of Twenty-fourth Street. Nothing prepared him for the sad condition of the Republic and the poor way of life found in the struggling "mud-stop" which was a part of the shipping routes of the world.

A person with more limited convictions and less determination would have taken the next boat to New Orleans — but not Benjamin Eaton. He had transferred from the church in Wisconsin to escape the severe weather, and his career in Texas was one he intended to follow. Until he arrived, the only Episcopal services in the Republic were conducted by Caleb S. Ives in Matagorda and a lay reader, Col. William F. Gray, in Houston. Henry B. Goodwin from Maryland had served Galveston and Houston until April of 1840, when he left to make a trip to England in "behalf of the church and the cause of education in Texas."

In spite of his disappointment in what he found in Texas, Eaton's better judgment caused him to plunge into the tasks at hand. He checked throughout Galveston and found about a dozen people who were interested in becoming a part of the new Episcopal movement. It was fortunate that those who committed themselves were people of means and willing to accept responsibility in the community and the church. These people from the eastern part of the United States and the British Isles were seeking a peace their religion had taught them, and they found in Benjamin Eaton a leader they could follow.

During the spring and summer of 1841, the efforts of Eaton and the congregations were so successful in securing subscriptions for a new church that a "neat Gothic structure 40 feet by 70 feet was in process to be completed by January next, and not to exceed in cost $4,400." The church was finished in June of 1842, even though the title was not transferred to Eaton as rector until April of the next year.

This church was actually the second one to which Eaton had received a title. The first one lasted hardly long enough to have a title drawn, having been destroyed by a storm three months after it was completed. There is a trace of humor in a later report made by one of the members, Oscar Farish, when he recorded what happened:

117

*TRINITY EPISCOPAL CHURCH, Galveston.*
*Organized 1842. Second building 1843. (Registrar's collection)*

The church was blown down, falling on a cow. Eaton
had just time to save his own life by crawling through a
window. After his great fright and exposure during the
night, I visited him the next morning as all his friends
did, and I shall never forget his sad, despondent looks,
but he soon recovered his spirit and energy. A singular
experience happened on that night. A sum of eleven
hundred dollars in gold was stolen from the Washington

Hotel situated on the ground on which now stands the Cotton Exchange. When the church was razed, the money was found behind the pillars of the church, the thief putting it there, no doubt, as the safest place of deposit and where it would be least likely to be found.

Farish did not make it clear whether or not the cow survived her religious experience or if the gold was returned to its rightful owner.

The rebuilt church was opened on Palm Sunday, 1843. In the midst of all the adversity suffered by the rector and congregation, a new member to the Episcopal movement, Charles Gillette, came to the rescue by raising money for the Galveston church before he settled in Houston.

The name Charles Gillette will be mentioned many times during the various reports on the Episcopal church in Texas. He had been ordained deacon and priest by the bishop of Virginia and soon volunteered to come to Texas. History has recorded the role he played in Houston, Galveston, and Austin in using his abundant talents to further the cause of the church.

The Board of Missions requested that Gillette delay his departure to visit churches in the United States to collect money to help rebuild the Galveston structure. By careful planning, Eaton was able to complete the building with the money Charles Gillette had been able to raise. When the rebuilt church was opened, Gillette attended, along with Caleb Ives from Matagorda, to share in the happy occasion with Benjamin Eaton and his dedicated congregation.

The year 1843 was a crucial time for the church in Texas. The threat of war with Mexico remained, the Indians continued to be restless, and other church groups seemed to be expanding faster than the Episcopal movement. After a survey of the diocese, Reverend Gillette made a report that eventually brought some action. He wrote that "the Presbyterians have about ten ministers in the country, the methodists have up to forty, the Roman Catholics have about six, and our own church has only three."

Another problem confronting them was the establishment of parochial schools, something Gillette felt was essen-

119

tial if the Episcopalians were to keep their children from the Catholic schools. Caleb Ives had established a school in Matagorda, but parochial training was lacking in Houston and Galveston. Due to his efforts and the encouragement of Bishop Polk, who had been relieved of his obligations in Texas but still visited the churches in the state occasionally, the schools were eventually established.

By 1850, Galveston had become the citadel of the Episcopal movement in Texas. It was only natural, then, that an effort was made to build a new church. Ground was broken on November 29, 1855, but it took two years to build, at a cost of about $40,000. When completed, the parish was not only in debt to the builders and financiers, but also to the rector for his salary. It was 1866 before it was possible to clear the debt and have the church consecrated.

Galveston became the home of Bishop Gregg in 1869 and was a focal point of the Episcopal church in the diocese. Trinity Church did not become a cathedral, as did St. Mark's in San Antonio and St. Matthew's in Dallas, but the generosity of its members made the congregation a vital tool for the bishop in developing a forward-looking missionary program. In all of the programs for outside purposes, Trinity Church and its individual members were at the top of the list of contributors.

Benjamin Eaton, who had been away for several years, returned as the rector of Trinity Parish on December 1, 1865. Then in the summer of 1867, another outbreak of yellow fever caused him to leave again, and they recalled the fearless service he rendered during the earlier epidemics.

John Owen, the beloved rector of Christ Church at Matagorda, was called on again to supply the parish on a temporary basis. He ministered faithfully to the victims of the fever until he contracted it himself and died in October. A tablet on the south chancel wall of the church commemorates the sacrifices of the two priests, John Goshorn and John Owen, who died ministering to victims of the epidemics.

Benjamin Eaton was back in the parish by mid-December of 1867, where he handled an increasing load of busi-

120

ness until one day in March of 1871, when he collapsed in a coma. He died that afternoon, and the congregation was very grieved. In his rectorship of over thirty years, he had helped build Trinity Church from a struggling and impoverished little group to a sound and prosperous congregation.

Trinity Church became more active under the new rector. After some delay, due to reluctance on the part of the vestry at St. Paul's Church in Selma, Alabama, where he had been stationed, Stephen M. Bird came to the Galveston church. He was a tall, youthful, good-looking man who had a special appeal with his approach in the pulpit. In March of 1873, less than a year after he arrived at Trinity Church, he presented the largest confirmation class that Bishop Gregg had presided over since he had been in the diocese, a class of forty-eight, in what was then the largest and richest city in the state.

Stephen Bird remained for twenty-two years. Under his leadership, the parish matured and moved forward. He was followed by Charles M. Beckworth, who began service in March 1895 and remained until December 1901.

There was a lapse of about ten months until the next rector accepted the call. Lay readers and visiting clergymen handled the services until Charles S. Aves arrived on October 7, 1902. He served until November 1, 1917, and then became rector emeritus until June of 1923.

It took almost three months to locate and call the next rector, Raimundo de Ovies, who started on February 24, 1919, and remained until the end of August 1927. He was replaced on September 1, 1928, by Edmund H. Gibson.

After Gibson left in 1962, he was replaced by Roger H. Cilly, who served until he became suffragan bishop of the diocese in 1976. He now lives in Houston. The rector as of 1980, John C. Donovan, began service in 1974.

The history of Trinity Church after the turn of the century includes programs that have played a vital part in the progress of the church and the twenty to thirty organizations that have been formed to carry them forward. The church by 1980 had been served by eight rectors and forty-two lay readers, and nineteen postulates had entered or were preparing to enter the ministry.

The congregation of Trinity Church has been filled with people who have made outstanding contributions in all walks of life. Their names have been recorded in the history of the church through their deeds and the contributions they have made to make the building a symbol of lasting beauty. The stained glass windows by Tiffany, the marble busts of former rectors Eaton and Bird, and numerous oil paintings of individuals and highlights in the progress of the church all add to the stability of the Episcopal movement.

Sources:
1. Morgan, "Trinity Protestant Episcopal Church 1841-1953."
2. Lawrence L. Brown, *The Episcopal Church in Texas 1838-1874.*
3. *The Texas Almanac,* 1980.
4. Personal conference with Lawrence L. Brown, professor emeritus of the Episcopal Seminary in Austin.

## ST. DAVID'S EPISCOPAL CHURCH
### Austin – 1859

St. David's Church was established on Tuesday, July 19, 1859, when the two Episcopal parishes in Austin, the Church of the Epiphany and Christ Church, agreed to unite. They had separated in 1856 when some of the more prominent members of the Church of the Epiphany withdrew because of the slavery issue. Charles Gillette from Houston was called to organize a new parish, and on December 20, 1856, Christ Church became a reality.

Edward Fontaine, a great-grandson of Patrick Henry, and the first rector in Austin, spoke out publicly about the gravity of the slavery issue, but he lost about twenty members just the same. A debt of $1,000 remained on the building, which the vestry assumed individually. The building remained the property of the original parish.

Charles Gillette, as rector of the second parish, Christ Church, held services in the new county courthouse. The congregation worshiped in the large courtroom shaped like an amphitheater and the choir sang behind a red velvet cur-

122

*ST. DAVID'S EPISCOPAL CHURCH, Austin.*

123

tain stretched across a platform where the judge sat on court days. The only known furnishings Christ Church had were two tall, silver-plated flagons they had received from the Ladies Missionary Society of St. Luke's Church in German-town, Pennsylvania.

The year 1859 was a trying period for Edward Fontaine, who as rector for Epiphany Church had returned to Austin on January 18, 1851. On Friday, July 15, 1855, his wife, who had been ill for several years, died and left their three sons for him to rear. Even with the help of his faithful black servant and sexton at the church, Jake Fontaine, it was a difficult job. With the problems that continued to arise in the church, Fontaine had more than he could handle.

In a letter to his old friend, Mirabeau Lamar, under whom he had served for one year as secretary of state for the Republic, he pointed out his feelings: "I am really tired of hard work and poor pay. I wish to leave the State . . . without selling my house, and phillibuster (sic) ecclesiastically in a new field, or retire and rest in an old, rich, and well-paying parish."

Before the year was over, Fontaine married a wealthy widow, Mrs. Susan Taylor Britton, at Jackson, Mississippi. They lived on her plantation. After he had served as chief of ordnance for the Confederate army in Mississippi, he continued his work in the church until his death on July 19, 1884.

In Austin, Charles Gillette continued to hold services for Christ Church in the courthouse. Since the congregation of the Church of the Epiphany had a building but no rector, it seemed logical to unite the two. After careful negotiations, St. David's was born.

The first Episcopal church in Austin dates back to April 7, 1853. The site chosen had a commanding view of the Colorado River and the hills beyond. It was located at what is now 7th Street and San Jacinto, across from the two-story mansion in which President Lamar had lived.

The cornerstone of the new church, which occupied the same location as that of the present building, was laid with an elaborate ceremony by members of the Austin

Lodge of Free and Accepted Masons, who were chosen by Fontaine because he was chaplain of the Grand Lodge of Texas Masons. According to a report in a local newspaper, *The State Gazette*, a large number of Austin residents and out-of-town visitors climbed the hill to witness the beginning of Austin's first stone church.

Before a church building was available, services had been held in the Senate chamber of the Hall of Congress, a drafty, one-story log structure with an eight-foot stockard around it as protection against the Indians.

Prior to the construction of the Church of the Epiphany, Gillette had been called to Austin from Houston in 1848 to make the first attempt to organize Christ Church. With no permanent clergyman available, the effort was doomed to fail. The way was still open for Fontaine, who provided the Episcopalians in Austin a place to worship five years later.

If St. David's is to be recognized as a product of a union resulting from a congregational split over the slavery question, then it must be remembered that it, too, became a victim of new alignments when the Civil War became a reality. On April 19, 1861, cannon fire on the state capitol grounds announced the fall of Fort Sumter. There was no longer a possibility of arbitration. The next day, Governor Edward Clark called out 3,000 troops in Texas.

It was evident by then that St. David's was split into two factions, with powerful social and political figures on both sides. On the Union side were A. J. Hamilton, former attorney general and congressman; Amos Morrill, a law partner of Hamilton and later chief justice of the Supreme Court of Texas; Elisha Pease, former and future governor of Texas, who left the state to go north during the war; and James H. Raymond, the first state treasurer of Texas.

It is well to note that Svante Magnus Swenson and his uncle, Svante Palm, although leaders in the Swedish movement in Texas and actively involved in the establishment of the Gethsemane Lutheran Church in Austin and the Palm Valley Lutheran Church in Round Rock, were members of St. David's who favored the Union position on slavery. They

125

found it wise to leave the state until after the war had ended. (More details about their activity is covered in the section on the Swedish movement.)

On the side of the South were members such as George M. Flournoy, an attorney general; William S. Oldham, who later was a member of the Confederate Congress; Judge Joseph Lee, chief justice under President Mirabeau Lamar; Gen. Thomas (Tom) Green, a veteran of the Indian wars; John G. Swisher, a banker on the Texas State Military Board, who later had a West Texas county named for him; and Dr. Samuel G. Haynie, an early medical doctor who had also been the postmaster, the mayor and a representative in the legislature from Travis County. He had also served the church as senior warden for sixteen years.

There were many others who could not agree with the attitude Gillette was taking in support of the Union. He resigned on October 1, 1866, and after he had closed out his affairs he moved his family to Ohio, where he was to take over a parish. *The Tri-Weekly Gazette* of Austin, with a dateline of March 27, 1886, carried a story when he returned briefly: "Mr. Gillette, former rector of St. David's Church, preached a farewell sermon last Sunday. We regret to lose him. Though differing on certain Church matters, we always believed him to be a pure-minded, conscientious, upright man, and we most cordially wish him every success in his new field."

One of the most prominent figures in the history of St. David's was Alexander Gregg, who became the first bishop and held that post for many years. He arrived on December 9, 1859, and spent several months getting acquainted with his people and the territory he would be covering. In early 1860 he moved his family, his household goods, and a few slaves to the capital. He soon discovered the differences on the slavery question between members of the church and Gillette. Even so, he managed to work with members of both groups and served the diocese well until May 20, 1891, when his last meeting with the council of St. David's took place. Seated in his new bishop's chair on that day, he was presented his impressive pastoral staff, which has continued to be carried by bishops in procession. Because of his health, a search for a successor began. In time, a Virginian from Bedford County, by way of Philadelphia, George Herbert Kinsolving, accepted the position that had been turned down by several ministers who had worked with Bishop Gregg.

Bishop Kinsolving arrived in Austin on November 18, 1892. He was received enthusiastically and soon purchased a house on Whitis Avenue near the home of retired Bishop Gregg. They became great friends, and the new bishop gave his feelings in a statement written by his assistant. He wrote of the older bishop: "I deemed it an unspeakable honor and privilege to offer this man my tribute of respect and love." Bishop Gregg, in poor health for a long time, died July 10, 1893.

After the resignation of Charles Gillette, the vestry of St. David's Church continued to keep Benjamin Rogers on a trial basis until spring, at his own request. On March 21, 1866, he received the call to be rector, beginning April 1.

Rogers met the challenges he received form his congregation. As a fearless preacher, he also began to denounce the poor conditions of prisons in the state, and especially the Travis County jail and the poor accommodations the prisoners were forced to tolerate there. He received such wide publicity that he became president of the Prison Reform Association and attended a world conference held in London, England. In this and other causes, he was far ahead of his time.

Rogers was a man of many talents. On January 3, 1870, at a meeting of the vestry, the members accepted a plan he had submitted which called for enlarging the building instead of constructing a new one. He was to serve as the architect, and Dr. Haynie would act as superintendent of the work. By following such a plan, a large amount of money was saved.

One system used by members of St. David's congregation that hasn't been mentioned in the records of some of the other religious beliefs was to collect pew rents for each year in advance. It was announced that a chart showing the

127

location of the pews of the church and the prices to be charged would be on display in a local drug store window. The parishioners could go there, select the pew of their choice, and pay the owner, Mr. Raymond, who was a parishioner himself. This method of auctioning the pews was better than trying to conduct the business in the church.

At a vestry meeting on March 11, 1872, Rogers said it was time for him to retire and asked that it become effective at Easter. Vestry members protested that no change was desired and not even a half dozen members would want him to leave. He agreed to stay under certain conditions, which basically involved following the policies his conscience dictated.

On December 5, 1874, Rogers surprised the vestry by announcing his resignation, to become effective at the end of the month. After he had gone, J. W. Phillips held services until the vestry called Thomas Booth Lee of Little Rock, Arkansas, to be rector. His term of service began on March 21, 1875, and continued until September 30, 1912.

Fortunately for all concerned, the turbulence of the Reconstruction period in Texas was over and the constitutional rights of Texans had been restored. During this period one of the foremost parishioners, Governor Elisha Pease, made marked progress in his efforts to develop a system of public education and a more humane approach toward caring for handicapped people, who had received little or no attention before. Governor Pease established a state hospital for the insane in 1856 and an institution for the deaf in 1857. He was called the "Father of Public School Education in Texas." The ultimate establishment of the University of Texas in 1886 fulfilled a dream held by Mirabeau Lamar and Edward Fontaine. With the backing of parishioners like Governor Pease, Lee was able to carry the growth of the church forward at a pleasing rate.

In 1885 the congregation exceeded the seating capacity of the church. A local architect and parishioner, A. M. C. Nixon, was employed to furnish plans to enlarge the church.

The old roof was removed and the walls were raised two feet. An imposing chancel and sanctuary were built on the north end behind three arches like those on the south. As the sanctuary was moved back to the north, the main entrance had to be moved to the south, which now has large double doors and broad stone steps.

On September 30, 1912, Lee died suddenly. *The Austin Statesman* related the news the next day in large headlines and gave a short view of his long service at St. David's. "During nearly ten years," the article stated, "[the church] was attended by the wealthiest and most influential families and it had the largest membership in the city. It is still one of the largest congregations and has maintained its old ascendancy."

Thus came the end of an era for St. David's Church.

Some parishioners in St. David's Church had never known any rector except Lee. For them to accept a replacement would be difficult. Some of his devoted followers left soon after his death and joined All Saint's Church, where William Hall Williams was rector. At St. David's, the communicant strength was reduced to 215.

Services at St. David's were held by lay readers, with occasional help from Bishop Kinsolving, until Milton R. Worsham accepted the position as rector. On December 12, 1912, he took over his pastorate and, according to the *Austin Statesman,* "He was quartered at the Driskill hotel because the church had no rectory then."

Reverend Worsham served well while he was at St. David's. By June 1916, the communicant strength had increased to 350 — the largest proportionate increase in the diocese. It came as a surprise, then, when he announced that he planned to accept a call from the Church of the Good Shepherd at Jacksonville, Florida. He served there for seven years until he died on April 14, 1922, at the age of forty years.

St. David's was without a rector for four months. Then, probably at the suggestion of Bishop Kinsolving, a fellow Virginian was called. He was Lewis Carter Harrison, who served seven years, from November 1916 until October 1923. In some ways, these were years of unrest as they comprised the war years and the following period of adjustment. Even so, progress in the church continued. Under Harrison's direction, a home east of the church which was owned by Theo Meyer was purchased as a parish house, where church school classes could be held.

Under the leadership of Harrison, the communicant strength reached 450. His accomplishments were summed up in his letter of resignation, which became effective October 1, 1923. He had accepted a call from Emmanuel Church at Brook Hill, a suburb of Richmond near his old home.

The next rector at St. David's was another Lee—Lenoir Valentine Lee. Also from Virginia, he served from June 1924 until September 1, 1928.

While Lee served as rector, a plan by D. K. Woodward, after many long and complicated transactions, was accepted and a charter was granted to St. David's Hospital on December 31, 1924. Dr. Joe Gilbert was its first director. A conflict over the enlargement of the old church and the construction of a parish house led Lee to offer his resignation effective September 1, 1928.

After an interim period of two months, Beverly Munford Boyd became rector on November 8, 1928. Like so many of his predecessors, he was a Virginian and had served two parishes there before he moved to Texas.

Just before the arrival of Boyd at St. David's, Bishop Kinsolving, who was eighty-seven years old and in poor health, asked that his dear friend, Clinton S. Quin, have full authority in the diocese.

Boyd served until his resignation on March 16, 1934, when he left to accept a post in North Carolina that lasted only one year. He then went to Richmond, where he remained until his retirement in 1963.

The first Texas-born rector to serve St. David's Church was James S. Allen, a native of Fort Worth. He was almost thirty-nine years old when he accepted the post, and he stayed for five years until he left the ministry, temporarily, in March of 1939. He later was rector of Christ Church in St. Joseph, Missouri, and of St. Andrews Church in Kansas City, Missouri.

St. David's came of age under Charles Abram Summers, rector for over thirty-six years.

130

In October 1975, the second native Texan came to serve as rector of St. David's. Laurens Allen Hall was born in San Antonio and graduated from the University of Texas at Austin. He previously served at St. Christopher's Church in League City.

Sources:
1. Barrett Tanner, *The History and Treasures of St. David's Church.*
2. Mrs. Doris M. Johnson, secretary to St. David's Church (frequent interviews).

## ST. MARK'S EPISCOPAL CHURCH
San Antonio — 1850

The oldest Protestant church building still in use in San Antonio is St. Mark's Episcopal Church. The grounds on which it is located were part of the Mission San Antonio de Valero, now known as the Alamo. The land was granted by the Spanish Crown, after the secularization of the property, to two converted Indians who had been dependents of the mission. The deed of the patent is dated 1793. St. Mark's Church then acquired the property in 1858 through gifts from early members, including William Vance and Samuel M. Maverick.

The first mission of the Episcopal church in San Antonio, Trinity Mission, was founded in 1850 by J. F. Fish, who was a chaplain in the United States Army. Services were held in an adobe building where the Gross Bank later stood. A lot was purchased on St. Mary's Street (then called Rincon) but was sold for a debt against it. After that, the congregation met in a rented hall, the basement of the "new" Presbyterian Church, and later in Wolfe Hall of Saint Mary's Hall at Martin and Navarro streets.

The early days of the church in San Antonio were difficult. Captain Fish was transferred to another station in 1852 and Charles Rottenstein, who had been a Methodist minister, took charge of the parish on April 1, 1853. Under his leadership, the membership increased from thirteen to fifty-two before he left in 1854 to go to Dallas. After that,

131

*EARLY CHURCH, St. Mark's, San Antonio.*

Trinity Mission was without ministerial leadership from 1854 until 1858, when it was officially discontinued.

Early in 1858, Lucius H. Jones of Seguin visited San Antonio and began to reorganize the congregation. He presented to the convention the application of St. Mark's Church in San Antonio for admission to the diocese. The Committee on New Parishes, after assuring itself that Trinity Mission was extinct, made a favorable report, and St. Mark's Church was received into the diocese on April 16, 1858. The following year, Jones resigned his post at Seguin and became the first rector of the church.

Bishop Gregg laid the cornerstone of the new church on December 22, 1859. During the next two years, the building fund continued to grow. Among those who were active in the effort to carry out the building plans were Col. Robert E. Lee and Samuel Maverick, who had signed the Texas Declaration of Independence. Colonel Lee had been stationed in San Antonio from 1855 to 1857 and then had returned in 1860 as commander of the Texan forces.

Unsettled conditions after the Civil War caused progress on the church to stop, and it was not finished until 1875. Again, one of those largely responsible for the completion of the building was Gen. Robert E. Lee, then a lieutenant colonel and once again stationed in San Antonio. In his biography, written by Chaplain Bob Lee, the account of General Lee's efforts can be found: "While in San Antonio, he interested himself with the good people of the town in building the Episcopal Church to which he contributed largely." The first name listed as a life member in the first Diocesan Missionary Society with a gift of fifty dollars was that of Robert E. Lee, a member of St. Mark's Church.

An early focal point in the history of St. Mark's was the arrival of Walter R. Richardson on June 1, 1868. He was a man of great vision who began to translate that vision into action.

The first step was taken in 1870 with the purchase of Wolfe Hall, where the congregation had been meeting. The new home was given a facelift with an attractive marble front to give it more dignity.

*ST. MARK'S CHURCH, San Antonio.*

In March of 1873, work on the new building began in earnest, and on Easter Sunday, March 18, 1875, the opening of the completed church was celebrated. The architect was one of the most famous of that period, who had designed Trinity Church in New York City. He was also the founder of the American Institute of Architects.

134

In 1874 western Texas was cut off from the Diocese of Texas, where St. Mark's had been placed originally by the General Convention, and the Missionary District of West Texas was created. Shortly afterwards, St. Mark's was made the cathedral church of the new district through concurrent action by the bishop, the wardens, and the vestry. It was then ratified by the congregation.

As a result Richardson became dean and never lost the title, although Bishop Johnson, after his election in 1888, preferred not to continue cathedral status for St. Mark's. As a church in the Diocese of West Texas, which had replaced the Missionary District of West Texas, St. Mark's has contributed greatly to the lay and clerical leadership of the diocese throughout its history.

The bell in the tower of the church was cast from the metal of a cannon found buried on the old homestead of Colonel Maverick, near the outer walls of the Alamo. On one side is a Texas star, enclosing the word "Alamo" and the dates 1813, 1836, and 1876 (the first two referring to incidents in wars with Spain and Mexico and the last one indicating the date the bell was cast and hung).

The church itself, after completion in 1875, was not altered until 1896, when certain changes were made to add to the convenience of the members and to make room for the new and larger organ that was installed. It was not disturbed again until 1949, when the present building program began and the seating capacity was extended to accommodate 120 more people. A new tower was added, the church was extended the desired length, and a much needed protected entrance was provided. The Steves eighteen-bell memorial carillon was placed in the new tower, and the entire property was repainted, redecorated, and put in the finest condition possible.

The present four-story parish house and the adjoining educational building, with an auditorium, classrooms and gymnasium, were built in 1947 while Dr. Rolfe P. Crum was rector. During the building program of 1949, the final part of the fourth floor, which had been an attic, was completed by the construction of ten new classrooms. In 1942 the

135

Children's Chapel was built, using part of the fourth floor, and has since provided a worship center for the children of the elementary department and church school. By 1950, the parish house and educational buildings were completed. All space is utilized to its maximum capacity.

A gift of a new chapel was made in the fall of 1949, and work began on it the following spring.

In 1939, under the leadership of Everett Holland Jones, who later became bishop of the diocese, St. Mark's community house was developed. Other Episcopal churches in the city joined the effort, and in 1951 it went under the sponsorship of the diocese and became a mission for Hispanic people.

Through its years of service, St. Mark's Church has established as parochial missions St. John's Church, St. Luke's Church, and St. Stephen's Church and has helped with the establishment of Christ Church.

In the middle 1950s, St. Mark's Church established a daycare center to help working mothers. It grew to a point where it was necessary to add a first-grade class.

Sources:
1. The Reverend David L. Veal, San Antonio, Texas.
2. *The Centennial Report, 1850-1950,* St. Mark's Church, San Antonio, Texas.


## ST. JAMES EPISCOPAL CHURCH
## La Grange – 1885-86

Resting among large liveoak trees on the banks of the Colorado River is the historic town of La Grange, the cradle of Stephen F. Austin's first colony. For years descendants of the original settlers have offered hospitality to people of many ethnic groups who have come to find new homes.

The focal point of this community can be found in several historic houses of worship, including St. James Episcopal Church, located on the corner of Colorado and Monroe streets.

The attractive frame building of unusual construction

136

ST. JAMES EPISCOPAL CHURCH, La Grange.

was designed by Richard M. Upjohn of New York and is an excellent example of the Queen Anne architectural style that has been Americanized. He also designed St. Mark's Church in San Antonio.

The first Episcopal baptisms were performed in 1852. For the next thirty years, missionary work was carried on before the parish was organized in 1885. The period between 1881 and 1891 was productive for the parishioners, despite the problems of reconstruction, drought, illness and bad crops.

Following the initial effort in the early 1850s, a steady decline occurred before La Grange and the parish experienced growth. A concentrated drive was started in 1973 to resume parish status for St. James, and after two years

137

Frank Fuller, a deacon, was ordained to the priesthood and became the seventh resident minister of the church.

In 1980 the congregation at St. James ranged between 130 and 150 members. The dedication and stability shown by the loyal parishioners is a tribute to the strong missionary work done by the Episcopalians during the formative years.

Sources:
1. *The Fayette County Record,* May 25, 1979.
2. Interview with Richard L. Barton, Sr., publisher.


## ST. MATTHEW'S EPISCOPAL CHURCH
### Dallas—1870

An Episcopal parish in Dallas was established in 1857, even though St. Matthew's first church was not erected until 1870. In the meantime, services were held in the old Dallas County Courthouse. Some of the records of the early Episcopal movement are not available, but they have to be interpreted as meaning the courthouse when the term "old stonehouse of Smith and Patterson" is used.

The first Episcopal service was in May of 1856, with George Rottenstein presiding. The faithful few who attended the first service never dreamed that the congregation they hoped to develop would ultimately become a cathedral serving an area of over a million people and form a diocese embracing all of North Texas.

Dallas in 1856 was hardly more than a settlement on the Trinity River. "Downtown" consisted of a number of wooden buildings, wooden sidewalks, and muddy streets. Domestic animals roamed the streets at will, and the owners were more difficult to control than the stock.

The "old stonehouse of Smith and Patterson" was located on Main Street, between Houston and Broadway. A temporary rail marked off the "chancel" from the rest of the bare second-floor space. Two dry-goods boxes covered with "orange calico" served as a reading desk and altar. Four people attended the first meeting.

ST. MATTHEW'S EPISCOPAL CHURCH, Dallas.

George Rottenstein became a legend in his own time. A native of Germany, he was baptized a Roman Catholic. He later became a Methodist and served as a minister for twenty-one years. While he was editing a church paper in Houston, his son was ordained as minister in the Episcopal church. This displeased the elder Rottenstein, so to convince the boy of his folly, he studied the history of the Episcopal church. In doing so, he decided that his son had been right. He was later ordained in the Protestant Episcopal Church and returned to Texas as a missionary.

At first he worked around San Antonio, but he had little success. Then he moved on to Corsicana, where he established St. Bartholomew's parish. Then the courthouse where he was holding services "took fire or rather was set on fire early in 1856." He moved to Dallas, where he hoped to find a place to hold services.

Rottenstein worked hard and was rewarded for his efforts. On St. Matthew's Day, September 21, 1857, the articles of association were drafted by the young parish. The proper officers were elected, and Rottenstein took the necessary papers to the Diocesan Convention at Austin in

139

May of 1858. The articles were ratified, but Rottenstein was transferred to Louisiana and the little parish of St. Matthew's was left without a rector.

During the next two years, the parish remained about the same. The annual assesment for the diocese was five dollars, and this was usually paid by the senior warden, J. M. Patterson. St. Matthew's church was lost when a fire destroyed the entire business section of Dallas on July 8, 1860. No further progress was made until the arrival of the newly consecrated bishop of Texas, Alexander Gregg, the following October.

Bishop Gregg found things in a sad state of affairs. The central section of town was a charred ruin, the records of the parish had been destroyed, and the parishioners were so scattered he could locate only six of them, all female.

He immediately arranged to hold services in the Masonic Hall, which had been saved from the fire. The results were far beyond expectation. The hall was crowded with people of all denominations, and some with no denomination at all. They had turned out to see what the new bishop was like.

The meeting infused new life into the parish immediately. Bishop Gregg confirmed several people and appointed Judge J. M. Patterson, a lay reader, to conduct public services until a minister could be brought in to take over the congregation.

In 1861 Texas withdrew from the Union and was plunged into war. As most of the able-bodied men left, Dallas was thrown into a state of confusion and poverty. It was crowded with refugees from other states, only a few of whom were capable of doing the necessary work. Dr. MaKaye was sent by the bishop to hold services, but at the end of the war he left, as did most of the refugees.

Shortly, Rottenstein returned to Dallas with his wife to take up the work he had left before the war. In November 1865, he started holding services in the auditorium of the courthouse. However, because of the severe cold, he was forced to move to a hall over a small brick store on the corner of Main and Jefferson, the site where the present Hall of Records is located.

140

The dedicated priest worked hard to rebuild the congregation, but his health was against him. The severe privations he had suffered during the Civil War told on him, and he died in February of 1868. Since there was no minister in Dallas at the time, he was buried in the Masonic Cemetery and the ritual of the Masonic Order was conducted over his grave.

Once again St. Matthew's was a church without a rector. The leaders acted on the advice of Bishop Gregg and offered the post to Silas Dean Davenport, a native of North Carolina who had come to Texas as a missionary. He had done church work in Marshall and Corpus Christi before he accepted the call from St. Matthew's in Dallas.

He arrived on a blistering day in August of 1868, with his three-year-old daughter. The town was growing, and the commercial activity indicated that it would eventually become the trade center of North Texas.

Things went so well at St. Matthew's under Davenport that plans were made for a permanent church building. A site was chosen on the northwest corner of Elm and Lamar and purchased by Bishop Gregg for $100. Under Rottenstein, a building fund had been started and this grew to $1,000. The fund continued to grow, and soon the building was started. It was a great occasion when the bishop came to lead the procession to the new site where the cornerstone was laid.

Dallas had no lumberyards and, at that time, no railroads. Ox-carts were used to bring the lumber from Jefferson in East Texas. The cost of the church was $6,000 and was borne primarily by the people of Dallas. Soon after it was occupied, a small rectory was built by the young men of Dallas as a gift to Davenport in appreciation for the work he was doing for the community. The church, although not quite completed, was occupied in the summer of 1870. In November, about the time the rectory was finished, a bell (still used today) was sent as a gift from merchants in New York.

St. Matthew's and Texas grew during the period following the Civil War until it became evident that the state, with

*ST. MATTHEW'S CATHEDRAL, Interior.*

such a vast area for missionaries to cover, should be divided into more than one jurisdiction. In the General Convention of 1874, the Missionary District of Northern Texas was established and Charles Garrett was elected the first missionary bishop of the new district. He arrived in Dallas on December 31, 1874, on the new T&P Railroad that had just started supplying service to the area. After some investigation, he selected St. Matthew's as his cathedral and named Davenport as his first dean.

In 1876, not quite six years after the first church was built, the building was outgrown. The lot where it stood was sold in March and a piece of property on the corner of Commerce and Kendell was purchased. During an attempt to move the old frame building, which had served as the first cathedral, to the new site, it collapsed in the middle of the street. Although carried piece by piece, to the new location and reassembled, the building bore no resemblance to the original.

Ground was broken for a new church on the corner of

142

Commerce and Kendell on April 17, 1876, and in early May, the congregation joined Bishop Garrett in laying the cornerstone.

The new cathedral, although not completed, was occupied on June 3, 1877. It was Gothic in style, with graceful arches and pillars that caused it to be frequently referred to by the press as "the finest church in Dallas." Although it served for thirteen years, the building was never completed. Soon after it was built, the congregation grew so large that it was considered inadvisable to add the tower.

The coming of the railroads had been a vital cog in the growth and development of Dallas, but for St. Matthew's Cathedral, one of them, at least, had some liabilities. The Santa Fe Railroad station was nearby, on Jackson Street. A train arrived every Sunday at noon, about the time the rector was warming to his sermon. Immediately, the cries of hotel runners, conductors, and the crowd in general, accompanied by the hissing and clanging of the engine, were carried into the church on clouds of steam and smoke.

Toward the end of the 1880s it was evident that something must be done. The thought was to sell the present lot and purchase a less expensive one in a better neighborhood. The difference in the two prices would then go into a building fund. The nearness to the railroad turned out to be a blessing, because the church location was sold to a commercial venture for $60,000.

A new location was purchased on the northeast corner of Ervay and Canton. Three years later, the adjoining lot was purchased for the new church. A $100,000 stone edifice of majestic proportions arose, and when it opened in 1895, far surpassed any other place of worship in the city.

It was decided that a fitting time to consecrate the new structure would be the twenty-fifth anniversary of the consecration of Bishop Garrett. This fell on December 20, 1899, and the services could not take place until the debt on the church was paid off. This would have been an impossible task except for the dedication of Dean Hudson Stuck, who had arrived in 1894. He gathered a few loyal supporters around him, and to the amazement of many, the money was raised. The consecration of the cathedral occurred on

143

schedule and was one of the most impressive ceremonies Dallas had ever seen.

Fifty-one years after George Rottenstein brought the Episcopal faith to Dallas, Harry Tunis Moore arrived in the city in April of 1907 to serve as dean of the cathedral. He was born in Delavan, Wisconsin, on October 4, 1874, the same month and year that Bishop Garrett had been elected as bishop of Northern Texas. He served as dean of St. Matthew's until 1917, when he was elected a bishop coadjutor for the Diocese of Dallas. Bishop Garrett, though still at the age of eighty, turned much of the routine work over to the new coadjutor, but his own efforts never stopped. He visited his people, baptized children, married young couples, and conducted funeral services.

Randolph Ray was called from College Station, where he had been working with the students at Texas A&M College and in the St. Andrew's Church of Bryan. Dean Ray had an excellent education and had abandoned a career as a writer to serve the church as a clergyman.

For thirty-four years the majestic stone church at Ervay had served the congregation of St. Matthew's, but because of a great shifting of the residential sections, a new one became necessary. Prior to this decision, Bishop Garrett had automatically become the presiding bishop of the Protestant Episcopal Church, when a death occurred and the office was left vacant. It was then that Bishop Moore became bishop of the Diocese of Dallas.

In 1927 plans were made for a new cathedral, and on June 22, 1929, the congregation was moved to St. Mary's College Chapel on the campus at Ross and Garrett. At the rate Dallas and the congregation were growing, a larger building in a good location would be necessary to meet the needs of the church.

St. Mary's occupied almost a city block and was located in the new residential developments of Highland Park and University Park. Plans were made for the chapel to be located there until a larger cathedral could be built.

At last it appeared that the cathedral would be safe from the encroachments of the city. The initial plans were

144

drawn but had to be set aside because of the stock market crash later in the year.

Dean Ray, after having seen the size of the congregation grow from 600 to 1,568 in five years, resigned in 1923 to accept a call to "The Little Church Around the Corner" in New York City. Other deans carried on until the depression was over. Then plans were made to retire the large debt that St. Matthew's had assumed with the acquisition of St. Mary's.

Gerald G. Moore began service as dean in October of 1941 and joined Bishop Harry T. Moore in guiding St. Matthew's through the war years. Through subscriptions by members and friends, the debt was paid by 1938.

Shortly after his arrival Dean Moore was able to reach a signal achievement with the building of the great hall, which has enabled St. Matthew's to provide the diocese and the immediate area with a center that meets every need.

The physical plant of the cathedral is more complete and in better condition than ever before. A two-year program was required to put the complex in the best shape possible.

On November 1, 1964, C. Preston Wiles, Ph.D., formerly the rector of St. Mary's Church and the president of St. Mary's Hall in Burlington, New Jersey, became dean of St. Matthew's.

Sources:
1. *St. Matthew's Cathedral 1875-1975.*
2. *St. Matthew's Cathedral, 100th Anniversary Celebration 1857-1967.*
3. *The Episcopal Churchman, Diocese of Dallas,* Vol. XXVIII, No. 3 (May/June 1980).

# VI

## THE METHODISTS

The Methodist movement in Texas took roots in 1815 during the Tennessee Conference, which was held in the Bethlehem Meeting House, near Lebanon, Tennessee. When the names were called of those to be admitted to preach on trial, Samuel Thompson from Missouri presented the name of William Stevenson.

Stevenson, in the Arkansas Territory at the time, later moved into Texas. He visited a place called Pecan Point, in Red River County, not far from where Clarksville is located. As a result, William Stevenson, in 1815, became the first Methodist preacher to hold services in Texas and the first to organize a congregation. According to the records, he was also the first Protestant minister to do so.

This society, or small church, at Pecan Point was the first Methodist, or Protestant, congregation organized in Texas. Amos Tidwell was the earliest recorded class leader. The village disappeared by the mid 1830s, and the church with it, eventually.

When William Stevenson organized the congregation at Pecan Point, the Mexican government was requiring all settlers to follow the Roman Catholic religion. Any other participation was illegal. Therefore, all Protestant services had to be held quietly in private homes.

William Stevenson had lived in Missouri, near the Moses Austin family, and he knew them well. After the Austin colony had been established in Texas, he wrote Stephen F. Austin, the son, to clarify the status of religion in the colonies. Austin wrote back in May of 1824:

"The Government of this nation has finally settled down into the Federal Republican system and the outlines of the constitution are copied from that of the United States, with the single exception of an *Exclusive Religion* in favor of the Roman Catholic, which is the law of the land, and as such, must be obeyed. And if a Methodist, or any other preacher except a Catholic, were to go through the Colony preaching, I shall be compelled to IMPRISON HIM."

Mexican authorities gave little attention to the area along Red River and the Sulphur Fork. But in the Redlands of East Texas the Mexican authorities were more careful, and Protestant preachers from Louisiana had to be more cautious.

A congregation was organized at Colonel McMahan's home in 1833 and a church was built. This time the organizer was James P. Stevenson, the son of William Stevenson, who was by that time a member of the Louisiana Conference.

William Stevenson wanted to send preachers, and to go himself, into the Austin and DeWitt colonies, but he hesitated to defy the law openly. But if he hesitated to bring Methodism further into the land, he didn't discourage it.

In June of 1824, Henry Stephenson (note the difference in spelling), who had preached along the Red River with William Stevenson, made a trip into southeast Texas and visited people in Austin's Colony whom he had known earlier. He may even have quietly made an attempt to see if preaching the Protestant faith was possible.

One account shows that Stephenson visited San Felipe, Austin's new capital, but was not allowed to preach—at least publicly. It is evident that services were conducted just the same, because John Rabb has written that Stephenson visited him, three miles from San Felipe, in June of 1824 and preached to a party of four families. He concluded his letter by saying: "Colonel Austin knew nothing of his preaching until after he was gone."

147

The first camp meeting in East Texas was held in 1832. It was conducted in Sabine County, near where the town of Milam is now located. This was part of the area little noticed by the Mexican authorities, and Needham J. Alford, a Methodist, and Summer Bacon, a Cumberland Presbyterian, combined their efforts.

There was some opposition after the meeting was announced, but this was overcome. One resident arrived with a long bull whip and declared that "he would whip the first preacher who took the stand." Alford took the challenge and stared him down. Little else was said.

While the meeting was in progress, the Mexican commander in Nacogdoches, Colonel Piedras, was informed about it. He asked if they were stealing any horses. When he was told "No," he then asked if they were killing anybody. Again he was told "No" and he replied, "Let them alone." After that, there was no more opposition to Protestant preaching in East Texas. The founders of McMahan's Chapel felt secure enough to build the first Protestant church in the territory the next year.

There was still opposition to the Protestant religion further south and west. Even with leaders such as Col. William B. Travis asking for ministers to be sent to serve the settlers, little was done until after Texas had won independence from Mexico in 1836.

On August 17, 1835, seven months before his death at the Alamo, Colonel Travis issued an appeal from his headquarters at San Felipe de Austin, Texas, to the New York *Christian Advocate and Journal,* a publication he had been receiving and read with interest. He complained about the Methodist church "which has bothered to send pioneers of the gospel into almost every destitute portion of the globe, and should have neglected so long this interesting country."

The war clouds were beginning to hang heavily over the land, and little more was done to promote the Methodist movement until Texas became a republic in 1836. After that, the Protestant movement was brought out in the open and the establishment of Methodist churches all over the state was under way.

148

Sources:
1. Walter N. Vernon, *Methodism Moves Across North Texas,* published by North Texas Conference Society, 1967.
2. Macum Phelan, *A History of the Expansion of Methodism in Texas 1867–1902,* published by Mathis, Van Nold & Company, Dallas, Texas.
3. R. E. Curl, *Southwest Texas Methodism,* published by The Inter-Board Council, The Southwest Texas Conference, The Methodist Church, 1937.
4. Special conference with Dr. W. C. Fancher, Jr., the Nacogdoches district supervisor of the United Methodist Church, Nacogdoches, Texas.

## McMAHAN'S CHAPEL
### Sabine County — 1833

McMahan's Chapel was founded in 1833 in the home of Col. Samuel D. McMahan, who had moved to Texas in 1831 from Tennessee. At first the organization was referred to as a small society; however, when secrecy as a Protestant group was no longer necessary, it openly became a church. It is considered the earliest Methodist church now active in Texas, and possibly the earliest Protestant one.

Records show that Samuel D. McMahan moved from a place known as Doak's Crossing in Tennessee to what is now Sabine County. At the time, it was a part of the San Augustine municipality, a unit of the Mexican government. When the new counties were laid out, McMahan's Chapel was left in Sabine County, even though it was only thirteen miles from San Augustine.

McMahan built his log house on a site at the top of a hill, a short distance east of the spot where the chapel was erected a few years later. Historians have pointed out that in 1832, while traveling by horseback through the dense woods between his home and San Augustine, Colonel McMahan stopped to pray. While doing so, he was converted. He immediately began a search for a Methodist minister to come and preach to him, his family, and his friends.

The request reached a circuit rider from Louisiana by the name of James P. Stevenson. He responded by making a preaching tour into the territory that is now known as deep East Texas.

149

*McMAHAN'S CHAPEL, near San Augustine.*

In July of 1833, Stevenson preached a series of sermons in the McMahan home. Several people were converted, and an effort was made to organize a church. Since the organization of a Protestant church was forbidden by the Mexican government, Stevenson prevailed on the leaders to postpone their efforts. However, on his return in September, he found that during his absence of less than three months, the Methodist group had grown and had continued to conduct classes and study groups. They were more anxious than ever to organize a church. So Stevenson conducted another series of services, and during the process he organized a Methodist church. The record stands that in September of 1833, McMahan's Chapel became the first Protestant church in East Texas, even though it was illegal in the eyes of the Mexican government.

Colonel McMahan was appointed the class leader, an office comparable to that of charge lay leader, in later years. The church was organized in his home and continued to meet there until Texas gained independence in 1836.

After Texas became a republic, the church grew rapidly. Waves of new settlers were flocking to Texas, and to accommodate this growth, a log church building was built in 1837 in sight of the McMahan home. Logically, the church was officially called McMahan's Chapel.

Colonel McMahan became one of the greatest religious and civic leaders of his time. He is credited with being one of the first recorded converts to the Protestant faith in Texas, and it has been pointed out that he was the first person identified as licensed to exhort, during the San Augustine quarterly conference held in 1837. Soon after that his son and four sons-in-law were also licensed to preach.

The first log building, a thirty-by-forty-foot structure, was used until 1872, when a frame structure was erected. The third building was erected on the original site in 1900, and it served the congregation until it was dismantled to be replaced by the present masonry chapel, erected in 1949.

Bishop A. Frank Smith, the presiding bishop of the Houston-San Antonio area, delivered the first sermon in the new chapel and conducted the opening ceremonies for the new building. He was assisted in the dedication program by Joe T. Tower, the father of former U.S. Senator John Tower, who, in 1961, became the first Republican senator elected in Texas since Reconstruction days.

During the early years, McMahan's Chapel depended largely on the leadership of its founder, Colonel McMahan, with the help and supervision of such pioneer preachers as James and William Stevenson, who visited from the Louisiana Conference. There were others, including Henry Stephenson, who continued to move further into the state and preached at Peach Creek in Gonzales County.

McMahan's Chapel is in a rural setting, located on more than fifteen acres of tree-shaded land with rolling terrain and well-kept lawns, an abundance of spring water and a picnic area with tables to accommodate visitors who come to see the famous little shrine.

Besides the regular services conducted at the chapel, an annual celebration is usually held in September, the month that McMahan's Chapel was organized.

Sources:
  1. Rev. W. C. Fancher, Jr., District Office of the United Methodist Church, Nacogdoches, Texas.
  2. *West Texas Conference Methodism on the March,* Lakeview Methodist Assembly, Palestine, Texas, 1960.
  3. Mrs. Virgie W. Spurlock, *The History of McMahan's Chapel.*

## COCHRAN CHAPEL UNITED
## METHODIST CHURCH
Dallas — 1856

The Methodist movement in Texas gained a strong outpost when Cochran Chapel was organized in July of 1856. Since then, a growing number of Methodists have worshiped there in the same location, which is now a part of Dallas.

An early settler, William M. Cochran, moved his wife and six children from nearby Peters Colony to a location closer to Dallas, near Bachman Creek. It was in his home that the first sermon was preached, and it became a tribute to Mrs Cochran, who was the first Methodist in the county.

Cochran died in 1856, three years after the move, and Mrs. Cochran was left to raise the children. She decided her land was ideal for a church. She did the surveying and set aside three acres for a Methodist church and a cemetery. A copy of the original deed is hanging in the church norvex as a reminder of Cochran Chapel's part in the early Methodist movement.

The deed was dated July 11, 1856, and the first building, a frame structure forty by thirty feet, was soon started. It was built from rough timber that had been hand-dressed after being hauled 150 miles from Jefferson in East Texas. Ox teams were used, and it took several weeks to complete each trip. The structure was finished in 1858, and Dr. J. W. P. McKenzie preached the sermon of dedication. The name Cochran Chapel had been suggested by a trustee in honor of the family who had helped make it possible.

Prior to the construction of the church, a prayer group had been formed and the five members, Mr. and Mrs. I. B.

*COCHRAN CHAPEL, Main Sanctuary, Dallas.*

Webb, Mrs. Nancy Jane Cochran, and Mr. and Mrs. M. F. Fortner, continued to serve the church for over twenty years.

In the early days of Cochran Chapel, prowling Indians and roving animals made it necessary for the men to take their rifles to church. These and other problems confronted the members, but they continued to move forward in their efforts to attract new people.

The efforts paid off when, in 1867, Cochran Chapel became the first church to hold a district conference. Bishop E. M. Marvin presided, and it was the first time most of the members had seen a bishop.

The congregation continued to grow. At the second quarterly conference, held May 18, 1883, a new building committee was appointed. Members were P. A. Winn, Eli F. Merrell, John Fields, H. Gibbs, J. H. Cochran, and W. P. Cochran. In 1885 the second church was built, with O. S. Thomas as the pastor.

The years and the weather caused the larger frame

153

*CHAPEL OF SILENCE, Cochran Chapel, Dallas.*

building to show alarming signs of wear. In 1924, when W. M. Bowden became the minister, he set out to correct the situation. An empty World War I barracks at Love Field was rented to serve as a place to worship while the church was reworked and converted into a brick veneer structure that was modern in every respect. The auditorium measured fifty-two feet by sixty-six feet and had a seating capacity of 300. There was also a choir loft, a balcony, a basement, and ten Sunday school rooms.

On May 10, 1944, seventy-seven years after the initial meeting, another district conference was held at Cochran Chapel. Dr. F. A. Buddin presided over the Centennial Celebration of the conference, and Bishop Ivan Lee Holt was the speaker.

By 1952, the building, located at 9027 Midway Road and Northeast Highway, was completely redecorated and theater seats were added. Individual members purchased the seats and received recognition from metal plates placed on an arm of each chair.

A variety of improvements came during the next twenty years. In 1972 a historical marker was presented by the Texas State Historical Association through the efforts of the Dallas County Historical Survey Committee.

In November of 1974, Meaders Hall, a small chapel, a bride's room, a church library, and a historical room were dedicated by the presiding bishop, McFerrin Stowe, under the efforts of the pastor, Robert Young. The seating capacity of Meaders Hall is 400 and is the center of many activities that bring members of the Cochran Chapel congregation closer together.

Sources:
1. Personal interview with Mrs. W. T. Baker, Dallas, Texas.
2. Dedication history prepared October 29, 1972.
3. *The Texas Methodist,* Cochran Chapel, United Methodist Church Edition, April 25, 1980.
4. *Memories Live On and On.*
5. *The Story of the Stained Glass Windows at Cochran's Chapel.*

## THE FIRST UNITED METHODIST CHURCH
### Austin – 1840

The history of the First United Methodist Church of Austin is a vital part of the history of the state. Since 1923, when the present structure was built at Twelfth and Brazos, it has helped to set the standards the government has come to live by.

Methodism came to Austin in the fall of 1839, only a short time after the community was established. John Haynie came to Texas from Alabama as a circuit rider and preached in the area between Bastrop and Austin. He avoided Indians because he refused to bear arms, and on occasion he had to swim his horse across the Colorado River to keep his appointments.

In November of 1839, Haynie served as chaplain in the House of Representatives at the first Congress of the Republic of Texas to meet in Austin. It was then that he organized the first Methodist group, the second Protestant congregation in the community. Fourteen members met in the home of David Thomas.

Haynie was followed as minister in 1841 by Josiah Whipple from Illinois, who conducted services in a bowling

155

*FIRST UNITED METHODIST CHURCH, Austin.*

alley on Congress Avenue for lack of a church building. He frequently preached with a pistol and a rifle in the pulpit because of the possibility of Indian raids.

Such Indian raids and possible Mexican invasions limited the growth of the Methodist movement in Austin in the early 1840s and caused a lapse in service between the time Whipple left in 1843 and Homer S. Thrall arrived in 1845. Thrall, who later wrote the first history of Methodism in Texas, found no congregation, so he preached in the hall of the House of Representatives. It was necessary for him to open a school to pay his expenses, even though he slept on the floor in a lawyer's office.

The motivation of Thrall was effective. The Methodists in Austin were reorganized, with Governor J. P. Henderson and a number of legislators as members. Texas had just joined the Union, and it was fitting that the first Methodist church building was started shortly afterwards — a frame building on the northeast corner of Congress and Cedar (now known as Fourth Street). It was dedicated on December 19, 1847, and served a series of ministers through 1852, when the next milestone of progress was passed.

John W. Phillips became the new minister in 1852. In January of that year a group of Austin physicians led a movement by doctors all over the state to organize a medical society. The Texas Medical Association was thus founded. Years later, the occasion was recorded for history when Park Davis Drug Company commissioned Robert Thom to do a picture of the white frame building with the doctors assembled in front. The original, painted from a description of the event as it had taken place, hangs in the library of the Texas Medical Association in Austin.

Josiah Whipple served his second call to the church from 1864 to 1868, when it was known as the Methodist Episcopal Church, South. His service included years of the Civil War and Reconstruction. The membership declined to seventy-seven, primarily because emancipated slaves, through the help of Isaac Wright, a minister of the Methodist Episcopal Church (North), formed their own congregation.

157

*TEXAS MEDICAL ASSOCIATION organized at early Methodist Episcopal Church, Austin.*

The new congregation became the Wesley Chapel Methodist Church, the oldest black Methodist church in Austin and probably in the state. With the help of the Freedmen's Aid Society, services were held in the basement of the church, which created racial tensions and produced a period of emotional strain between the two groups.

While John W. Phillips was still pastor, and shortly after the Texas Medical Association was formed, the original building was sold to the Christian church. The Methodist group moved to a red brick building on the corner of Mulberry (now known as Tenth Street) and Brazos. They stayed at that location until the newer building of 1882 was sold to the Austin Labor Temple Association.

Work began on the present building on June 23, 1923. The cornerstone was laid that day, and Ben H. Powell, representing the Grand Master of the Grand Lodge of Texas, served as master of ceremonies. E. R. Barcus, the minister at the time, helped plan the first unit that was open for worship on December 1, 1923. Bishop James E. Dickey preached the first sermon.

The first unit of the building, which was the basement, contained an auditorium, thirty-one Sunday school rooms, classrooms, a ladies parlor, a kitchen, a nursery, and restrooms. The superstructure above the basement, which contained the sanctuary and additional rooms, was opened for services on Sunday, December 16, 1928.

The Annual Conference in 1940 was the beginning of a real growth period for the First Methodist Church in Austin. Mrs. John Robbins and Ben H. Powell were the delegates who selected Kenneth Pope as the new minister. The dynamic leader, who later became a bishop, began his service with a congregation of 1,986 members. When he left in 1949, it had increased to 3,451.

Ground was broken on July 18, 1951, for a new Educational Building at the same Tenth and Brazos location. It was completed in August of 1952 at a cost of $215,000. Then, in April of 1965, the First Church received a facelift that involved new glass doors to replace the outmoded wooden ones. In 1980 the stately and dignified complex

159

stands as a silent sentinel near the Capitol building, only a short distance away.

Among more recent ministers, former associate pastor Bruno Schmidt retired in order to serve as the editor of the *Texas Methodist Historical News.* The associate pastor as of 1980 was Scott R. Somers, with Dr. Jack D. Heacock as minister.

Sources:
1. Interview with Rev. Bruno Schmidt, former associate pastor of the First United Methodist Church of Austin, and editor of *The Texas Methodist Historical News.*
2. A Bicentennial Gift, *History of the First United Methodist Church of Austin.*

## THE FIRST UNITED METHODIST CHURCH
Crockett — 1839

The pride and dedication that developed in the historic little deep East Texas town of Crockett during the early days of the Republic carried over into the infant Methodist congregation and became a part of it. Much of the early history of Crockett is found in the history of the church.

For nearly twenty years, the Methodist movement in Texas developed behind closed doors. Since participation in Protestant services was prohibited by Mexican law, any activity had to be controlled and conducted without publicity. The Methodist Episcopal Church of the United States, inclined to publicly respect the law, refrained from answering the call of Col. William B. Travis and other officials for ministers. This did not stop the Methodist families who came to colonize Texas. They practiced their faith in seclusion and buried their dead without the presence of an ordained minister.

As early as 1815, the records show that Methodist circuit riders were coming from the Arkansas Territory and the Louisiana circuit to serve settlers along the Red and

*FIRST UNITED METHODIST CHURCH, Crockett,
original brick building.*

*FIRST UNITED METHODIST CHURCH, Crockett,
current building.*

161

Sabine rivers. There is no indication, however, that they ventured as far inland as Crockett during the early years.

One colonist who activated the Methodist movement in Houston County was John Andrew Box. He had worked in the church in Alabama and, according to some sources, "was a devoted layman who labored on the circuit."

John Box arrived in Texas in 1835, along with his father, three brothers, a sister, and their families. The records show he was granted a head-right on Cochina Creek, just east of the present town of Kennard. The next year he purchased a head-right from Frank Johnson, which took in the southwest section of Crockett. After serving with Sam Houston at San Jacinto, he settled the Johnson property and left his oldest son, William, to take care of the farm at Cochina.

John Box apparently ministered to the Methodists in Houston County before ordained ministers arrived. A daughter, Mrs. Rowena Box Davidson, is remembered to have said that her father preached in the townsite of Crockett when only two families lived there. The homes of the Box families became the stopping places for the ministers and the bishops who came later.

After Texas became a republic in 1836, the entire area was fertile ground for missionary work by all Protestant groups. Dr. Martin Ruter, the president of Allegheny College in Pennsylvania, Littleton Fowler, a native of Tennessee, and Robert Alexander, also from Tennessee, all volunteered to come to Texas as soon as the new government had taken over. All three men were commissioned in April 1837 as missionaries by Bishop Elijah Hedding, who was in charge of the foreign missions of the church.

Houston County was a part of the large territory traveled by Littleton Fowler. He visited settlers and conducted services there. Making his headquarters at McMahan's Chapel, he moved across the area to establish churches at San Augustine, Nacogdoches, Washington-on-the-Brazos, Houston, and Brazoria. He arrived in Houston while Congress was in session and on November 21, 1837, was elected chaplain of the Senate. When the Grand Masonic Lodge of

Texas was organized the next year, he was elected Grand Chaplain. A month later, upon the death of Dr. Martin Ruter, who was the superintendent of the Texas Mission, Fowler succeeded him as head of the mission.

Crockett received an appointment at a new Methodist church in the Texas Mission when the conference met at Nachez, Mississippi, on December 4, 1839. At the time, the state was divided into two districts. Crockett was in the San Augustine District.

The first pastor assigned to Crockett was Henderson D. Palmer of Alabama. He may have known Littleton Fowler, who was an agent of La Grange College, where he had attended school. Nevertheless, Fowler found him teaching school in Nacogdoches in 1838 and made him a class leader before giving him a license to preach in July of that year.

The *Texas Methodist Centennial Yearbook* gives this account of the event:

"The first man to be licensed to preach in Texas, according to the records, was Henderson D. Palmer, who was licensed by Littleton Fowler at Box's Fort, Nacogdoches County, on July 7, 1838. Palmer became a well known traveling preacher, and died a member of the Trinity (North Texas) Conference in 1869."

Palmer not only organized the church at Crockett but he met his future wife there, the daughter of a local minister, John Wilson.

According to the records, the Methodist church at Crockett was organized shortly before Christmas of 1839. Henderson Palmer, as the pastor, John Wilson, a local minister, and Littleton Fowler, as the presiding elder, met with a group of prospective members headed by John Box, J. R. Bracken, Charles Ellis and James Brent, along with their families, to make plans for the new church.

After the church had been chartered, Palmer organized a Methodist church at the little community of Shiloh, about eighteen miles from Crockett. Stephen Box, the father of John Box, donated three acres of land to be used for religious purposes. Brush arbors were constructed and

163

camp meetings were held each year. Families would go to Shiloh in the summer and camp for two or three weeks while attending services and visiting. This practice continued until after the turn of the century.

In 1840 the General Conference authorized the Texas Mission to become an annual conference, and several new ministers were admitted on trial. In the process, Henderson Palmer was moved to Jasper and Daniel Carl was appointed as the second minister for the young Crockett church.

The Methodist congregation was the first church organized in Crockett. At first, meetings were held in private homes. Then, for a number of years, a union church was shared with several other denominations. The small building then used was across the street from the present Methodist church, on Seventh Street. The only site the church has ever had was purchased from Col. John Long in 1858.

The first church, a large frame building, was constructed on the present site in 1864. The minister at that time was Harvin W. Moore, the father of Judge Leroy L. Moore, who served for many years as superintendent of the Methodist Sunday school.

Mrs. Gail Q. King recalled the first church in her *Scrapbook* as "a long wooden building painted white, lighted by swinging lamps, which burned kerosene and occasionally went out if the sermon was too long, and they frequently were. It was heated by wood stoves and was very cold most of the time. The organ was one that had to be pumped, but we always have had faithful organists in our church and for the most part, good music."

The Texas Conference was divided in 1844, with Crockett becoming a part of the East Texas Conference. It remained that way until the conferences were merged again in 1902. Crockett had the distinction of being the host church for the East Texas Conference's annual meetings four times during those years (in 1862, 1871, 1877, and 1888).

In July of 1897 a building committee was organized and the frame building was moved across Goliad Street to the Moore property until a brick church was constructed.

164

The cornerstone was laid September 1, 1901, and the church was finished in 1902.

The general conference of 1902 merged the East Texas Conference and the Texas Conference. Crockett had the distinction of hosting the first meeting of the reunited Texas annual conference, which was held the first week in December 1902. Bishop E. R. Hendrix presided, and the new sanctuary was a fitting place for the occasion.

An impressive pipe organ has been a vital part of the church in Crockett. Massive pipes of irregular length reach almost to the ceiling in some places and produce a tone and volume that keeps pace with the rest of the church. Mrs. Ruby DeCuir was the organist for many years. Her father, Harvin W. Moore, was minister of the church in 1862. Mrs. Wilma Sexton Foote later served as organist, with Mrs. Mark Ellis assisting.

A growing church school made the construction of an educational annex necessary. It was completed in 1924 under the pastorate of C. W. Hughes. Gail Q. King, Sr., was chairman of the building committee, and Mrs. G. H. Henderson was president of the Woman's Missionary Society. The women of the church, under Mrs. Henderson's leadership, made it possible to include a basement with a kitchen so they could have church dinners. They paid their proportionate cost, as designated by the building committee, by serving the Lion's Club luncheons and operating a country store downtown.

Ground was broken in 1953 for a fellowship hall and single-level classrooms. Mrs. Jack Barbee was president of the Woman's Society of Christian Service at that time. Women of the church wanted another kitchen, and their rummage sales under the chairmanship of Mrs. R. J. Spence raised the money required to completely equip the new facility. John Spinks was chairman of the board of stewards at the time, with J. G. Beasley as chairman of the building committee and Raymond Cornelius as vice-chairman.

Under the leadership of Earl Cantrelle, a building committee was formed and work was begun on the renovation of the sanctuary in September 1976. Pat Kelley was chairman of the administrative board. The United Methodist Women, under the leadership of Mae K. Maxwell, with the assistance of Bertha Sanders, accepted the responsibility of redecorating the children's wing of the education annex.

The sanctuary, completed in 1978, reflects the craftsmanship of the late Homer Argall. The beautiful stained glass windows, made in Czechoslovakia, were placed there when the structure was completed in 1902.

The choir director in the 1980s was E. S. (Stew) Dorsey, a descendant of the pioneer Box families, the son of Dr. and Mrs. E. S. Dorsey and the grandson of Mrs. Hattie Box Murchison.

The First United Methodist Church of Crockett, a historic landmark in a historic town, is on the move still, with Rev. Earl Cantrelle as pastor (as of 1980).

The list of pastors of the First United Methodist Church in Crockett from 1839 to 1980 include the following:

| 1839 | Henderson D. Palmer | 1862 | Harvin W. Moore |
|------|---------------------|------|-----------------|
| 1840 | Daniel C. Clark | 1864 | George S. Gatewood |
| 1841 | Nathan Shook & | 1865 | Samuel Lynch |
|      | James H. Collard | 1866 | H. B. Phillips |
| 1843 | James H. Collard | 1867 | Francis M. Stovall |
| 1844 | M. H. Jones & | 1870 | W. C. Collins |
|      | Wm. K. Wilson | 1872 | A. M. Box |
| 1846 | Jacob Crawford | 1873 | John C. Woolam |
| 1847 | John C. Woolam | 1875 | D. M. Stovall |
| 1848 | Jefferson Shook | 1877 | D. P. Cullen |
| 1849 | C. Box | 1878 | J. B. Hall |
| 1850 | John Powell | 1879 | C. P. Cullen |
| 1851 | William W. George | 1880 | N. T. Burks |
| 1852 | Samuel C. Box | 1881 | J. W. Johnson |
| 1853 | Alfred Leroy | 1883 | J. R. Wages |
|      | Kavanaugh & | 1885 | W. A. Sampey |
|      | J. McMillen | 1886 | B. R. Bolton |
| 1855 | William P. Sanson | 1890 | J. T. Smith |
| 1859 | Samuel Lynch | 1891 | J. L. Dawson |
| 1861 | James A. Scruggs & | 1893 | L. M. Fowler |
|      | W. C. Collins | 1894 | John S. Mathis |

| 1897 | A. S. Whitehurst | 1930 | P. T. Ramsey |
|------|------------------|------|--------------|
| 1899 | J. A. Beagle | 1931 | Terry W. Wilson |
| 1900 | Ellis Smith | 1933 | John V. Berglund |
| 1902 | E. L. Crawford | 1934 | Bob L. Pool |
| 1903 | Geo. A. LaClere | 1935 | F. D. Dawson |
| 1904 | H. A. Hodge & | 1937 | O. W. Hooper |
|      | H. M. Whaling | 1938 | H. L. Munger |
| 1905 | C. E. Smith | 1940 | H. V. Rankin |
| 1906 | Irvin B. Manley | 1944 | R. L. Lemons |
| 1907 | James W. Downs | 1948 | C. L. Williams |
| 1908 | F. M. Boyles | 1949 | Leslie LeGrand |
| 1909 | Geo. W. Davis | 1955 | James H. Heflen |
| 1912 | D. H. Hotchkiss | 1957 | Vernon Cornelius |
| 1915 | C. U. McLarty | 1958 | C. A. West |
| 1918 | C. B. Garrett | 1962 | E. Jewel Strong |
| 1921 | E. A. Maness | 1965 | L. B. Broach III |
| 1924 | C. W. Hughes | 1970 | Jim H. Rhodes, Jr. |
| 1925 | C. A. Lehmberg | 1974 | E. J. Davis, Jr. |
|      |  | 1976 | Earl Cantrelle |

Sources:
1. L. B. Broach, Ramon Callaway, Georgia M. Spinks, *A Short History of the First United Methodist Church of Crockett.*
2. Rev. Earl Cantrelle, Mae K. Maxwell, Pauline Dunklin, *Update of Church History.*
3. Conversation with Mae K. Maxwell.
4. Author Frank A. Driskill, who was baptized in this church and served on Board of Stewards in 1933.

## THE FIRST UNITED METHODIST CHURCH
## Nacogdoches – 1837

Reports handed down from one generation to another seem to indicate that at least one Methodist service was conducted in Nacogdoches before 1821. According to accounts of the early circuit riders, the sermon probably was preached by William Stevenson, who came into Texas from the Arkansas Territory. It is known that he spent some time in Red River County and organized a congregation at Pecan

*RED BRICK METHODIST CHURCH, 1910, Nacogdoches.*

Point, near Clarksville. It should be noted, however, that this church did not survive.

The present congregation traces its origin to Littleton Fowler, who as a missionary to Texas preached in Nacogdoches in October of 1837. Before the end of the year, he founded a Methodist "society" of eighteen members.

In December of 1838, the Texas Mission of the Methodist Church became a district of the Mississippi Conference, and Littleton Fowler was appointed the presiding elder of the Texas District. Samuel A. Williams became the first minister formally appointed to the Methodist society in Nacogdoches.

A number of ministers followed Williams and services

were continued in Nacogdoches, even without a church building. The congregation met at a variety of places and became the largest and most active Protestant group in the community.

In 1860 a church building was finally constructed on two lots near the corner of Hospital and Pecan streets (then called Mulberry), and this building remained in use until 1887. The site of the present sanctuary was then secured, just across the street from the original building. The second and larger wooden church burned in 1907.

The congregation decided on a brick structure to replace the building destroyed by fire. Three years later, in the fall of 1910, the new sanctuary was ready for occupancy. Until then, J. W. Mills, who had been the minister during the building period, held services in the Old Opera House, the Ingraham Building, and in the Cumberland Presbyterian and Baptist churches. For fifty-seven years the brick Methodist Church with the beautiful stained glass windows added prestige as a landmark.

This church participated in the establishment of a second Methodist congregation, west of town. The new church was called "Perritte Memorial," in honor of the presiding elder, H. T. Perritte. The church, located at 1025 Durst Street, was completed in the fall of 1925 and opened its doors with seventeen charter members.

The first Methodist Bible Chair established at a Texas State Teacher's College was a result of Perritte's efforts. With the help of his successor, J. Ed. Harris, the dream of the popular minister was finally realized, even though he did not live to see it come true. Classes began on January 3, 1929, in the home of his widow. Later, the Macon Gunter Bible Chair was named for a Stephen F. Austin student who was killed in World War II. Through the years, directors of the Wesley (Gunter) Bible Chair have worked closely with pastors and stewards of the First Methodist Church in all areas of worship.

In 1936, while C. W. Lokey was minister, the W. W. Hazelwood home on Mound Street was given to the church for use as a parsonage. Until then, a frame building ad-

169

*FIRST UNITED METHODIST CHURCH, Nacogdoches, current building.*

*FIRST UNITED METHODIST CHURCH, Nacogdoches, interior.*

170

jacent to the church had housed the families of the ministers. The brick home served as a parsonage until the present modern structure on Raguet Street was completed in 1973.

With the First Methodist Church free of debt in 1965, the Quarterly Conference planned a new sanctuary and selected a building committee to handle the work. James Heflin was the minister at the First Church throughout the building years. The Church Conference approved the plans for the new building, drawn by two local architects, Carl Maynard and John Greer, in November of 1967. The last service was held in the old sanctuary that month. While the building was in progress, services were held in the Banita Ballroom of the Fredonia Hotel, across the street from the present structure.

Dr. Kenneth W. Copeland, the resident bishop of the Houston Area, Texas and Gulf Coast Conference of the United Methodist Church, delivered the opening sermon in the new sanctuary of the First Methodist Church of Nacogdoches on Easter Sunday, April 6, 1969. He was assisted by James Heflin, the pastor.

The completed complex projects a combination of dignity and beauty. Robert H. Robinson as pastor has carried on the long tradition of the historic church.

The Nacogdoches County Historical Committee secured a marker for the church through the Texas Historical Commission. The bronze plaque, dedicated in 1977, commemorates the congregation that has existed since 1837 as the first Protestant church in a city abounding in Texas history.

Sources:
  1. James L. Nichols, Jr., *Some History of the First United Methodist Church of Nacogdoches.*
  2. *The Daily Sentinel,* Nacogdoches, Texas, Saturday, April 6, 1969.
  3. Macum Phelan, *Early Methodism in Texas.*
  4. Conference with the pastor, Robert H. Robinson.

*FIRST UNITED METHODIST CHURCH, Houston.*

## THE FIRST UNITED METHODIST CHURCH
### Houston – 1841

The early Methodist movement in Texas challenged the Mexican government and, through circuit riding ministers, laid the groundwork for increased Protestant activity when restrictions on religious activity were removed.

Frequent requests for Methodist ministers to be sent to Texas while it was still a Mexican territory had come from Col. William B. Travis and other leaders involved in colonization. These appeals prompted the General Conference of the Methodist Episcopal Church, which was in session in Cincinnati, Ohio, in May of 1836, to issue a call for volunteers for missionary work.

Dr. Martin Ruter, who resigned as president of Allegheny College in Pennsylvania to accept the challenge, received an appointment as superintendent of the Texas Mission. This came in April of 1837, when Robert Alex-

172

ander, of the Mississippi Conference, and Littleton Fowler, of the Tennessee Conference, also received appointments as missionaries to Texas. Bishop Elijah Hedding, who was in charge of the foreign missionary work for the church, made the appointments.

Robert Alexander, twenty-six years old at the time, was the first of the three to come to Texas, but it was Littleton Fowler who was responsible for the Methodist movement in East Texas that included San Augustine, Nacogdoches, Crockett, and Houston. He established a residence at McMahan's Chapel and covered the large area by horseback. His circuit extended from the Sabine River on the east to beyond the Colorado River on the west. Mrs. Fowler frequently accompanied him, also on horseback, since the distance traveled was over a thousand miles and required at least two months to cover.

Littleton Fowler arrived in Houston while Congress was in session, and on November 21, 1837, he was elected chaplain of the Senate. When the Grand Masonic Lodge of Texas was organized in April of 1838, he was elected the grand chaplain. It was only a month later that Dr. Martin Ruter, who was the superintendent of the Texas Mission, died and Fowler was named to succeed him.

Some accounts credit Littleton Fowler with founding the first church in Houston, but further research seems to indicate that this is not true. There is evidence that the first Methodist church was organized by Jesse Hord in the spring of 1839, about a month after William Allen had organized the Presbyterian Church, the first church in the city. Rev. Mr. Hord had been assigned to the Houston Circuit, after the Mississippi Conference had met on December 5, 1838, and a special district for Texas, called the Texas Mission District, was set up. The appointment came on December 10, 1838, when a number of ministers met in a log cabin in San Augustine, Texas.

On Christmas Eve, Hord met with the Presbyterian minister, William Allen, and made arrangements for "harmonious preaching in the city." He visited Congress the same day and was assured "of the importance of the gospel

173

being preached in Texas." On Christmas Day, he traveled to Richmond and was in and out of Houston after that. With twenty appointments to cover he had little time to spend in any one place, but several sources indicate that he had enough time to organize a church (in April of 1839).

In some areas, Thomas Summers has been given credit for organizing the first Methodist church in Houston, in 1841, but evidence seems to support the 1839 date. The most substantial argument in favor of the earlier date is that Houston was given a regularly appointed minister for 1840, a year before the Summers effort developed.

Houston and the First Methodist Church grew together, but the year 1839 was not good for either of them. Two significant events would hinder them both. First of all, the capital was moved to Austin, and Houston became a town of uncertainty, boredom, inactivity, and vacant houses. The other disaster was the epidemic of yellow fever, which took the lives of 240 of the 2,000 residents, including John K. Allen, the younger of the two brothers who founded the city. He was only twenty-eight years old when he died. In spite of these difficulties, including worthless currency, the situation improved in 1840.

On December 4, 1839, the Mississippi Conference met in Natchez and two districts were created in Texas. Littleton Fowler became the presiding elder of the San Augustine District and Robert Alexander was appointed to the Rutersville (West Texas) District. Edward Fontaine was sent to Houston, while Thomas Summers went to Galveston.

At the General Conference, which met in May of 1840, the Texas Conference was established. The first meeting was held on Christmas Day of that year at Rutersville, and a Galveston district was created. Samuel A. Williams was named the presiding elder and Thomas Summers served a dual post in Galveston and Houston. He began the building program in Galveston in 1841, which was not completed until January of 1843.

In the 1842 conference, Galveston and Houston were divided. Richard Walker was sent to Galveston, while Summers remained in Houston. It is thought that Robert

174

Alexander, who acted as president of the conference in the absence of the bishop, specifically requested Summers to do the same thing in Houston that he had done in Galveston.

Thomas Summers spent much of his time traveling throughout the United States, raising money to pay off the debt of the Galveston church and acquiring additional funds for the Houston Building program. He was transferred to the Alabama Conference before he could see the new building opened for worship, which occurred on May 11, 1844. Josiah W. Whipple was sent to Houston in his place.

During the seventeen-year period from the building's completion until the beginning of the war, the church in Houston merely existed at times. However, at other times it seemed to flourish. The size of the congregation, and especially the Sunday school, seemed to depend on the quality of the minister and his ability to attract members. Under the Methodist system of rotation, at least fourteen ministers occupied the pulpit during that period.

The Houston Methodists were without a church building during and after the Civil War. It is believed that it collapsed during a storm. The exact date is a matter of conjecture, but the little brick church that had been the pride of the city since 1844 simply fell down. The date had to be some time before the beginning of the war, because the congregation used the African-American church that had been built on the adjoining block in about 1851 until the hostilities began. After that, services were held at the Lutheran Church. Thus it was that the Houston church emerged from the war without a building, with a membership that was scattered, and with all of the problems that faced those who had supported the cause of the South.

After the war ended, plans were made to rebuild the church. William Rees was sent as pastor in 1865, and he remained until his death from yellow fever in 1867. During his service there, and with the driving force of the building committee chairman, Charles Shearn, an effort was launched to raise funds to build a place to worship. It was

175

occupied for the first time on March 31, 1867, with a debt on it of $1,000, which was later paid by Mr. Shearn. Sometime afterwards, the new structure picked up the name of "Shearn Church." It was a plain, roughly-finished building with no Sunday school rooms. At least, though, the congregation had its own church again.

As Houston continued to grow, so did the Methodist movement. From an original congregation of less than twenty members, it grew to about 12,000 in 1980, making it the largest church in Methodism. As the congregation has grown, new buildings have been built to keep pace with the times. Much of the growth has taken place since World War II.

The church building is located at 1320 Main Street, in the heart of the city. The sanctuary was built in 1910, and the educational building was added in 1928. While other churches have moved to the suburbs, only the First United Methodist Church and the Episcopal Cathedral remain to represent Protestantism downtown. The church has become financially strong, having become free of debt in 1978.

Although nearly $3 million has been spent in the past two decades for remodeling and redecorating, the outward appearance of the buildings remains the same. Even in a business area as massive as downtown Houston, the majestic Methodist complex on Main Street gives an appearance of being in complete command.

The Texas Annual Conference has met at the church every year since 1939, with only three exceptions. It met in Dallas with the other conferences in 1966, in Galveston in 1974, and in Nacogdoches in 1975. A majority of the ministers in the Texas Conference were ordained at the church's altar.

The groundbreaking for the Quillian Memorial Center took place in March 1957, after more than $600,000 was spent on the facilities. Included is a large gymnasium, which also serves as a banquet hall, skating rink, and auditorium. A stage is situated at one end, and on the sides are tables for billiards and table tennis. The lounge area has a large kitchen which is completely furnished, even with a massive barbecue pit. There are several classrooms, and outside there are tennis courts, picnic tables, charcoal grills, and a swimming pool. With the addition of the Bintliff Chapel, completed in 1973 to take the place of the old chapel that had served the church for so many years, the facilities of the First Church leave little to be desired.

Dr. Charles L. Allen, a nationally-known minister, became pastor in August 1960. He has been invited to preach all over the United States and has written thirty-two books which are best-sellers in the field of religious books. The 1981 staff included Dr. D. Orval Strong, Rev. Frederick Marsh, Rev. Robert Stevens, and Diaconal Minister, Mrs. Mildred Parker.

Sources:
1. Lewis H. Grimes, *Cloud of Witnesses* (A History of the First United Methodist Church of Houston).
2. D. Orval Strong, *Supplement to A Cloud of Witnesses.*
3. Newspaper articles supplied by Bill B. Hedges of Galveston, Texas.


# TRAVIS STREET
# UNITED METHODIST CHURCH
La Grange — 1839

The Methodist movement arrived in the area that is now Fayette County, Texas, in 1824, before it was legal to establish a congregation other than one of the Catholic faith. Henry Stephenson, a circuit-riding preacher from Arkansas, had come through to speak to different groups.

In 1837, after Texas had won independence from Mexico, Dr. Martin Ruter was sent to Texas, along with two other Methodist ministers. Dr. Ruter died the following year, but his dream of a Methodist college was realized when Rutersville College, the forerunner of Southwestern University, was established in the town also named after him, Rutersville.

A year after Dr. Ruter died, Robert Alexander, one of

*TRAVIS STREET METHODIST CHURCH, La Grange.*

the two other ministers who came with him, was appointed to the Rutersville Circuit which included La Grange. The first services were held under brush arbors and later in the homes of members.

The first Methodist Conference in Texas was held in Rutersville on Christmas Day, 1840, and it was there that the Texas Conference was organized.

In 1844 the Methodist Episcopal Church was split into "Northern" and "Southern" churches over the question of slavery. The La Grange church became a part of the "Southern" branch and remained there until the three major branches of Methodism were reunited in 1939.

The first Methodist church building in La Grange was erected in 1851 in the 100 block of South Washington. It was a frame building, and the bell from the old courthouse was brought to the new church. Two years later, James E. Ferguson, a graduate of Rutersville College, was named pastor. At the time, the membership was made up of 147 white and 18 black members.

The Civil War and a yellow fever epidemic took a pronounced toll on the membership, but in 1866 the church was moved two blocks south on Washington Street to a newly purchased lot and was remodeled. An organ was added, and the first bell from the old courthouse again hung in a newly designed cupola.

In 1883 the lot where the present church is situated was bought and a new church building was erected. Bishop Linus Parker came from New Orleans to preside over the dedication. Again, the old courthouse bell was brought to the new church, where it still rings every Sunday to call the members to worship.

La Grange was transferred to the West Texas Conference in 1910, and J. E. Lovett became the first appointment from the new alignment. He was followed the next year by W. R. Keathley. After the union of the three main branches of Methodism in 1939 to form the Methodist Church, the West Texas Conference became the Southwest Texas Conference. That was the year that the Methodist church in La Grange celebrated its 100th anniversary. The pastor was S. M. Bailey.

In 1964 the Travis Street Methodist Church celebrated its 125th anniversary with the dedication of a historical marker. The church was also entered into the state archives as a recorded Texas Historical Landmark. The little church at nearby Winchester was added to the La Grange charge shortly thereafter.

In 1968 the Methodist Church and the Evangelical United Brethren Church united to become the United Methodist Church. The La Grange church followed suit and became the Travis Street United Methodist Church.

Among the earliest settlers in Texas to be converted by the Methodists was John Rabb. He was converted at the Caney Creek camp meeting in 1834. Dr. Martin Ruter made notes in his journal about his visits with John Rabb, which took place in 1838, shortly before Ruter's death.

The oldest membership roll still in the possession of

179

the church reveals that a local preacher by the name of A. G. Beaumont joined the church on February 8, 1863. It is not clear whether he was licensed to preach in the La Grange circuit.

The Travis Street United Methodist Church of La Grange has a long and productive history. It is significant, then, that this conservative and historic community, made up of several ethnic groups, should be one of the first in Texas to offer the pulpit to a female minister. While the change did not come without a lot of soul searching, the new pastor, Shirley D. Hill, in 1980 began rendering an outstanding service to the entire community.

Sources:
1. Interview with Linda McGill, secretary, Travis Street Methodist Church, La Grange, Texas.
2. *The Centennial Booklet 1839–1939.*


# THE McKENZIE
# MEMORIAL METHODIST CHURCH
## Clarksville — 1838

The First Methodist Episcopal Church, South, was founded in Clarksville, Texas, in 1838 by John L. Lovejoy and Dr. J. W. P. McKenzie.

Dr. McKenzie had been sent as a missionary to the Choctaw Nation in 1836, at Fort Towson, Indian Territory. The records further indicate that Dr. McKenzie crossed the Red River and founded three Methodist societies. The boundaries between Texas and Arkansas were not clear then, and these societies were in an area under the jurisdiction of Miller County, Arkansas, from 1830 to 1836, and afterwards in Texas. The societies in Texas were at Jonesborough, DeKalb, and Clarksville.

The exact date for the construction of the first building is not clear, but it was located on East Church Street and was used until 1855. It was then sold to the black Baptist church, the "Zion Travelers."

180

*McKENZIE MEMORIAL United Methodist Church, Clarksville.*

A new two-story building was erected just across the street from the present Masonic Hall. The church, located on North Locust Street, resembled the current Masonic Hall and then served as a meeting place for the Masonic group, who used the second floor of the new building.

While D. J. Martin was pastor, he was the leader in the organization of the Ladies Aid Society, which took place in 1882. It was the first women's organization of any kind in Clarksville. The ten charter members helped erect a parsonage and pay off a $500 debt on the church by raising their dues of one dollar per month and by giving dinners and holding other types of fund-raisers.

The church obtained its first musical instrument in the early 1880s, an organ that was normally used in the home. Mrs. Mary Eliza Kelly was the first organist. At about the same time, Col. T. W. Gaines became the first Sunday school superintendent of the church that was to serve the community until after the turn of the century.

In the early 1890s the church was remodeled. An

181

inclined floor was installed, the first in town, and new colored glass windows were purchased. The church was redecorated in the inside and painted on the outside.

Later in the nineties, the Junior and Senior Leagues were organized. Already the church had a program of Wednesday night prayer meetings. To get to the services, members walked on boardwalks and carried individual lanterns, since there were no streetlights. The kerosene lanterns were replaced by electricity in 1898, when B. S. Silvey built the first electric light plant in Clarksville.

Each year a revival meeting was held and many new converts were added to the membership. By 1900, the congregation had outgrown the building, so plans were made to erect new quarters. It was to be a red brick veneer building with a sanctuary, a Sunday school assembly room, and small classrooms. The choir room of the church in use was to be the primary room.

The so-called "church parlors" were on the second floor. A room at the south end was the pastor's study, and a large room in the center was the parlor. A small room at the head of the stairs served as the kitchen, with a wood-burning cookstove and a large pantry that separated the kitchen from the parlor. A furnace in the basement heated the sanctuary, but woodstoves were used on the second floor.

The new church was named McKenzie Memorial Methodist Church, South, in honor of Dr. J. W. P. McKenzie, the founder. New stained glass windows were donated by members, and the Ladies Aid Society purchased wall-to-wall carpeting for the sanctuary and the aisles of the Sunday school department. The old stained glass windows and the bell were sold to the Christian Church of Detroit, Texas. The former building was sold to the Lennox Brothers, and the money was used in the construction of the new facility.

There was still a debt on the building when T. J. Beckham arrived as pastor in 1906. He was anxious to have the church dedicated, so with the help of the board of stewards, the money was raised. Dr. G. C. Rankin from Dallas delivered the sermon dedicating the building.

In 1913 the annual North Texas Conference was held

at McKenzie Memorial Church. This was the high point in the seventy-five-year history of the congregation. Then World War I, the Depression that followed, and the general decline of the cotton industry began to slow down church activity and cause it to mark time. About 20,000 people from Red River County moved elsewhere to earn their livelihood. Even so, the members of the congregation did not give up in their efforts to carry their church forward.

In the early 1940s, the E. P. Black family gave McKenzie Memorial a pipe organ. Delivery was delayed two years because of the war, but it was finally dedicated in June of 1945 by Bishop Charles C. Selecman. Grants of land were given during the mid-century period, and a new parsonage was erected. The parsonage north of the sanctuary had been in use for over forty years. In this period of growth new carpeting was placed in the sanctuary. Land was also purchased and a home was built for retired ministers. L. B. Tooley was the first occupant, but a few years after his death, the property was transferred to the North Texas Conference. Late in the 1950s, the church was air-conditioned.

A trust fund was set up in the fifties to function when it became necessary to build a new sanctuary, which appeared to be in the near future. An acceptable bid of $236,000 for a new sanctuary and educational building activated the project, and in June of 1976 the cornerstone ceremony was held. The same white marble stone used in 1901 for the new building on Delaware and Broadway streets was placed in the north wall of the structure near the main entrance. The wording on it was not changed.

With a membership of approximately 500, it took a certain amount of boldness to borrow the money needed for the new program. Even though there was concern by some, most of the members resorted to pledges and the indebtedness was significantly reduced.

McKenzie Memorial United Methodist Church is the second oldest institution in Red River County with a continuous history. It was founded 100 years after John Wesley's initial efforts in London, which marked the begin-

183

ning of Methodism. On Heritage Sunday, May 24, 1980, McKenzie Memorial celebrated the 252nd anniversary of the Methodist movement and the 142nd year that the Clarksville church has served the community.

Sources:
1. *A Short History of the McKenzie Memorial Methodist Church.*
2. Joe Pinson, Church Historical, Supplement to the Short History from 1970–1979.
3. *The Texas Almanac,* 1980.

*FIRST METHODIST CHURCH, Liberty, built in 1854.*

# FIRST UNITED METHODIST CHURCH
## Liberty — 1840

The foundation for the Methodist movement in Texas was structured between 1815 and 1836, before it was legal to practice a religion other than Catholicism. Circuit riders out of the Arkansas Territory and the Louisiana Circuit came to preach in private homes and to hold meetings under large shade trees. Then, when the freedom of religion was included in the constitution of the New Republic, the Protestant movement began to grow.

Late in 1840, the first Protestant sermon in the Liberty area was delivered by Hugh Fields, a Methodist minister from Mississippi who traveled by horseback. Services were held in the log courthouse in Liberty and attracted a capacity crowd. The message apparently inspired some of the Protestants, because later in the year a Methodist society was organized.

On Christmas Day in 1840, Bishop Beverly Waugh of Baltimore convened the first session of the Texas Conference of the Methodist Episcopal Church. The conference was held at Rutersville, in Fayette County. It was the first time a duly constituted Annual Conference of Methodist Ministers had ever assembled in the Republic of Texas.

The first minister to be appointed to the Liberty Circuit was John C. Woolam, who came in the spring of 1841. In December of that year at the second Texas Annual Conference, it was reported that the Liberty Circuit had a total membership of seventy-seven. Of these, fifty-seven were white and twenty were black. By December of 1842, the number had increased to 136 white members and thirty-seven black.

Early religious services in Liberty were held in the log courthouse and then in the frame building that replaced it. Most likely, services were also held in some of the homes, since there is no record of a church building before 1846.

On April 11, 1846, a committee of the trustees of the Methodist Episcopal Church asked permission to erect a building in Church Square. Permission was granted, and a

185

log church was soon erected on the northeast corner of the designated area.

As was characteristic of some of the early Texas towns, a separate area was set aside for church buildings. In Liberty, a block in the inner town had been designated as the Plaza Igesia Parroquial (Parish Church Square) by the general land commissioner of Texas in 1831, José Francisco Madero. At that time, such designations were only for Catholic use.

The log church was destroyed by storm. Before it could be rebuilt, the town trustees of Liberty granted a petition by John M. Odin, bishop of the Galveston Diocese, for the construction of a Catholic church on the Church Square. The petition was granted on November 26, 1853.

In late 1854, the Methodist church acquired from a native, John Skinner, a tract of land that fronted on Main Street with Cos Avenue on the side. This location (where the present church sanctuary stands) was where the second building, a small, one-room frame structure, was built.

The first Sunday school at the Liberty church, according to minutes of the East Texas Annual Conference, which convened in Marshall on November 21, 1855, consisted of four teachers and twenty-five pupils. This same report listed fifty-three white members in good standing, ten white members on probation, with sixty-five black members in full connection and thirty-three on probation. This was the first time the black membership exceeded the number of white members.

During 1859, the Liberty church provided for the first time a parsonage for its pastor. The exact location is not recorded, but it is assumed to have been near the church, because part of the original land purchased was to have served that purpose.

The church bell was salvaged from a steamboat, the *Black Cloud,* which had sunk about three miles north of Liberty, in the Trinity River. On a sled drawn by a yoke of oxen, a resident by the name of Joseph Richardson brought the bell to the church in the 1860s and installed it in a cupola on the roof. It was subsequently installed in the

*FIRST UNITED METHODIST CHURCH, Liberty, today.*

187

belfry of the 1904 church, where it gave out its deep, rich tones until it was moved to the tower of the new church in 1930. It has been in use in the Methodist church for over 100 years.

As was the case with most of the early churches in Texas, a split developed over the slavery question. By the end of the Civil War, in 1865, the reported church membership was at a low of thirty white and thirty-five black members. However, by 1868, with the "carpetbag" rule in full swing, the membership had increased to 183, with no black members listed.

The postwar years brought many problems for the Liberty church, including financial struggles that all but destroyed it. In the end, through legal manipulations and complicated financial transactions, the church was saved.

In 1892 the Woman's Missionary Society was organized. It has been a driving force behind the progress of the church and currently operates as the Woman's Society of Christian Service.

The same year, a new parsonage was built on church property, north of the church where it faced Main Street. After a new building was erected in 1904, it was moved to the west side of the church and faced north on Cos Avenue.

The 1904 structure was the third Methodist church building in Liberty. It was a two-room frame building located at the site of the present education building, at the corner of Main Street and Cos Avenue. The cornerstone for it was laid on November 17, 1904, with Masonic services.

The first choir was organized in 1908 while A. J. Anderson was pastor. Laura Stevens was the first director, and Florence Calhoon served as the organist. It was reorganized in 1925 with Mrs. J. C. Huddleston as director and Mrs. Fred Hackenberger as accompanist. That same year, the Epworth League, the forerunner of the Methodist Youth Fellowship organization, was formed.

In 1927 a new parsonage was constructed — the third one — in the 2000 block of Webster Avenue on land donated by H. O. Compton. The next year, Miriam Partlow became the choir director and served in that capacity for the next forty years. In 1925, T. F. Calhoon resigned as Sunday school superintendent after having served for twenty-seven years.

By 1930, it became necessary to enlarge the church again. A building committee made up of J. Frank Richardson as chairman, Charles W. Fisher, vice-chairman, R. G. Partlow, Ray Partlow, and H. O. Compton planned the construction. The first services were held in the new building in January of 1931. By 1939, the indebtedness had been paid off and the church was dedicated by Bishop A. Frank Smith, while R. C. Terry was pastor.

In 1949, under the leadership of Chester Steele, efforts were made to start another expansion program to meet the increasing needs of the congregation. The intent was to convert the old 1930 building into Sunday school rooms and to build a new sanctuary and fellowship hall. A gift of land by the W. S. Partlow family was the beginning. Then a building committee made up of W. D. Partlow as chairman, Mrs. Charles W. Fisher, Sr., as secretary and Bill Daniel, Dr. A. L. Delaney, Martin Hargraves, J. F. Richardson, M. E. Shelton and W. Z. Trotti as members conducted an extensive financial campaign. Charles W. Fisher, Jr., served as general chairman. The effort was a complete success, with an additional tract of land given by E. B. Pickett, Jr.

On August 9, 1953, the fifth sanctuary constructed by the Methodists in Liberty became a reality as the first services were held. On September 6, Bishop Smith preached at the formal opening.

In August of 1959, a new parsonage was purchased in the Oak Forest Addition, the fourth to be owned by the Methodists. The next year, the parsonage property on Wabster Avenue was sold to the First Baptist Church, and in 1961 the sanctuary was dedicated by Paul E. Martin, resident bishop of the Texas Conference. By then, the church was free of debt.

Because of the Methodist system of rotating ministers, the church at Liberty was served by eighty-six different pastors between the founding date in 1840 and 1972. One of those was J. G. Hardin, who served as a supply minister in

189

1858–59. He was the father of John Wesley Hardin, a notorious Texas outlaw who had been named after the founder of the Methodist movement. When young Hardin took an examination in Round Rock and received a high school diploma and a certificate to teach, he had sixteen notches on the handle of his gun. As a teacher during a brief career near Corsicana, he reportedly received excellent attention and had no problem with discipline.

Sources:
    1. Charles W. Fisher, Jr., *The Methodist Church of Liberty, Texas.*

    2. Conference with Robert H. Robinson, former pastor, now at Nacogdoches.

    3. *Texas Almanac,* 1980.

    4. Conference with Charles W. Fisher, Jr.

# VII

## THE PRESBYTERIANS

The Texas Presbyterian Churches are represented by three branches: the Presbyterian Church, U.S. (Southern Presbyterian); the Presbyterian Church, U.S.A. (Northern Presbyterian); and the Cumberland Presbyterian Church. In 1943 the three churches had a combined membership of 104,210 communicants who were served by 621 ministers and licentiates. The three groups have much in common and have tended to work more closely together as the years accumulate.

The Cumberland Presbyterians began work in Texas when Sumner Bacon came in 1829 and in 1833 when Milton Estell organized Shiloh Church near Clarksville.

When Texas became a republic, a problem of disunity prevailed as the old school-new school controversy took shape. In 1834 an old-school minister, Peter Fullinwider, joined Stephen F. Austin's colony at San Felipe to teach school and do religious work. In 1838, Hugh Wilson organized the first old-school church near San Augustine. The Brazos Presbytery was organized near Old Washington in 1840, and within ten years every community in Central and South Texas had become aware of the presence of the Presbyterians. The Synod of Texas was organized with three presbyteries at Austin in 1851.

The new-school group diminished, and by 1865 the breach between the two rival groups was healed and the entire new-school group was added to the old-school synod. The Texas Synod of the Presbyterian Church, U.S., exceeded both of the other church groups combined, following the Civil War.

The Texas Synod of the Presbyterian Church developed Austin College, Schreiner Institute, Austin Presbyterian Theological Seminary, an orphanage at Itasca, and state conference grounds at Kerrville.

The Presbyterian Church, U.S.A., in the 1940s supervised and supported two orphanages and Trinity University.

One unusual feature of the Presbyterian church is that, in spite of its three denominations within a denomination, it maintains unity and peaceful co-existence. It is not unusual for the three groups to meet and worship together, sharing the same building and same pastor while maintaining three separate rolls of members.

Source:
1. *Handbook of Texas,* Vol. II.

191

*MEMORIAL PRESBYTERIAN CHURCH, San Augustine.*

## MEMORIAL PRESBYTERIAN CHURCH
San Augustine — 1838

The Memorial Presbyterian Church of San Augustine was first organized as Bethel Presbyterian Church at Goodlaw's schoolhouse about four miles west of San Augustine.

The oldest Presbyterian church in Texas with continuous existence was begun June 2, 1838. Hugh Wilson organized the congregation with twenty-two members, including two slaves that belonged to one of the charter members.

The charter members were James Sharp and wife, Isabella, Joseph Sharp and wife, Martha, Robert Hibbets and wife, Margaret, Mrs. Elizabeth Erwing, Mrs. Mary McEiver, Mrs. Polly Nicholson, Mrs. Elizabeth Dunham, H. B. Alexander, and wife, Peggy, James and Elam Alexander, Mrs. Catherine Darb, Mrs. Adeline Stodart, Mrs. Ann McKnight, John Polk and wife, Synta, Miss Amanda

Polk, and Jack and Hannach, the two slaves belonging to James Sharp.

In 1887 a new sanctuary was built in time for the church's fiftieth anniversary and was renamed to honor the early pioneers. Funds for erection of the building, still in use in 1980, were collected from all over the Synod of Texas.

Fannie Rankin gave the new church three new pulpit chairs. The hand-made pulpit was used for many years and has been retained as a table for the guest book. Two of the original hand-made pews are in a little room to the right of the sanctuary. The wainscoting in the sanctuary is part of the construction of the first church building. Several old books are part of the church library, and a copy of the early minutes of the church is displayed on the old communion table in the front of the sanctuary. The original minutes are in possession of the Presbyterian Historical Foundation in Montreal, North Carolina.

Among the pastors to serve the church, other than the organizing pastor, are D. A. McRae, who was pastor from 1880 until 1920, and George A. Templeton, who served until his death in 1980.

Dr. J. C. Oehler and John Thomson erected large cement lettering in front of the church property to call attention to the fact that Memorial Presbyterian is the oldest Presbyterian church in Texas in continuous existence.

Sources:
1. Ezekiel Cullen Chapter, Daughters of the Republic of Texas, San Augustine, The Cradle of Texas.
2. Memorial Presbyterian Church (Resolution of the Presbytery of Eastern Texas, June 1888).
3. Conference with Sam Malone, editor, The Rambler.
4. Conference with Winnie Nicholson.

*FIRST PRESBYTERIAN CHURCH, Houston.*

## FIRST PRESBYTERIAN CHURCH
Houston – 1839

On March 31, 1839, the First Presbyterian Church was organized in Houston. Although there was for some time confusion as to the priority of the dates for the organization of First Presbyterian Church and the Christ Episcopal Church, there seems to have been eventual concurrence that the First Presbyterian is the older of the two churches. The Houston Weather Bureau had stated that First Presbyterian had been organized on Easter Sunday, 1839. According to Christ Episcopal Church records, that church was established the day after Easter.

In 1839 the history of the Presbyterian Church in Texas was begun at San Augustine and Gay Hill. In May of the same year, Presbyterians had established a Sunday school in Houston. W. W. Hall, M.D., a friend of Sam Houston and first Presbyterian minister in Houston, was first chaplain of the Congress of the Republic of Texas. It is believed that David G. Burnet, president of the Republic, started a Sunday school which was closed when the president's duties took him away from Houston.

William Youel Allen, a Presbyterian missionary, arrived at Allen's Landing (Main Street at Buffalo Bayou) on March 31, 1838, and established a new Sunday school with three or four teachers and twenty-six pupils.

Allen traveled around Houston, going as far as Galveston, Velasco, Quintana, Brazoria, Columbia, Richmond, and Gay Hill in his efforts to spread the gospel.

The Board of Missions, soon convinced by reports of the potential for religion in the Republic of Texas, sent money and ministers to the new frontier. The area was declared to be within the domain of the vast area described in the Great Commission.

In the Senate chambers in Houston on March 31, 1839, Allen, after a sermon based on Psa. 122:6, invited those who were interested in organizing a Presbyterian church in Houston to remain after the dismissal. He then read the following as a basis for ecclesiastical organization:

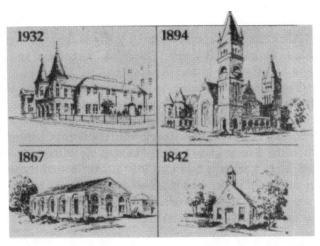

*FIRST PRESBYTERIAN CHURCH, Houston, first buildings.*

For the purpose of promoting Divine Worship, and our mutual edification in the knowledge and practice of piety, we whose names are hereto subscribed, do agree to associate ourselves together as a Presbyterian Church, upon the following principles viz:

1st. We believe the Scriptures of the Old and New Testament to be the word of God, the only infallible rule of faith and practice.

2nd. We sincerely adopt the Confession of Faith of the Presbyterian Church in the United States of America as containing the system of doctrine taught in the Holy Scriptures.

3rd. We adopt the form of Government and Directory for worship as laid down in the Constitution of the Presbyterian Church in the United States of America.

To the above agreement, the following persons subscribed their names: A. B. Shelby, Miriam Shelby, J. Wilson Copes, James Bailey, James Burke, Sarah Woodward, Isabella R. Parker, Edwin Belden, Harris G. Avery, Sophia B. Hodge, and Jannett Scott.

On July 5, 1840, trustees awarded a contract to Dr. Daniels for the erection of a church building on the corner of Main Street and Capitol Avenue. This original building was of pine, shaped like a cracker box with a gable roof, and covered with shingles. The building, painted white both

196

inside and out, featured stained-glass windows. On one side of the vestibule was the church library, with stairs going up to the "choir loft" on the other side. The pulpit was at the west end of the church, and the pews were of pine stained in mahogany and oak. A chandelier in the center of the church and the wall lamps were fueled with whale-oil. The first bell ever rung in Houston was installed in this building.

J. W. Miller arrived by steamer on Sunday, December 22, 1844, and preached his first sermon in Houston that night. The congregation at that time had thirteen members. W. Y. Allen described these people as "mixed in their religious views." He described Houston as being on the edge of a forest where wolves were often heard. He complained of the weeds which overran the town in summer and of the unpainted houses which appeared to have been "erected in a hurry." He spoke of a navigation problem which occurred when the north wind would blow and thus would impede travel to Galveston because little water remained in the bayou.

Having lost its first edifice in a fire, the congregation completed a brick building fifty-four by eighty feet in size. Constructed with much uncertainty and difficulty during the latter part of the Civil War, the building was estimated to have cost about $25,000 in "U.S. currency value."

First Presbyterian's third building was erected at the northwest corner of Main Street and McKinney Avenue during the pastorate of Dr. William Hayne Leavell, the son of a Baptist father and Presbyterian mother in South Carolina. This building served the congregation for fifty years and grew significantly under the pastorate of Leavell and his successor, Dr. William States Jacobs, a "tall, handsome man of much ability."

When the church at Main and McKinney was destroyed by fire, the recently selected pastor, Dr. Charles L. King, led the congregation in locating a new site at 5300 South Main Street. A building was erected there in 1948–49. Dr. King set a good example for the congregation during those times of fiscal hardship by having his salary reduced by $1,000 per year.

197

When Dr. King accepted the status of pastor emeritus, Dr. John William Lancaster was selected as the new pastor. Like some of his predecessors, Dr. Lancaster, as a man of capability and effectiveness, began leading one of the state's most historic churches. He was assisted by the emeritus pastor and by Pastors Larry Dean Allen, John F. Tolson, and Joseph O. Rand, Jr., in the oversight of the more than 3,000-member church.

Also on the church staff during Dr. Lancaster's service were June G. Owen as executive assistant; Leo V. McGuillen, church business administrator; director of music Ava Carapetyan; and organist M. Keith Ross. Carla N. Harrel served as director of youth ministry; the child care coordinator was Debra Hill Townsend; and Novaline Sentell was director of Christian education.

First Presbyterian has an outreach program which sends several missionaries to foreign lands in Brazil, Zaire, and Korea.

*FIRST PRESBYTERIAN CHURCH, La Grange.*

Sources:
   1. Church publication *(The Buildings and some of the men who have ministered in First Presbyterian Church of Houston, Texas)*, compiled and edited by Walter Scott Red (the seventh of Dr. S. C. Red's eight children); from *A Brief History of First Presbyterian Church of Houston, Texas,* by Dr. S. C. Red, church historian.
   2. Clara Alice Beaver, archivist.

## FIRST PRESBYTERIAN CHURCH
## La Grange – 1848

La Grange, as a part of Stephen F. Austin's colony, attracted many different ethnic groups. Many of the members of First Presbyterian Church came from the United Kingdom, as the names of its members and ministers indicate.

Beginning with five members in 1848 and its first pastor, Daniel Baker, the church grew to 164 members by 1974 with only a slight increase by 1980.

This congregation built one of the first church buildings in Texas which was still in use by another religious group in 1980. In 1852 the church building, which the Presbyterians constructed as a union church, was used by other religious groups. Later, at a public auction in 1883, the Presbyterians purchased the Baptists' interest for $200.

After using the old structure for more than one hundred years, the Presbyterians erected a new building and sold the old church house to St. Paul's African Methodist Episcopal Church. The old building was moved from its original location to Guadalupe Street. Its features included ornate half-paneling in the foyer, original wainscoting, pews, chairs, beaded ceiling, and a square piano. A loft or gallery originally accommodated slave members of the church.

The Presbyterian Church in 1980 was served by pastor W. Frank McElroy, Jr., assistant pastor Bryan McDowell, clerk of session Richard T. Halpain, organists Ann Moss and Dorothy Jones, church secretary Darlene Bramblett, and custodian Sarah Johnson.

199

Elders serving on session in 1980 were D. Jack Redus, Malcolm Snodgras, Mary Louise H. Schmidt, Phyllis O. Graham, and Jan Talen. The wife of former State Representative Charles Jungmichel has been active in the affairs of the historic church.

The following pastors have served La Grange's First Presbyterian Church:

| | |
|---|---|
| 1848–1852 | Rev. Daniel Baker, Founder |
| 1853–1855 | Rev. Rob't. F. Bunting, Pastor |
| 1856–1860 | Rev. Joseph Boone, Stated Supply |
| 1861– | Rev. Sidney S. Murkland, Temp. Supply |
| 1862–1868 | Rev. Rob't. M. Loughridge, Stated Supply |
| 1868–1874 | No pastor |
| 1874–1876 | Rev. Oliver B. Caldwell, Pastor |
| 1876–1884 | No pastor |
| 1884–1885 | Rev. Philip Hensley, Stated Supply |
| 1885–1888 | Rev. Oliver B. Caldwell, Stated Supply |
| 1889–1890 | Rev. Jas. A. Montgomery, Stated Supply |
| 1890–1900 | No pastor (almost closed down) |
| 1900–1907 | Rev. Thomas Hickling, Stated Supply |
| 1908– | Rev. T. C. Johnston, Revivalist (added 36 new members in one meeting) |
| 1910–1913 | Rev. William James, Stated Supply |
| 1914–1918 | Rev. Matthew Arnold, Pastor |
| 1918–1919 | Rev. Leonard W. Matthews, Pastor |
| 1920– | Rev. G. T. Bourne, Interim Supply |
| 1920– | Rev. Robert M. Hall, Interim Supply |
| 1921–1922 | Rev. W. H. Fuller, Student Supply |
| 1923–1924 | Rev. John L. Dickens, Evangelist |
| 1925–1926 | Rev. William C. Tenney, Stated Supply |
| 1927–1928 | Rev. Martin Luther Lathan, Pastor |
| 1928–1934 | Rev. Charles A. Nash, Pastor |
| 1935–1949 | Rev. Guy B. Duff, Pastor |
| 1950–1951 | Mr. J. Lem Tittsworth, Student Pastor (Pastor 3 months, 1951) |
| 1952–1955 | Rev. C. Percy Owen, Pastor |
| 1955–1957 | Rev. Martin H. Thomas, Pastor |
| 1958–1965 | Rev. H. Troy Jarvis, Pastor |
| 1965– | Rev. Frank McElroy, Jr., Pastor |

Sources:
1. *Fayette County Record,* May 25, 1979.

*WALNUT GROVE PRESBYTERIAN CHURCH, McKinney.*

2. Conference with Richard L. Barton, Sr., publisher.
3. Church Bulletin, June 22, 1980.
4. Conference with Assistant Pastor Bryan McDowell.
5. Telephone conference with Pastor Frank McElroy.
6. Conference with School Superintendent Fred Weaver and his secretary, Joellen Jaluska.

## WALNUT GROVE PRESBYTERIAN CHURCH
## McKinney – 1851

Walnut Grove Presbyterian Church, in Collin County, was begun thirteen years before the county was organized.

In eastern states word was circulating that Texas was a good and new land in which a better moral climate could be provided than in larger populated areas. In 1848, W. B. Ware and five other men and their families came to Texas from Tennessee. Down the French, Hayes, Tennessee,

201

Ohio, and Mississippi rivers, the group traveled in a boat sixteen feet wide and fifty-six feet long. They brought with them their livestock, furniture, wagons, and food supplies. Landing at Jefferson, the pioneers traveled in wagons to Walnut Grove, located between the present cities of McKinney and Denton.

With the help of his five children and his slaves, Ware constructed a log-cabin church which measured eighteen by twenty feet. This structure served a vast area as the only schoolhouse and church. Because of a structural fault in the roof, the building tended to sway in the middle. For several years people called it the "swayback" church.

When Joseph Rhea moved to Walnut Grove from Tennessee, he constrained the people to build a larger structure — one that measured thirty by thirty-two feet. As the church grew, D. M. Crutchfield donated land for a larger building. R. C. Grace became pastor and also published a newspaper called *The Walnut Grove Banner*. Subscription for the publication was twenty-five cents per year.

In 1896 the Walnut Grove Presbyterian Church built a new facility about one-half mile north of the first log church site. One hundred twenty-one years after its origin, the church was still active. The new church was built of cypress lumber hauled from Jefferson, many miles away, at a cost of $1,425.

Most of the members of the church made a living from farming. With meager income and maximum frugality, poorer families used gourds for utensils. The people had learned much from their predecessors, the Caddo Indians. They learned which berries and roots were good for food and medicine. There were many bears and deer as well as fish and birds, which, with little effort, were available for the dinner table. Some of the men of the church worked for Rhea's Mill, located only one-half mile north of their house of worship.

While the Rheas were away fighting for the Southern cause in the Civil War, they hired a Northerner to run the mill. As the war ended, the "Yankee" was ready to celebrate the victory as he called in Walnut Grove residents to a lavish banquet at the mill store. As the people were seated around the banquet table, which was arranged in the middle of the store, a most unusual deed of Christian charity was about to occur. The notorious James brothers were assuming the role of "Robin Hood."

Three uninvited and unexpected men wearing guns entered the store. They assured the people that no harm would come to them and that all they wanted was some food. With a pewter sugar bowl taken from the store, the men filled flour sacks with flour and sugar, thanked the group politely, and rode off toward Denton. If a man at a log house along the way answered the door call, the James brothers would fill his hat with flour or sugar. If a woman came to the door the benevolent bandits would fill her apron with flour or sugar. They used the newly acquired pewter sugar bowl from Walnut Grove as a dipper.

Camp meetings at Walnut Grove Church allowed the release of religious ferver and the socialization of old and new friends. Camp meetings and church-going of days gone by did not have as many attractive forces competing against them for people's time as exist today.

Although the church is small, it still meets regularly. By 1980, Mrs. Robert (Norma) Furr had served the church as organist for fifty-nine years and her husband had been a ruling elder for forty-eight years.

Near the church building and among beautiful walnut trees are the shaded tombs of the people who once were the substance of Walnut Grove Presbyterian Church.

Sources:
1. Bryan House (H. S. Essay), *Early Years at Walnut Grove.*
2. Conference with Rev. F. K. Mullendore, pastor, Prosper Presbyterian Church.
3. Mrs. Sammie Carey, secretary to Prosper I.S.D. Superintendent Bill Loggins. (Conference and copy services.)

*FIRST PRESBYTERIAN CHURCH, Tyler.*

## FIRST PRESBYTERIAN CHURCH
Tyler – 1870

First Presbyterian Church in Tyler was organized on
Sunday morning, April 3, 1870. The organizational meet-

ing was held in the corner of a Methodist church with the following people participating: Revs. S. F. Tenney and W. N. Dickey and Elders N. S. Brooks and J. M. Shelby, along with members Mrs. J. M. Shelby, Miss Rachel Shelby, Mrs. Margaret Simmons, S. T. Newton, August Niblack, and Mrs. Mary Niblack.

William N. Dickey, pastor of a Rusk Church, had traveled to Tyler several years earlier in order to seek out Presbyterian families in the area in anticipation of organizing a new congregation. On first investigation it appeared that no Presbyterians lived in Tyler. Finally, however, he located the Augustus Niblack family, Georgia Presbyterians who had moved to Tyler several years earlier. From that family, Dickey learned of other Presbyterians in the area. He then obtained permission to use the Methodist Church two Sun-

*FIRST PRESBYTERIAN CHURCH, Bonham.*

days each month since Tyler was only a "half-station" in Methodist work. Dickey returned in 1871 to Rusk in order to resume his work there, leaving the church substantially organized with twenty-five or thirty members, two elders, and one deacon.

Other early pastors to serve the church included W. W. Brim, J. H. Wiggins, W. R. McClellan, and Robert Hill, who served with the longest tenure (1915 to 1946).

Dr. James A. Jones, pastor in 1980, was assisted in his work with the 110-year-old church by associate pastors L. P. McCord and Jim Collie.

Sources:
1. *Tyler Courier Times,* April 2, 1980.
2. First Presbyterian Church (Tyler) bulletin, April 13, 1980.


## FIRST PRESBYTERIAN CHURCH
Bonham — 1872

The First Presbyterian Church, U.S.A., of Bonham was organized in August 1872 by C. M. Shepperison, an evangelist. The church was organized with fourteen charter members. H. L. Parmalee, Robert A. Ross and Orville Caldwell were elected elders, and J. W. Newman and J. R. Cashions were elected deacons. During its first year the membership was enlarged by the addition of Dr. J. L. Buchanan, John A. Price, Frank A. Ramsey, J. P. Holmes, and V. A. Ewing.

Ruling elders of the church in its earlier years were Samuel McFarland, Burwell Cox, O. H. Caldwell, W. A. Evans, Thomas Latta, R. E. Martin, J. F. Battle, R. E. Allen, J. R. McKee, T. S. Tefteller, P. B. Maddrey, W. D. Balthrop, J. F. Sadler, J. B. Vernon, E. F. King, W. T. Smith, N. C. Bradford, H. L. Rodgers, M. V. Gray, W. D. Scarborough, H. D. Tillers, R. M. Lusk, and Smith Lipscomb.

The beautiful wooden church building is now over 100 years old. It is the only church in the Bonham area with a spire and belfry.

206

*FIRST PRESBYTERIAN CHURCH, Fort Worth.*

Source:
  1. Juanita C. Spencer, *Bonham and the Town of Bailey Inglish.*

## FIRST PRESBYTERIAN CHURCH
### Fort Worth – 1873

On May 25, 1873, the Fort Worth Presbyterian Church (Southern Presbyterian) was officially begun with ten members. Among some of the prewar pioneers was Mrs. W. P. Burts, whose husband was the second physician to arrive at the frontier village (in 1858). He was also Fort Worth's first mayor.

The history of the church is very much like the history of the town. Coming from the north were Capt. and Mrs.

207

B. B. Paddock, who arrived in Fort Worth the same month the Presbyterian group was first visited by an evangelist. Youngest officer in the Confederate army, the captain had decided at age twenty-eight to start a new life of adventure in Texas. As editor of the city's newspaper and charter member of the church, Captain Paddock was one of the town's most influential leaders. Another charter member was Capt. S. P. Greene, who led the volunteer fire department and served as clerk of the session when the church organization was completed on April 27, 1874.

At first, the church met upstairs over Knights' Livery Stable at Third and Calhoun streets. W. W. Brim was called to the church in 1877 as its first regular pastor. In that year, the church erected the first building on Jones Street between First and Second streets.

When the railroad made Fort Worth the westernmost railhead, the town began its rapid growth. With this growth came all-night saloons, dance halls, gambling houses, and hotels. One hotel was owned by C. A. Daniel, a Cumberland Presbyterian. For four years the Cumberland Presbyterians had held services at the Masonic Hall the first Sunday of every month.

In 1878 a new graduate of Trinity University rode his horse into Fort Worth as an enterprising magazine salesman. A. H. Stephens, the young man, checked into Daniel's hotel. Stephens agreed to stay over the weekend and preach if Daniel could get as many as twelve people for his audience. This meeting resulted in the organization of the Cumberland Church of Fort Worth on September 15, 1878. Hotel owner Daniel was a charter member, along with Julian Feild, a businessman who had established himself in Fort Worth in 1845.

Young Stephens remained with the congregation and helped obtain donations for a building and lot at Fifth and Taylor streets. Donations brought into Fort Worth by Stephens from outlying ranches included cattle and hogs that could be exchanged for money. When the building was completed, the young magazine salesman, after a little more than a year in Fort Worth, decided to leave for theological studies in the seminary.

There was a uniquely successful cooperation between the Southern and the Cumberland Presbyterians in Fort Worth. In 1888 the imposing structure was built at Fifth and Taylor, fifteen years later than the Southern Presbyterians had built their first modest structure to house the congregation. In 1906 the General Assemblies made it possible for Cumberland Presbyterian and the Presbyterian Church U.S.A. to unite. The two groups did so and changed the name to Taylor St. Presbyterian Church, U.S.A. On January 30, 1916, both church groups, meeting separately in their buildings only seven blocks apart, approved articles of federation and the church was incorporated as First Presbyterian Church of Fort Worth.

Now the merged groups had one pastor, one group of officers, one piece of property, and one church program. But in some ways they remained two congregations with maintenance of two denominational rolls, two separate records, and equitably divided "basket collections."

Among other pastors and leaders were William Caldwell, French McAfee, Dr. Arthur E. Holt, a congregational minister, James K. Thompson, Robert F. Jones, and Dr. C. A. Hickman.

Dr. Robert F. Jones, on the Sunday prior to the congregation's move into its new $2 million structure on December 23, 1956, had the following definition for a church's purpose:

> What is it that makes a church great? Not soft seats and subdued lights, but strong courageous leadership — past and present. Not alone their tall towers with the bells, but the lofty vision of the people. Not the amount of money received, but the amount of service rendered in Christ's name. Not a large membership, but God's direction and power. Not what we have done in the past, but what we are doing now and will, under God's grace, do tomorrow.

Source:
1. *Church Directory (Centennial Edition) 1873–1973*, First Presbyterian Church, Fort Worth Texas.

*PRESBYTERIAN CHURCH, Prosper.*

## PROSPER PRESBYTERIAN CHURCH
### Prosper — 1878

Prosper Presbyterian Church is not as old as some Presbyterian churches in Texas, but it has some historical features which are unique. It is not as old as the La Grange Presbyterian Church, begun in 1852, nor as old as the Presbyterian church which met in the temporarily closed Catholic church in Victoria between the years 1836 and 1840.

On July 7, 1878, R. H. Hacker, together with a small group of members, organized the church as the McAdew congregation, Cumberland Presbyterian Church. The church first met in the Pleasant Valley School House, which would be used for a period of fourteen years (1878 to 1892).

The first church building was erected in 1892 on a lot donated by Mr. and Mrs. James B. Bell. A one-room building with two doors and several windows, the building was painted white on the outside and the interior was unfurnished. The church was furnished with an organ, a pulpit, and long hand-made pews. It was heated by a woodstove and lighted by kerosene wall lamps.

The church building was moved to Rock Hill in 1896, and the name was changed to Rock Hill Cumberland Presbyterian Church. In 1899 one of the church's greatest revivals added many new members to the church while L. J. McGee was pastor.

A. P. Mohard, Sr., had the distinction of serving the church as elder for sixty-one years and was senior elder at the time of his death in March 1959. Other elders of the church in its early years were John Yarnall and C. E. Beanland.

With the changing times, the church was moved in 1902 from Rock Hill to Prosper, Texas, on a lot donated by Mr. and Mrs. J. L. Baker. Two years later the church experienced another great revival when many responded to the preaching of John Bone. The next year Bone became the church's first full-time resident preacher at a salary of $600 per year.

In 1905 the women of the congregation were encouraged to assist with the church's work and missions. Soon after, the "Ladies Aid" was organized and was later known as the "missionary society" and finally the "Prosper Presbyterian Women's Association." The group helped with furnishings for the church and redecorating of the sanctuary. Over the years the church has been enlarged and modernized by improving the heating and air conditioning and adding brick veneer to the outside.

F. K. Mullendore, the thirtieth pastor to serve the church, began his tenure in 1965. He has been active in civic affairs of his community and has served a two-year term as mayor.

During its first hundred years of existence, the church has changed its location three times and its name three times. The presbytery to which the church belonged changed its name four times (White Rock, Guthrie, Dallas, and Trinity). In October of 1979 another name was adopted when it merged with the presbytery of the covenant of the Presbyterian Church U.S.A.

211

As a result of the merger of denominations, the church has been Cumberland Presbyterian, Presbyterian U.S.A., and United Presbyterian in the U.S.A.

Sources:
1. *A History of the Prosper Presbyterian Church 1878–1960*, compiled by Mrs. H. L. Sterling; *From 1960–1978*, compiled by Mrs. Jaunice Stanton, with assistance from Mrs. Arnim Johnson (100th Anniversary Church Publication); *Memorial Lists*, compiled by Mrs. Sherrill Huston.
2. Conference with Rev. F. K. Mullendore.

## MADISON SQUARE PRESBYTERIAN CHURCH
### San Antonio – 1882

*MADISON SQUARE PRESBYTERIAN CHURCH, San Antonio.*

While the first churches were built when their community was very small and the location was once ideal, their locations have been rendered less desirable because of population shifts and growth. Some churches, however, have preferred to stand their ground.

When Madison Park Presbyterian Church was founded, San Antonio had a population of 20,000 people. In 1938 the congregation, after deliberation, decided to retain its location and stay in its old building, which is a cornerstone of "upper San Antonio."

It was in the early 1940s that this church played a major role in getting Trinity University moved to San Antonio. This relocation proved to be an advantage to higher education, to San Antonio, and to the church.

212

Leaders of the church were also leaders in the development of the city. The G. W. Brackenridge family, whose activities and charities did so much for San Antonio, were members of this church. Brackenridge was treasurer for the first board, and his sister was elected the first president of the Ladies Aid Society. Mrs. John French and Mrs. Anna Colby helped with financial needs of the church in reconstruction of the tower, installation of a bell, and construction of a Sunday school building.

The Historical Marker, placed in 1977 by the State of Texas, records the following words about the church's history:

On December 1, 1881, the Rev. William Buchanan came to San Antonio as a missionary of the Presbyterian Church of the United States.

With support from the military community and other persons of northern background, he began to hold services, at first in a fire station, and later in a downtown Lodge Hall. On February 18, 1882, he acquired the present site, then in an outlying district known as "Upper San Antonio." On the next day, February 19, he organized the Madison Square Presbyterian Church. Members of the Brackenridge, Buchanan, Hill, Irvine, Konkle, McLane, Raymond, and Vanderlip families signed the Charter Petition. In the following month, the congregation began meeting here, on its own site, in a temporary chapel.

This Gothic revival edifice of rusted stone was completed in 1883. Severely damaged in an 1886 windstorm, it was rebuilt by 1895. In later years, the interior has been extensively remodeled, and an educational building has been added.

Members of the demised Grace Cumberland Church joined this congregation in 1906. The Madison Square Church has been active in local mission work, and in 1942 helped bring Trinity University to San Antonio.

W. P. Lytle, D.D., was pastor as of 1980, with Edwin Riske, D.M.A., as organist-choirmaster, Loren Stenberg as

213

director of Christian education, and Samuel L. Terry as pastor emeritus.

Source:
1. Copy of Application for Sanctuary to be entered on the National Register of Historic Places. (Provided by Mrs. A. R. Dietzmann, church secretary.)

# VIII

## ETHNIC CHURCHES

### THE CZECHS

The Czech people are derived ethnically from a Slavic population living continuously in Bohemia and Moravia and in parts of Austria, Hungary, and Poland since the fifth century, B.C.

Moravian Karl Postel visited Texas in 1828 and wrote stories about it, which influenced several persons to immigrate. A Czech, Frederick Lemsky, who later taught music in Houston, played "Won't You Come to the Bower?" at the battle of San Jacinto. In the late forties a notable Czech, Josef Ernst Bergman (Horak), settled at Cat Spring in Austin County.

With an inherent aptitude toward husbandry and handicraft, the Czechs gravitated to the richest soils in the state, settling the blacklands from Denton to Brownsville. Ninety percent of the Czechs live in thirty-two continuous counties. Counties which lead in Czech populations are Fayette, Lavaca, Austin, Burleson, Williamson, Wharton, McLennan, Fort Bend, Bell, and Victoria. Czech communities bear such appropriate names as Frydek, Praha, Tabor, Nada, Pisebs, and Raznov.

Approximately seventy percent of the Czechs are Roman Catholic. Among their top priorities upon arrival in

Texas was the establishment of their own church and school.

Czechs have supplied leadership in such towns as Temple, La Grange, Caldwell, Taylor, Sealy, Bellville, and Smithville.

Source:
1. *The Handbook of Texas*, Vol. I.

## ST. MARY'S CATHOLIC CHURCH
### Frydek (San Felipe) – 1883

Several Catholic people, mostly of Czech origin, settled in and around San Felipe in 1852. The first family to arrive whose name is recalled was August Mlcak with his son, Anton, and daughters, Antonio and Frances. When the Mlcaks arrived in Galveston, their sole possessions, other than the family luggage, were two twenty-dollar gold pieces. Another name recalled was that of Joe Zelezik.

Most of these people came from the Czech part of Silesia, and from Moravia, where Frydek was the seat of government and center of the district.

The Frydek church began, it might be claimed, in 1883. In that year two priests, Francis Pridal of Brenham

*ST. MARY'S CATHOLIC CHURCH, Frydek (San Felipe).*

216

and Joseph Chromick of Fayetteville, made trips to the home of John Pavlicek, where Mass was celebrated.

In about 1887, the Sealy Catholic Church was built. The Frydek people were then affiliated with the Sealy church, while the burial place was in the San Felipe public cemetery nearer their homes. In 1890 the Czech Catholics started their own cemetery on land donated by John Pavlicek.

In 1907, Frank Machan, pastor of Immaculate Conception, Sealy, directed the building of a Catholic school to serve children from Frydek and Sealy. This building was erected in Frydek in order to serve as a school, a sisters' home, and a church. The grounds for the building were next to the cemetery. The school-church was blessed on May 20, 1908, by the Most Reverend N. A. Gallagher on the same date that St. Mary's became a mission parish of the Sealy church.

The schoolteachers were Sisters of the Order of Divine Providence of San Antonio. Pastors serving the Frydek church from its beginning were William Skocek, M. A. Dombrowski, Monsignor Joseph A. Valenta, Paul Nemec, John Kolas, A. W. Nesvadba, F. J. Klobout, Father Klinkacek, and Innocenc Raska.

Father Lad Klimicek moved to Frydek in 1944 and served until his death in 1970. During his tenure, the

*OUTDOOR ALTAR, Frydek Catholic Church.*

217

Frydek church grew into a village of its own. A grotto of thanksgiving was built honoring the sixty-seven young men who were called into the service of World War II, all of whom returned safely to their church home. A new rectory, a youth center, and a scouthouse were later constructed. A large, sheltered open-house recreational area was also built. After Father George Binhard served the church for a short time, Father Bernard Snock arrived in July 1970, and celebrated his first decade with the church in 1980.

In 1972, Frydek built a large, beautiful new church, its third church building to serve the predominantly Czech community.

Sources:

1. *St. Mary's Catholic Church, Frydek, Texas, Dedication Memorial and Parish Picture Book.*

2. Conference with Mrs. Gladys Sodolak.

3. Catholic Archives, Austin, Texas.

## ST. MARY'S PARISH
### Praha — 1855

St. Mary's Parish was established in 1855 on a hillock in Fayette County — 5,834 miles from Prague, Czechoslovakia, for which the home of the parish was named.

For its first years after organization, the church was served by Father Victor Gury, who came periodically from Frelsburg to administer the sacraments and celebrate Mass in the homes of parishioners.

A small frame house was built in 1865, and Mass was offered there at midnight on Christmas Day by Father Joseph Bikowski. Then, in 1866, a small frame church building was erected on a twenty-acre site, donated by Mathias Novak, and a cemetery was begun. Ten years later, a second frame church was built in the same location.

On November 20, 1895, a large and imposing stone church was dedicated by Bishop John A. Forest under the title of Assumption of the Blessed Virgin Mary. On this

*ST. MARY'S CHURCH, Praha, near Flatonia.*

*INTERIOR, ST. MARY'S CHURCH, Praha.*

same occasion confirmation was administered to 342 persons.

A year after completion of the church, a school was opened under the direction of the Sisters of Divine Providence, who continued in charge of the school until 1913. The Sisters of the Incarnate Word and Blessed Sacrament conducted the school for the next six decades, until it was closed in 1972.

From this parish have grown parishes in Moulton, Flatonia, St. John, High Hill, Hostyn, Schulenburg, Cistern, Ammonnsville, and Wiemar.

This is the only parish in the United States which follows the custom of honoring the Blessed Mother in a *Prazka Paut,* or homecoming, by observing August 15, the Feast of the Assumption, with an all-day celebration, regardless of the day of the week.

It was a historic event on April 18, 1966, when Josef Cardinal Beran, the exiled primate of Praha, Czechoslovakia, visited the parish. To commemorate this event, a monument was erected in front of the church to honor the archbishop who had been confined in a Communist prison for eighteen years. Cardinal Beran, moved greatly by seeing the monument, said: "Here you people in Praha, Texas, have erected this to my memory and yet in my own country my own people will not receive me." At day's end, the old priest attended a dance at the Pavillion.

Mrs. Lyndon B. Johnson was present for dedication of a historical marker for the church on July 7, 1967. The president's wife also visited the cemetery and the graves of nine young men of the parish who gave their lives during World War II.

In the past, St. Mary's Parish averaged 100 or more baptisms a year, but during recent years, as people have left rural areas to find employment in the cities, the parish baptizes only three or four each year. One hundred families under the direction of Father Marcus A. Valenta comprised the 1980 membership of the parish.

Sources:
   1. Catholic Archives, Austin, Texas.
   2. *Houston Chronicle,* September 1, 1868.

# THE DANES

## ANSGAR EVANGELICAL LUTHERAN CHURCH
Danevang – 1895

The first Danish colony arrived in Texas in 1894, when land was bought by the Dansk Folkesamfund, the Danish People's Society. This colony had hoped to preserve on the fertile coastal plain the Danish culture and language. Earlier, Christian Hillebrandt and his family had combined a cattle drive and move into Texas in 1830.

A branch of the Danish Lutheran Church was interested in the project as a means of propagating the faith the settlers had known in their homeland. A church dispute had begun in Denmark, and around 1870 the Evangelical Danish Lutherans in America split into two groups, not too friendly toward each other.

It was the Danish Evangelical Lutheran Church which supported the Texas colony and which followed N. T. S. Gruntvig – clergyman, philosopher, poet, and historian. This group, the low-church side of Danish Lutheranism, came to be known as "happy Danes." The other group, the rivals, were known as "holy Danes," "gloomy Danes," or the "Home of the Inner Mission people" – a much sterner group. Many of the society's members were in the north central United States, where most of the Danes had first settled, such as Illinois, Wisconsin, Minnesota, Iowa, North and South Dakota, Nebraska, and Kansas.

J. C. Evers, as part of a three-man committee, was appointed by the folk society to investigate Texas lands. He was to determine if the land was worth its advertised price of $9 per acre and if the area was suitable for settlement by the Danish people.

A favorable report on the area was made by the com-

*LUTHERAN CHURCH, Danevang.*

mittee. Evers negotiated a contract to buy 8,000 acres the first year and successively to extend the purchases to 25,000 acres. A man could obtain as many as 320 acres. Of the first seventy-eight families to move to Danevang, only two claimed the full acreage available for each man.

With the sale of the first 8,000 acres, the land company promised to give 160 acres for a school and church site.

Some of the Danes came directly from Denmark, although Evers did most of his recruiting in the north central states. Jens Peter Olson, who changed the spelling of his name from Olsen to appear more American, was the first of the colonists to arrive and buy land. Olson, who came from Holbaek, Sjaelland, was soon followed by over seventy initial families whose names included Mogensen, Larsen, Rasmussen, Madsen, Hansen, Krag, Thomsen, Lykke, Andersen, Nygaard, Hermansen, Treumen, Christinsen, Wind, Roun, Berndt, Petersen, and Jorgensen.

The Olsons moved to Danevang from Kansas in January of 1895, riding in a railroad freight car with their daughter, family belongings, furniture, and livestock. When they got to Rosenberg on their way to El Campo (Danish colony, El Campo, Texas, as Danevang was first called), the family was moved into a passenger car.

The first colonists had arrived in time to witness a bleak and disheartening scene. The beautiful grass-covered plain had suffered from a vast fire. The lush prairie grass was reduced to black ash. Following the fire there was excessive rain and flooding. Some of the cattle brought in by the Danes died of starvation. The new settlers experienced much difficulty in adjusting to the new land. The settlers complained of the black mud, the overflow of rivers, and even the bedbugs. One family complained that even after putting the four bedposts in pans of water, the bugs would climb to the ceiling and drop on them.

The lands were fertile and cotton proved to be a good money crop. The men raised pigs, then smoked bacon by the traditional Danish method in a barrel. They sold the bacon along with surplus dairy products processed by the women.

The settlers built their houses on blocks of sufficient height to avoid the flooding and to make the houses cooler in the summer.

F. L. Grundtvig and Evers visited the colony in 1895, at which time Grundtvig held church services in Mads Andersen's home.

Ninety-three families had purchased over 9,000 acres by the end of 1895, and more families were coming from Schleswig or the islands of Fyn and Sjaelland, as well as most other parts of Denmark.

Forty acres were provided for the church at a cost of one dollar, with a restriction that if the congregation ever seceded from the Danish Evangelical Lutheran Church the land would be forfeited. In 1895 the Danes built a community meeting hall, a post office, a weather station, and a school. The postmaster was the weather observer.

The Lutheran congregation used the meeting hall for church services, with Pastor L. Henningsen in charge. Later the people built their first church house, a wooden frame structure with a large, high steeple, in 1908–09. The church bell was rung not only on Sundays but also at sunrise and sunset.

The first ministers were native Danes, and they were

multi-talented men. One of the early ministers, S. H. Madsen, served as a doctor and repaired watches and sewing machines in order to supplement his pastor's salary of $15 per month.

It is said that Agersklv Petersen was one of the "most Danish" of the pioneers. Danish was spoken in his home as the children enjoyed the folk tales of Hans Christian Andersen or the Brothers Grimm.

In 1900 the Galveston storm ravaged the coastal plain, and the people of Danevang suffered the loss of their cotton crop. Another storm in 1909 did much damage, and in the storm in 1945 the church building was almost completely destroyed. A building, much like the first, was erected and continues to serve the sturdy and tenacious Nordic people as their forebears were once served.

Other Danish people have settled in significant numbers in the following counties: Lee, Bexar, Galveston, Dallas, Grayson, Harris, Limestone, Travis, Bosque, Williamson, Gillespie, and Brazoria.

Although the first years were difficult for the pioneers in a new land, a descendant proudly remarked, "We are the sons of Vikings." The poet Ove Nielsen wrote:

> Gone is the Viking who battled the wave,
> But never his spirit will rest in the grave.
> We are Americans, fruit of the Danes,
> The blood of the Viking is warm in our veins.

Sources:
1. John L. Davis, *The Danish Texans* (The University of Texas Institute of Texan Cultures at San Antonio).
2. Correspondence with Verner A. Petersens.
3. Telephone conference with Pastor Donald Kenning.

*ST. LOUIS CATHOLIC CHURCH, Castroville.*

## THE FRENCH

## ST. LOUIS CATHOLIC CHURCH
### Castroville — 1845

Castroville was named after the founder, Henri Castro, who, while operating under an empresario contract with the Republic of Texas, set out to establish a colony of 600 families or single men over seventeen years of age. He had not originally set out to establish a colony specifically of

Alsatians, but due to the lack of cooperation from France, he found it necessary to turn elsewhere to meet this quota. To do so, he spread out across Central Europe, where he found fruitful grounds, especially in the Rheinish provinces of France and Germany.

Not all of the original colonists were of French extraction but the majority of them were Alsatians. And it is their culture that the little town retains today.

The German flavor was there too. While local Chamber of Commerce brochures describe the town as "The Little Alsace of Texas," there are citizens who can, if they choose, speak a language that is very Germanic but is not German. It is actually a South German dialect with a few words derived from the French, along with a smattering of Americanisms. Although technically a French territory since 1648, Alsace had remained in culture a German entity.

The Gothic cathedral in Strasbourg, Alsace, although quite beautiful, is something of an oddity in that it has only one steeple in place of the conventional two, which is the hallmark of German churches. Before World War I, the Prussian administration in Germany proposed the building of a second steeple to the cathedral in Strasbourg so that the odd appearance could come to an end. The people involved refused. They contended that their cathedral had been that way for 500 years and they liked it the way it was. The church in Castroville likewise has only one steeple.

Despite the many hardships that faced them, the immigrants in Castroville held on to the new homes they had carved out of the wilderness. They built small stone houses with high pitched roofs soon after their arrival and then laid the cornerstone of the St. Louis Catholic Church.

Prior to that time, Vicar-General Jean Marie Odin, the chief administrator of the Catholic church in Texas in the 1840s, realized that there were not enough priests in the state. He therefore went back to France to try to recruit more. His efforts enjoyed success and he recruited some priests who were to serve at Castroville, including Claude

Marie Dubois, who later succeeded him as bishop of Galveston.

Odin's special concern was to provide for the numerous German-speaking Catholics in the diocese. Immigrants from Central Europe were literally pouring into Texas, and colonies were being founded in New Braunfels, Fredericksburg, and Cat Spring — along with the various settlements of the Castro colony. Therefore, it is understandable that Odin was extremely happy when in early 1845 an Alsatian priest, Father John Gregory Pfanner, offered to serve as parish priest at Castroville.

For a priest, Pfanner had unusual ambitions. He was interested in making money and he teamed with the other priests, Father Lienhard and Father Jean Roesch, to recruit families to come to Texas. They were to receive land grants for each family or adult male they brought. In the end, their efforts paid off well.

The three priests arrived in Castroville in February of 1845 with their colonists. Father Pfanner encouraged development of the community and especially the construction of the church that had come to a standstill soon after the cornerstone had been laid by Dr. Odin on September 12 of the previous year. With not one but three priests to direct the work, it seemed likely that the efforts of the early colonists could be redirected and progress could be made toward a spiritual revival of thinking and work.

Unfortunately for the Catholics of Castroville and for the prestige of the church, Father Pfanner did not channel his energies in the proper direction. He involved himself in secular activities, some of which were suspect if not dishonest. He was ultimately indicted by grand juries in San Antonio and Victoria for fraud and murder. His guilt or innocence was never proved, but he left the country in August of 1846 for Mexico and never returned.

The Catholics of Castroville were left without a priest, and the colonists became demoralized. Castro began to fear that he would lose much of the land he had been awarded if too many of the immigrants decided to leave. To protect himself, and to build morale, he offered the colonists who owed him money the chance to pay off their debts by working on the church. They responded well, and in their spare time they completed it. Vicar-General Odin dedicated it on November 9, 1846.

Even though the church had been finished, it remained idle, with the exception of an occasional visiting priest. This lasted until January of 1847, nearly two and a half years after the founding of Castroville, when one of the most remarkable men in the history of the Catholic church in Texas arrived to take over. Recruited by Odin, twenty-nine-year-old Claude Marie Dubois began the difficult task of overcoming a negative reception because of the problems of the previous priest.

The people of Castroville responded to Dubois' efforts and soon he had more than he could do. Other than his work in Castro's colonies, which besides Castroville included Hondo, LaCoste and D'Hannis, he was responsible for the Catholics in Fredericksburg, some eighty miles north of San Antonio, and in New Braunfels, thirty-five miles east of San Antonio and fifty-five miles from Castroville. To help in the formidable task, Odin sent Mathew Chazelle to Castroville as Dubois' assistant. He stayed until his death from pneumonia and exposure on September 1, 1847. Father Dubois was alone again, but a man of his character and spirit was not to be denied, so he carried on.

Early priests in Castroville all labored under trying conditions. Dubois' next assistant was Father Emanuel Domenech, and together they labored to hold up under the most difficult circumstances.

Famine, drouth, and plague had to be contended with. A cholera epidemic struck in 1849 and also raged in Fredericksburg and New Braunfels. Many deaths were recorded before it disappeared as suddenly as it had come. The last death from this epidemic was recorded in Castroville on May 30, 1849.

The first church in Castroville had long since been outgrown, so a new one was completed in time for Easter in 1850. Stained glass windows that depicted events in the early life of St. Louis were found in Galveston and installed

229

in the church. The church was described by a contemporary writer as "an elegant stone building which would do credit to a wealthier community."

This church was soon outgrown and plans were under way, five years after its completion, to build still a third building. It was finally completed and the first Mass was celebrated there on August 25, 1870. With moderate changes and additions, it remained as first constructed until a complete renovation was started in October of 1972. The rededication was held on June 24, 1973.

Castroville today is a picturesque town that is a blend of the ranch life and hunting and fishing of southwest Texas with the heritage that many of the residents received from those who came from the French-German province of Alsace.

Gerald Hubertus, pastor at St. Louis as of 1980, after replacing Larry Stubben, functioned as an advisor to the St. Louis Parish Council, which was formed in 1970 to generate a new awareness among laymen of their responsibility to share in the work of the church.

Sources:
1. Interview with Rev. Gerald Hubertus, pastor.
2. Gittinger, Rihn, Haby, and Sanvely. *The St. Louis Church, Castroville.*


# THE GERMANS

Unlike most other ethnic groups, the Germans who have contributed so much to Texas cannot be identified with a single religion. There are over half a million Texans who are at least one-half German, and they are both Catholic and Protestant.

"Wanderlust" brought a few Germans into the area as early as 1749, as accounts indicate activity along the Red River in what is now a part of Bowie County. However, the record of those who came that early is not clear. It was not until early in the 1800s that a real effort was made to settle the Texas territory that belonged to Mexico.

The first account of German settlers in Texas covers the period between 1815 and 1820. Three Durst brothers (originally spelled Darst)—John, Joseph, and Jacob—came to Texas from Louisiana and settled in Nacogdoches. They had been born in Spanish Missouri of parents who had come from Germany about the time of the American Revolution. Two of them, John and Joseph, were to figure prominently in Texas history.

No mention is made of religion among the German people during those early days. Since the Protestant religion could not be practiced legally until after 1836, it is likely that they didn't participate in services. It is known that the descendants of the Durst brothers were Methodists.

The German colonists landed either at Galveston or Indianola. Most of them moved inland toward Yorktown, New Braunfels, and Fredericksburg. The distinctive architecture of the Germans—including the Catholic, the Lutheran, and the Methodist churches—have dominated the countryside and the small towns that extend into the Texas Hill Country. A stranger passing through can sometimes determine which churches are German by whether or not they have twin steeples. Twin steeples were traditional and a constant source of argument between the French and the Germans in the border provinces of Alsace and Loraine.

Many German immigrants and their descendants have followed the Methodist beliefs. Whether they were Methodists before they came is not clear. Some accounts show that Methodist officials met incoming ships and offered their services to the immigrants who were in search of new homes.

The first Methodist church in the Texas Hill Country was founded in Fredericksburg in 1849 as a German mission. Other similar charters were granted in Mason and Junction. Two of the charter members of the German Methodist Mission in Fredericksburg were Johann and Margaretha Durst, who quite likely were descendants of the Durst brothers from Nacogdoches.

231

The Catholic movement was strong in Central Texas among the Germans, but on the surface, it appears not to be as strong as that of the Lutherans or the Methodists.

The Germans have blended so well into the pattern of life in Texas that it is not possible to separate their religious efforts from other nationalities. No attempt is being made to list separate churches under a discussion of their movements, except the Lutheran churches in Seguin and Fredericksburg, which still deserve the German classification.

Like other ethnic groups, while contributing so much to the state's general prosperity, the Germans have continued to preserve their proud heritage through social and cultural events that have grown in popularity through the years. Most Texans enjoy the German music and folk songs and dances that dominate these events. And there is no question about the popularity of the German sausage and pastry delicacies that draw thousands of visitors to events such as the *Wurstfest* in New Braunfels, which is held each year at the end of the harvest season.

The Christmas tree tradition was brought to the state by the German settlers who came in the mid 1840s.

Sources:
1. *The German Texans* (Institute of Texan Cultures, San Antonio, Texas).
2. Newspaper clippings from the Eckhardt and Kleberg files.
3. Personal interviews with residents of Yorktown, New Braunfels, and Fredericksburg.

## EMANUEL'S LUTHERAN CHURCH
## Seguin — 1870

Although the first congregation at Emanuel's Lutheran Church was not organized until January of 1870, local Lutheran work dates to 1851, when Seguin was part of a missionary circuit served by Pastor Theobald G. Kleis. After Kleis moved to Pennsylvania several years later, brief pastorates were followed by long vacancies which were not conducive to successful missionary work. It was not until

*FIRST CHURCH SCHOOL, parsonage,
Emanuel's Lutheran, Seguin.*

the first German Evangelical Lutheran Synod, organized in Houston on November 10, 1851, sent Pastor Johannes H. Wohlschlegel as a full-time missionary that any progress was made toward establishing a congregation.

Wohlschlegel came late in 1869 and preached his first sermon in September of that year. During the following months, he gathered a nucleus of nineteen families. On January 30 he organized Emanuel's Church.

On January 31, 1870, the day after the first meeting, a lot was purchased for $400 and recorded in the courthouse. On February 21, three weeks later, work on the new church got under way. It was completed in less than six months and was dedicated on August 14. George W. Schmitt had been elected by the seventeen charter members to supervise the construction.

Wohlschlegel was pastor and teacher. He taught school five days a week, but soon he found he could not subsist on the small salary he was receiving. He preached his final ser-

233

EMANUEL'S LUTHERAN CHURCH, Seguin.

EMANUEL'S LUTHERAN, interior.

234

mon there on November 27, 1870, and left Seguin for Ross Prairie.

Emanuel's Lutheran was at that time independent, since it had not joined the Texas Synod of the Lutheran Church. There was a question of whether or not an attempt should be made to attract another pastor, but a young German Methodist lay minister, Theodor Mumme, offered to serve for a year. He preached a trial sermon on January 1, 1871, and the next day the congregation met and elected him as pastor, at a salary of $100 a year. He remained more than three years.

During that time, a contract was made with the State of Texas for the rental of the church for a "free" school at $150 for ten months. It was signed by John Schmitt as trustee and by J. C. Degress, the superintendent of public instruction in Texas. As a result, the old frame church became the cradle of the public school system in Seguin. The arrangement lasted from 1871 to 1885, and Mr. Werner was the teacher while Mumme served as pastor.

In 1872 a bell was purchased at a cost of $175. This necessitated adding what the minutes call "a second story" to the small tower. The bell, which is still being used, was inscribed as follows: *"Deutsche Evangelish Lutherische Emanuels Kirch – Seguin, Texas – 1872."*

A serious dispute arose in the congregation in 1873 and divided it into factions. The dispute continued into the following year and finally resulted in a sharp split. Theodor Mumme and ten charter members, including the elders and trustees, left and organized what later developed into the Austin Street Methodist Church.

A lawsuit resulted, since those who left felt they had a right to the property. However, because of a clause in the constitution stating that in case of such a split the property should remain in the hands of those loyal to the Lutheran Confessions, the judge ruled in favor of Emanuel's.

The membership, which had been reduced by more than fifty percent, reorganized immediately and elected new elders and trustees. On July 12, 1874, E. Giese was called as pastor. He had been called as a teacher and then agreed to preach. He stayed only one year. John F. Frehner of New Braunfels, a circuit rider from the Texas Synod, conducted occasional services and tried to hold the group together. During the vacancy of two years, Mr. Rhode and Mr. Wagner were the teachers.

In February of 1877, Frehner moved to Seguin and began bringing the dispersed members together. He also revived the daily school, teaching five days a week. At first he taught in his home and later he taught the state-supported school in the church.

On September 6, 1886, the congregation became a member of the Texas Synod. It was during this time that Franz Weisskoppf was serving as pastor. He began in 1884 and remained until 1897. The Synod affiliation was terminated in 1890 when Weisskoppf and the congregation withdrew from membership. Emanuel's was without membership to a Synod until 1924, when it rejoined the Texas Synod under Pastor Jannsen.

When Texas Lutheran College, formerly called Lutheran College, was moved from Brenham to Seguin, the growing enrollment increased the attendance to Emanuel's Church to a point that a new and larger sanctuary had to be built. The old church was torn down, and until the new one could be completed, services were conducted in the old Presbyterian Church on South Austin Street.

The second church was dedicated July 6, 1913. It served the congregation until 1956, a period of forty-three years. By coincidence, the first church also served for forty-three years, from 1870 to 1913.

In 1955 the church roster showed 1,700 baptized and 1,344 communicant members. The Sunday school had an enrollment of 629, and it was evident that more space was needed.

The Church Council was authorized to proceed with definite plans, and work on a new building began on December 27, 1955.

The present church, along with the educational building and equipment, cost nearly half a million dollars. Cruciform in shape, the structure was built in modified contemporary Gothic style. It has a seating capacity of 850 and contains enough classrooms to house sixty different groups. Underneath the church is a large fellowship hall with a kitchen and stage, where 600 guests can be seated at tables. There is also a special reception room, choir robing rooms, and a special nursery.

The more recent pastors who have shared in the growth and development of Emanuel's Lutheran Church are Dr. E. J. Braulick (1945–1957), H. L. Anderson (1957–1962), LeeRoy Brandes, associate pastor (1957–1962), H. A. Heineke, interim pastor (1962–1963), Daniel F. Schorlemer, Milburn Franke, and John Schwartz, Jr., whose terms of service have been interwoven and have carried Emanuel's past the centennial year of 1970. Every pastor, beginning with Dr. Braulick, has been associated with Texas Lutheran College, either as a teacher or as a student. The pastor as of 1980 was Chester M. Patten.

*ZION LUTHERAN CHURCH, Fredericksburg.*

237

Sources:
1. Interview with Pastor Chester M. Patten.
2. *The Centennial Story 1870–1970.*
3. *Emanuel's Lutheran Church Directory, 1980.*

## ZION EVANGELICAL LUTHERAN CHURCH
### Fredericksburg – 1852

When Fredericksburg, Texas, was founded on May 8, 1846, there was not a Lutheran congregation or a Lutheran pastor in the state. Six families in the new colony of Lutheran faith who banded together under the leadership of a layman, William Schumaker, a tailor and book-dealer from Wuppenthal, Germany, were determined to hold on to their Lutheran heritage. The met in a small rock house near the *Vereins-Kirche.*

The *Vereins-Kirche* (community church) was built soon after Fredericksburg was founded. A society for the protection of German immigrants in Texas, known as the *Mainzer-Adelsverein,* was responsible for the church and made it the central point in the colony. It was the first public building to be constructed and served as a town hall for political meetings, a schoolhouse, and a fort against the Indians. It also served as a church with assurance from the *Adelsverein* that people of all faiths could hold their worship services there. The dedication was held in 1846 and festivities lasted all day – a worship service in the morning, a *Volksfest* in the afternoon, and a ball in the evening.

From the beginning, the Lutherans were not satisfied with the minister who preached and taught at the *Vereins-Kirche.* Through their lay leader, Schumaker, they started a search for a Lutheran minister. They heard of one by the name of Schneider, who lived in Victoria. He accepted the invitation to come to Fredericksburg, but the Lutherans were disappointed when they found out he was an ardent Methodist missionary. Some of the less faithful followed him when he set out to organize the Methodist group.

The loyal Lutherans tried to follow a pastor of the Evangelical Protestant Church by the name of Gottlieb

238

*ZION LUTHERAN CHURCH, Fredericksburg, today.*

*SECOND ZION CHURCH building, Fredericksburg, 1908.*

239

Burchard Dangers, who served in the *Vereins-Kirche* from 1849 to 1869. He, too, was disappointing, and again the Lutherans pulled away from the community church.

It was 1850 before the first Lutheran pastors came to Texas, eleven in all. On November 10, 1851, Luther's birthday, they organized the First Evangelical Lutheran Synod in Texas, located in Houston. One of the founders, Pastor P. F. Zizelman, the first secretary of the Synod, arrived in San Antonio in 1852. After a series of hardships and a period of illness, Zizelman accepted the call to organize the Zion Congregation in Fredericksburg in September of 1852.

On Monday, September 27, 1853, a building site was purchased for $45 at 151 West Main Street, then known as San Saba Street. The first rock church, fifty feet long and thirty-six feet wide, was completed in 1853. It was the fulfillment of a dream long held by the Lutherans in Fredericksburg. The second church was built in 1884, and the third building came in 1908. In each case, extensive renovations were made before new structures came into being.

The present church stands on the original site, fondly referred to as "on a knoll in the valley." It was secured in 1852, but the outward appearance has changed considerably through the years. In 1884 the first addition to the church was undertaken, under the guidance of Pastor R. Fiedler. The walls and windows were raised two feet, the frame tower was raised ten feet, the interior received a ceiling, and a balcony was added.

During the pastorate of I. Glatzle, the church was thoroughly rebuilt and renovated for a second time. An extension of twenty-five-by-fifty feet was added, with an altar space, so that the church took on the form of a cross. A massive tower of stone, designed by Adolph Wehmeyer, was added to the front of the building. Because his exterior dimensions for the tower were used for the interior, he subsequently referred to the building as "the steeple with the church."

The third renovation of the church was undertaken under the pastorate of F. A. Bracher in 1939. The pulpit

240

that had been donated by the Charles Kuenemann family was lowered and rebuilt, the church was repainted, and the altar niche was redecorated with scriptural passages and symbols. A baptismal altar, donated by the family of Pastor F. A. Bracher, was added and cathedral lights were installed. All the improvements were completed under the supervision of the building committee led by Alfred Neffendorf and Clements Kneese.

In 1953, during Pastor G. W. Sager's ministry, the annex was added to the east wing of the church, to be used as an educational building. It had been planned since 1941, but construction was delayed because of World War II.

The next renovation was completed in 1960. A new high altar was added, but the base of the old altar, which had been a gift of the Ladies Aid Society, was retained. The esteemed "Christus" statue was placed in a high central panel.

Hand-carved figures of the four original symbols were added and religious symbols were placed at various vantage points on various trusses and corbels. The pipe organ was rebuilt and chimes were added. New pews and windows, with many furnishings, added to the increasing beauty of the stately building.

During Pastor Kermit Menking's years at Zion, which extended from 1963 to 1977, additional improvements were made. The church subsequently was led by Wuthrich, a native of Taylor.

Sources:
1. Interview with Pastor Ardene A. Wuthrich.
2. *The 125th Anniversary, 1852–1977, Zion Evangelical Lutheran Church*, Fredericksburg, Texas.

## FIRST PROTESTANT CHURCH
New Braunfels — 1845

*By Rosemarie Leissner Gregory and Myra Lee Adams Goff*

The history of First Protestant Church is simultaneous with the history of New Braunfels.

The sequence of events leading up to the founding of New Braunfels in 1845 began with conditions in Germany. The industrial age was dawning; consequently, many skilled craftsmen were finding their work no longer in demand. There was overpopulation and wages were very low. Also, heavy taxation followed the Napoleonic wars.

Available land in Texas and an opportunity for economic betterment were beckoning forces to the industrious Germans. With economic prosperity could come social improvement and finally a say in political concerns.

In 1842 a group of noblemen formed Verein Zum Schulz deutscher Einwandrer in Texas (Society for the Protection of German Immigrants in Texas), also referred to as *Adelsverein* (Society of Noblemen). In March of 1844, the *Verein* was reorganized and came under the protection of Duke Adolf of Nassau. Prince Karl of Solms-Braunfels was appointed commissioner-general of the Society and was instructed to go to the Republic of Texas to prepare for the arrival of the immigrants.

Although Germans had settled in other parts of North America for want of religious freedom, none had gone to Texas for that reason. The *Verein* in its constitution assured that schools and churches would be available. To that end, Prince Karl contacted the Superior of the Order of the Holy Redeemer in Baltimore, the Right Reverend Father Alexander, and sent traveling expense money for a Roman Catholic priest to join the colony. This did not happen immediately.

Similar conditions which caused many Germans to take on unknown challenges in a new land also brought a highly educated theologian to North America, the Reverend Louis Cachand-Ervendberg of the Evangelical faith. Having landed in New York in 1837, the Reverend Ervendberg first made his way to the German settlement of Teuto on Salt Creek, fifteen miles west of Chicago, Illinois. There, in 1838, he married Marie Sophie Dorothea Louise Muench, who had come to America in 1836 with her uncle.

242

Together the Ervendbergs moved to Texas in 1839, settling briefly in Houston, where Reverend Ervendberg founded the first German Protestant congregation. By 1841, Pastor Ervendberg had small German congregations at Cummins Creek, Westmuenster, Blumenthal, Industry, and Cat Spring in Austin and Colorado counties.

In the summer of 1844, Prince Karl met the Reverend Ervendberg in Industry (Austin County) and appointed him an official of the *Verein*. In that capacity the Reverend Ervendberg became the first pastor of the "Deutsch Protestantische Gemeinde en Neu Braunfels," the German Protestant Congregation of New Braunfels.

Reverend Ervendberg met the new arrivals on the coast and held the first worship service there on December 23, 1844. The following evening, Reverend Ervendberg conducted Christmas Eve services. For the occasion Prince Karl had an oak tree lighted with many candles and strung with bags of candy and gifts for the children. Communion was served on Christmas Day. These three services, conducted in the camp at Lavaca Bay, began the history of First Protestant Church.

The first church service in New Braunfels was conducted on March 21, 1845, by Reverend Ervendberg in a grove of trees at the foot of what now is known as Sophienburg Hill. This was the day that the settlers finally arrived from the coast. The site for New Braunfels was purchased some weeks earlier by Prince Karl and named for his ancestral home, Braunfels, on the Lahn River in Germany.

Reverend Ervendberg conducted divine services regularly, according to the rites of the German Protestant Church, approved by the *Verein*. The congregation constituted and incorporated itself on October 5, 1845, making the present church the oldest corporation in New Braunfels. The charter of incorporation, issued to the congregation on October 15, 1845, by the Republic of Texas, is still in existence in the files of the church.

The rules for the German Protestant Church in Texas were drawn up by Reverend Ervendberg. These were followed and on October 5, 1845, a three-member church board was chosen. Those elected were George Kirchner, Heinrich Bevenroth, and Heinrich Schaefer.

The board held its first meeting Sunday, October 12, 1845. The pastor was the presiding officer. Hermann Seele was appointed secretary, and from that day until his death on March 18, 1902, a period of fifty-six years and five months, he served the congregation in that capacity. During the meeting the board also decided that a church would be built. All members who were in a position to do so were asked to haul the cedar logs. The board obligated itself to set an example by working as a body on construction of the church in order to expedite its completion as quickly as possible. The floor of the church was to be made of caliche and clay and constructed by the members.

The school promised by the *Verein*'s constitution initially was under the auspices of the colonial council. Reverend Ervendberg received permission from the council for Hermann Seele to assist him with the school, which began August 11, 1845. The pastor planned the curriculum, and on warm, sunny days the school took place in the same grove of trees where the first service was held. When the weather was bleak, school met in the Ervendbergs' small cabin, which was the first house completed in the settlement. By March 1846, with the completion of the log church, school was being held there. Although nondenominational, the school came under the auspices of the church board until 1853, when a city school was established.

Twenty deaths were listed in New Braunfels in 1845. The tragic year of 1846 recorded 348 deaths in the parochial register. With such great loss of life, there were sixty orphaned children. Members of the church helped the pastor and his wife place two large tents where the present church stands today. With the help of a competent matron, the Ervendbergs cared for the orphans. Relatives or friends took all but nineteen. The Ervendbergs took on the responsibility of the remaining children.

With the additional members in their household, a larger home was needed. By 1848, Reverend Ervendberg obtained a charter entitled "Western Orphan Asylum" but

244

popularly called *"Waisenhaus."* Parishioners helped with supplies and with the construction of the home, which was located on 200 acres about five miles from New Braunfels above the Guadalupe River. The Reverend Ervendberg continued ministering to the church until January 1851.

The log church served the church until the 1870s. (A large cross in the present sanctuary was made from original logs of the church.) In 1875, during the Reverend August Schuchard's tenure, the cornerstone for a new church was laid with this inscription: "Jesus Christ Yesterday, Today, and in Eternity." The limestone structure was built directly behind the log church, and until March 16, 1879, services continued as usual in the old structure.

The stone structure, originally built without a tower, was complete in 1881 and the log church was torn down. In 1888 the congregation decided to build a tower, which was three stories tall with an eighteen-foot spire above the third story topped by a globe and arrow.

The stone church's interior was completed in July of 1893. Shortly thereafter, three new bells were given to the congregation. The bells were hung in the tower and first rung on Saturday, May 11, 1895, in observance of the fiftieth anniversary of New Braufels. From that day on, these great bells have rung, bringing news of joyous and sad occasions. The bells are sometimes rung independently and sometimes together in harmony. They are rung on the hour throughout the day and night, and at the beginning of every church service.

The original small bells brought from Germany by Carl Schaefer under the direction of the *Verein* hold a revered place in the history of the church and the community. They are in a place of honor in the musical portion of First Protestant's heritage rooms.

Music is an important tradition in the community, and the church carries out this tradition. Early in the life of the church a cantor led the singing of hymns. The first mention of a choir is in the minutes of July 1880. The first organ, built by F. Heusinger of Williamsburg, Pennsylvania, was dedicated in June of 1869. Another organ was bought from

Edward Pfeifer and Son of Austin in 1897. The first English choir was formed in July 1926. In 1924 the beginnings of the present organ were purchased from George Kelgen and Son of St. Louis. Over the years the organ has been moved, renovated, and enlarged. Presently the organ has a set of pipes of twenty-four ranks. The organ underwent a complete renovation in 1992 and will add more ranks as space permits.

Mrs. Ella Springer Mornhinweg was director of the German choir for twenty-eight years and served as the organist. Her husband, the Reverend Gottlob Mornhinweg, served First Protestant for fifty-six years, from 1899 until his death. During his tenure the Seele Parish House and the two-story brick parsonage were constructed.

The first efforts toward raising funds for the enlargement of the stone church were begun under the Reverend Edwin Berger. The actual construction and renovation took place under the Reverend Carl Burkle. Marvin Eickenrohdt served as architect for the project, which was completed in 1956.

Perhaps the stained art glass windows of First Protestant Church are the single most outstanding element for melding the old and the new. Of the thirty-four windows in the present sanctuary, twelve are from the old building. The renovation of the church provided the opportunity to move the windows and place them chronologically to depict the life of Christ.

The windows, with their rich vibrant colors, tell the story of Jesus Christ from "The Nativity of Christ" through "The Ascension." Other windows depict various biblical symbols appropriate to the area in which they are placed. Perhaps the window that is most outstanding is the chancel window above the altar. Rich in Christian symbolism and beautiful in colors, the round window is five and a half feet in diameter and contains 969 pieces of art glass. In the center Jesus with hands outstretched looks down at the congregation with the message, "My Peace I Give Unto You."

As with other churches with a particular ethnic background, the needs of the people bring about an inevitable change. At times the transition from a German-speaking to

246

an English-speaking congregation was not an easy one. Originally all services, singing, and reading materials were in German. During World War I, the public schools converted to teaching in English and the use of German was deemphasized. This change affected the church as well. First Protestant honors its past by conducting German services on Christmas Day, Good Friday, and by emphasizing German hymns and chorales during the Heritage Sunday services. The oldest organization in the church, the *Frauenverein* (Women's Organization), organized in 1892, continues to hold the majority of its meetings in German.

Although the Deutsch Protestantische Gemeinde en Neu Braunfels has gone from affiliation with the Evangelical and Reformed Church to the United Church of Christ (a merge of the Evangelical and Reformed and Congregational Christian), the purpose is the same: First Protestant United Church of Christ of New Braunfels dedicates itself to the glory of God.


## THE GREEKS

Greek immigrants to Texas came later than immigrants of other nationalities, but they were able to blend into the economic structure and participate in the growth that followed. They brought with them a pride that is matched only by the contributions they made after they were settled.

The Greek movement began in Dallas before the turn of the century. By 1915, one hundred fifty families had come into that area. By 1950, that number had increased to 2,000 people. (That total had doubled by 1980.)

In spite of the early start and a continued growth in the Greek population in Dallas, the center of activity for Texans of Greek extraction is Houston. There are an estimated 6,000 in the Port City (1980) and the number is still growing.

San Antonio is the third largest center of Greek Texans. The settlement began around 1890, with only limited membership. By the end of World War I, a small group of

*HOLY TRINITY Greek Orthodox Church, Dallas.*

restaurant owners and salespeople had formed the nucleus of a Greek community that continues to grow at a steady pace. Even so, San Antonio continues to rank behind Houston and Dallas in Greek population.

From these established centers, young people with Greek heritage have spread across the state to become a part of the Texas tradition.

Source:
1. *The Greek Texans,* Institute of Texan Cultures, San Antonio, Texas.

# HOLY TRINITY GREEK ORTHODOX CHURCH
## Dallas — 1915

Although Greek immigrants began to come to Texas before the turn of the century, the first Greek church was not established until 1915. The Holy Trinity Greek Orthodox Church, located on the corner of Sanger and Riggs streets, was established in Dallas, with Daddios Lekkas as the first minister.

The first congregation started with seventy-five families, but by 1950 growth indicated the need for a new church building. By then there were 2,000 families in the Greek community who participated in making the new structure possible. It stands today as a monument to those who have contributed so much to Texas.

The first Greek Festival was held in 1958 to further project the Greek culture and to preserve traditions. Funds raised through the carnival-like project were used to further promote the church as the center of the Greek community.

*ANNUNCIATION Greek Orthodox Church, Houston.*

249

In 1972 the church interior was completely redecorated with icons and murals by artist John Geris.

Source:
1. *The Greek Texans*, Institute of Texan Cultures, San Antonio, Texas.


## ANNUNCIATION GREEK ORTHODOX CHURCH
Houston – 1917

Greek immigrants arrived in Houston at about the same time as they arrived in Dallas, but again the thrust of the movement was not until after 1900. During the first years of the new century, Greek immigrants took advantage of the opportunities they found in the fast growing Houston area.

One of the first things they did was to organize a church. Father Angelopulus of New Orleans conducted the first morning service in the Christ Episcopal Church for a congregation of fifty charter members. Little else was done to encourage continuing religious services for the Greek community until 1916, when a new surge of interest developed to encourage the building of their own church.

In 1917 the Annunciation Greek Orthodox Church was established with about thirty families in the congregation. It was a modest chapel, constructed of wood, that was drab looking on the outside. On the other hand, it sparkled inside with a jewel-encrusted altar and crystal chandeliers. At the first services, men sat on one side and women on the other.

In 1952 an imposing stone church and auditorium were completed, and in 1967 the Palemonakos Educational Building was added. Also in 1967, the Houston church was elevated to the status of a cathedral and became headquarters of the Eighth Diocese, moved from New Orleans. Houston is now the acknowledged center of Greek Orthodox activity in the Southwest, and the congregation is the focal point in a variety of activities.

Since 1967, the parish has held an annual Greek Festi-

250

ST. SOPHIA Greek Orthodox Church, San Antonio.

val to help keep the Greek heritage and culture alive. Each year tens of thousands attend and enjoy the food, music, and fun.

Source:
　　1. *The Greek Texans,* Institute of Texan Cultures, San Antonio, Texas.

## ST. SOPHIA GREEK ORTHODOX CHURCH
### San Antonio – 1927

A few Greek immigrants arrived in San Antonio at about the same time that they were settling in Dallas and Houston, but it was not until after World War I that a Greek community in the Alamo City began to develop. Even then, their ability to blend into the economic structure that

251

already existed was so good that the increase in numbers was not readily noticed.

At first, their religious needs were taken care of by visiting Greek Orthodox priests who held services at St. Mark's Episcopal Church. It wasn't long, however, before the need of a full-time priest became evident. The realization developed when the Greeks found themselves having to wait for a priest to arrive from Dallas to conduct a funeral.

In 1924 the Greek-American Democratic Club was founded and an effort was made to raise money to build a church. By 1926, plans for the Byzantine-style structure were well along, and the following year the St. Sophia Greek Orthodox Church was completed. Father Emmanuel Pamos became the first pastor.

By 1960, the congregation was made up of more than 500 members, which represented about 125 families. This group continued to grow, and on Greek Independence Day, March 25, the day in 1821 that Archbishop Germanos of Patras proclaimed Greek independence from the Ottoman rule, 1,500 people gathered at the Casino Club for a concert, a flag-raising ceremony, patriotic speeches, and a dance.

Like other Texas Greek communities, the one in San Antonio gained new life when the first festival was held in 1961. It was called a Funstival, and like those held in other areas of the state it was a fund-raising affair and continues to grow.

San Antonio leaders in all areas are numbered among the Greek people. One of those to receive recognition was Dr. Timothy Caris, who became acting dean of the medical school at the University of Texas Health Sciences Center. Dr. Caris has served as attending physician at Bexar County Hospital and has been professor of medicine and associate dean for Continuing Medical Education at the school since 1976.

The interior of St. Sophia is colorfully decorated with icons painted by a long-time pastor, Ergon J. Zografos. The minister in 1980 was James Karagas, assisted by John Stehling, a deacon, and Gregory Roth, chaplain.

Sources:
1. Material supplied from church records.
2. Personal interviews.
3. *The Greek Texans,* Institute of Texan Cultures, San Antonio, Texas.

# THE JEWS

Jewish Texans are descended from immigrants who came from Western Europe, Bavaria, Alsace, France, and Germany. They began coming as early as 1850 and continued until the end of the century. At first, they settled in the more concentrated areas because they were basically business and professional people, but today they live in towns and cities throughout the state.

*FIRST JEWISH SYNAGOGUE in Houston.*

253

*TEMPLE BETH ISRAEL, Houston, early 1920s.*

Houston was the first to have a Jewish synagogue, but Dallas followed twenty years later to develop the largest congregation in the state. Galveston, because of accessibility through its port, received many Jewish immigrants after the Civil War.

## TEMPLE BETH ISRAEL
Houston – 1854

In 1980, Temple Beth Israel in Houston observed the 126th year since it was chartered in 1854. Members of the congregation examine with pride its history, its dynamic present, and the future they hope will parallel the progress being made by the city that has offered them a home for so many years.

In 1850, Houston was a community of about 2,400 people. Today that number exceeds two million. In 1859, Beth Israel had a congregation of twenty-two families. In 1980, the records showed a membership of about 1,500

254

*CONGREGATION BETH ISRAEL, Houston, 1925.*

*CONGREGATION BETH ISRAEL, Houston, present synagogue entrance.*

255

families, in the nation's fifth largest city where about 27,000 Jews reside.

Immigrants from Western Europe, Alsace, Bavaria, France, and Germany made up the first Jewish congregation in Houston, in 1859. Congregation Beth Israel received its first charter that year, even though several informal groups had been meeting as far back as 1854.

The 1850s was a pivotal period for Houston, both economically and politically. By the 1860s, Houston had become the leading town on the Texas coast, and Beth Israel had managed to keep pace. By then, the first Jewish cemetery had been established and a religious school was in operation.

The synagogue was the center of all activity for the Jewish people. Before 1870, services were held in a frame building on LaBranch Street, between Texas and Prairie streets. In 1866 the decision was made not to repair that building but to erect a new one.

In June of 1870, a parade of more than 1,000 participants marched down Main Street, led by Schmidt's Brass Band. The marchers made their way to the site of the new synagogue on Franklin Avenue. There, a suitable ceremony was held with proper Masonic honors, and the cornerstone was laid. Four years later, the temple was completed.

During the years that followed, Beth Israel members underwent some changes in the beliefs they had been following, and some of the congregation, primarily the Polish and Russian members, left to establish the Congregation Adath Yeshurum because they disagreed with the reform movement.

After the turn of the century, Dr. Henry Barnston became Beth Israel's rabbi. The highly educated native of England became a respected leader throughout Houston, as well as the Jewish community. It was under his direction that Beth Israel again entered into a building program.

In 1908 a new "Romanesque" temple was dedicated, having been constructed at the corner of Lamar and Crawford. Then, after World War I, when Houston became a major port and many of the oil and gas industries had established their headquarters, another move by Beth Israel was made.

This time, in 1925, the temple was built at the corner of Austin Street and Holman Avenue. Many of the present members of the congregation have memories of this building. They remember the eloquent sermons that Dr. Barnston preached, and they recall the kindergarten teacher, Mrs. Mirian Browning, who taught them their first concept of God.

When Dr. Barnston retired in 1943, Temple Beth Israel had a membership of 807, the largest in history. It was fortunate for the congregation that they were able to replace him with Rabbi Hyman Judah Schachtel, who was called by the temple president, Irvin Schlenker, "the peerless pulpiteer." Throughout his period of service, until he became an active rabbi emeritus, Rabbi Schachtel was a dynamic leader.

As Houston's Jewish population continued to grow and move toward the suburbs, Beth Israel's leadership saw the necessity to make a similar move. In 1964, under the leadership of I. S. Brochstein, the temple purchased land on North Braeswood, where the beautiful and functional structure that opened its doors in 1967 continues to serve as a base for those who respond to the needs of its people.

In June of 1975, Rabbi Samuel Egal Karff, the third senior rabbi of Congregation Beth Israel, arrived. He became a strong leader who reflected the openness, the richness, and the variety of the city as a whole.

Sources:
1. *The Beth Israel Story: A Celebration 1854–1979*, Congregation Beth Israel, Houston, Texas.
2. Correspondence with Stanley J. Singer, director of administration, Congregation Beth Israel.

*TEMPLE B'NAI ISRAEL, Galveston.*

## TEMPLE B'NAI ISRAEL
### Galveston — 1870

Although there had been neighborhood meetings in the home of Isadore Dyer, and later in the Temperance Hall, a temple was not provided for the Jewish people in Galveston until 1870. Named B'nai Israel, it is the second oldest in the state (Beth Israel in Houston, dedicated in 1854, is the oldest). Because of its location in a port city, B'nai Israel became one of the most active congregations in the state.

Years before a synagogue was built in Galveston, a Jewish Cemetery Association was organized. That was in 1852, two years before there was a synagogue in Texas. The plot of land for the cemetery was donated by Isadore Dyer and in 1866, the Hebrew Benevolent Society was chartered to purchase additional land for burial purposes. It soon became evident that there were enough people in Galveston of the Jewish faith to require a synagogue.

The cornerstone for the original temple was laid on June 9, 1870, with M. P. Tucker, the Grand Master of the Masonic Order in Texas, conducting the ceremonies. Rabbi Jacobs of the Portuguese Synagogue of New Orleans conducted the religious services.

The first acting minister of the temple was Alexander Rosenspitz, who remained until 1871. Then Abraham

258

Blum, a Frenchman, became the second minister and the first official rabbi. He served from 1871 to 1885. Rabbi Joseph Silverman began service in Galveston on May 16, 1885. When he left to accept the position of junior rabbi of Temple Emanuel in New York City, Temple B'nai Israel received Henry Cohen, who remained for sixty-two years.

Rabbi Cohen was born in London on April 7, 1863. He was ordained a rabbi in 1884. After his first synagogue in Kingston, Jamaica, in the British West Indies, he went to Woodville, Mississippi. Then, on May 18, 1888, the man who was to write much of the Jewish history in Galveston was called to B'nai Israel, where he felt "he could make a contribution."

Indeed he did. He survived two storms, one in 1900 that did severe damage to the synagogue, and another on August 15, 1915. On both occasions, large repair bills for the building were incurred, but Rabbi Cohen was equal to the task. He continued to give his services in a variety of programs, the primary one being the Galveston Information Bureau, founded by Jacob H. Schiff to promote the welfare of Jewish immigrants.

In January 1928 the cornerstone of the Henry Cohen Community House of Congregation B'nai was laid, and the building was dedicated on November 18 of that same year. The inscription read: "Erected in honor of Dr. Henry Cohen's forty years as Rabbi of the community."

The man who was a classic example of religious leadership that cuts across all nations and all doctrines did not live to see the temple now located on 30th Street and Avenue O in Galveston. Rabbi Cohen died June 12, 1952. The man who had elected "to stay in Texas" had done his work well. Plans moved forward to erect the new center of worship that has become a symbol of his leadership.

The Masonic fraternity, comprising the Grand Lodge of Texas, and Harmony and Tucker Lodges of Galveston, again conducted ceremonies of laying the cornerstone on June 9, 1954. Masonic leaders of the city participated, and Rabbi Sidney Wolf of Temple Beth El in Corpus Christi gave the cornerstone address.

*TEN COMMANDMENTS in Hebrew, Emanu-el, Dallas.*

Sources:
    1. Mrs. Henry M. Stern, *The History of Temple B'nai Israel.*
    2. The Henry Cohen Memorial, Galveston, Texas, February 25–27, 1955.
    3. Congregation B'nai Israel.
    4. The Harris and Eliza Kempner Sanctuary, April 11, 1975.
    5. Personal interview with Marcus Wells, former active member now living in Round Rock.

# TEMPLE EMANU-EL
## Dallas – 1872

Although Temple Emanu-El is not the oldest Jewish house of worship in Texas, it is the largest. Founded in 1872, fifteen years after Temple Beth Israel in Houston was chartered, it is situated on a twenty-acre tract of land at the corner of Northwest Highway and Hillcrest Road in Dallas.

The present temple was chartered in February of 1957. The first synagogue, located on the corner of Ervay and St. Louis streets, was dedicated in 1899. The next was moved to Harwood and South Boulevard in 1916 and served the Jewish community well until it was outgrown and the present facility was put in operation.

*TEMPLE EMANU-EL, Dallas.*

*TEMPLE EMANU-EL, present synagogue.*

261

Temple Emanu-El was designed by Dallas architects Howard R. Meyer and Max M. Sandfield. The consulting architect was William W. Wurster of Berkeley, California, and the art coordinator was Gyorgy Kepes of Cambridge, Massachusetts.

The sanctuary has 728 permanent seats and can be fitted out to accommodate 1,000 people. When combined with the Louis Tobin Auditorium, it will seat 2,500. In addition to the sanctuary, which is used for all major religious services, there is the David Lefkowitz Chapel, which is open daily for private meditation, as well as for weddings, funerals, and children's services.

The sanctuary has a domed ceiling that is seventy-two feet high and is lighted by seventy-two fixtures that are extended from above. There are forty-seven classrooms in the building to accommodate 1,600 children for religious instruction. The program involves an elementary program, a middle school, and an upper division school. A multipurpose adult program helps keep the Temple Emanu-El family properly informed and positively identified. School classes are held primarily on Saturday and Sunday mornings.

Temple Emanu-El is a congregation which teaches and practices Reform Judaism.

The Alex F. Weisburg Library houses 6,000 volumes of Judaism history, theory, and philosophy; while the Charlotte and Martin Weiss Youth Rooms provide recreation for children of all ages.

The rabbi as of 1980 was Gerald J. Klein.

Much of Temple Emanu-El's earlier history centers around Rabbi David Lefkowitz, who served the congregation from 1920 until 1949 and then became rabbi emeritus, serving until his death in 1955. Another great leader was Rabbi Emeritus Levi A. Olan.

Sources:
1. Interview with Elizabeth Thermond, secretary to Rabbi Klein.
2. Booklet, *Welcome to Temple Emanu-El.*
3. *History of Temple Emanu-El,* prepared by the office of Rabbi Klein.

*TEMPLE BETH-EL SYNAGOGUE, San Antonio.*

# TEMPLE BETH-EL
## San Antonio – 1874

Temple Beth-El in San Antonio is the third oldest congregation of the Jewish faith in Texas. The Reform Temple in Houston and Dallas preceded it.

Jewish activity abounded in San Antonio at least twenty-five years before a synagogue was built. This activity was interrupted by the outbreak of the Civil War, and about all that held those who remained together was a Jewish burial ground that had been started in 1855. The Civil War disrupted the growth of the Jewish community in San Antonio because, like so many of their fellow Texans with Germanic or Central European roots, they did not approve of slavery. To show their objections, many of them left the state.

By 1870, Jewish leaders began thinking of establishing a formal congregation and a synagogue. An article in the June 16, 1935, issue of the *San Antonio Express* stated that a handful of Jews had been holding religious services as early as 1872. These meetings, which were held in the old Ruellman Hall, opposite Joske's on East Commerce Street, were conducted by members of the Hebrew Benevolent Society which had been formed in 1856. One purpose of the group was to provide burials for indigent Jews in the San Antonio area.

During those meetings in the early 1870s, the Society purchased from Mrs. Mary Maverick a piece of land on the northeast corner of Travis and Jefferson streets. This seemed to indicate they were serious about a synagogue.

There were reports, although the meetings were not recorded, that a group of Jewish men were meeting to organize a formal congregation. Then in 1874, meetings of subscribers to a building fund were held in the Odd Fellows Hall. Plans were made to build a synagogue which would cost about $11,000–$12,000. Most of the time there were twenty-seven to twenty-eight men in attendance. Leo Veith was chosen temporary president, while B. Oppenheimer was named temporary secretary.

The following week, on June 4, 1874, a second recorded meeting was held in the home of Louis Zork to draft a constitution and by-laws for the new congregation. Three more meetings were necessary to complete the organization, for which Louis Zork served as the presiding officer. On June 17, 1874, the constitution and by-laws to govern the new congregation, now named Temple Beth-El (House of God), were unanimously adopted.

The meeting went back to the Odd Fellows Hall, where on July 5, 1874, the final and permanent organization of the congregation was completed. Sam Mayer was elected president, L. Zork was named vice-president, B. Oppenheimer was nominated to serve as secretary, and Solomon Deutsch was selected as treasurer. The trustees were M. L. Mortiz, M. Goldfrank, M. Koenigheim, A. Michael, and Mayer Halff. A building committee was appointed and a fund-raising organization was named. The last of the formal business was to pass a resolution to join the newly formed Union of American Hebrew Congregations of the United States, an organization of the new Liberal branch of Judaism. On September 27, 1874, the congregation voted to adopt the resolution.

The new synagogue building was finally completed, and September 10, 1875, was set for the formal dedication. A new organ was purchased and a resolution was passed asking "that the Israelites of San Antonio be respectfully requested to close their places of business during the dedication ceremonies at Temple Beth-El from Friday evening, September 10, 1875 at 4 P.M. until Saturday evening."

According to Frances Kallison, who has made an in-depth study of the founding of the congregation, "At the hour, on that date, the key was formally presented to the president of the congregation, the doors were thrown wide open, and the dedication services were begun, conducted by I. K. Guthein, assisted by Alex Rosenspitz."

The synagogue has had only two locations in San Antonio, the present one at Belknap and Ashby streets, and the original one on the corner of Travis and Navarro streets. There were two buildings on the first site.

The present building was completed and dedicated in 1927. The synagogue sits on a hill, and its red tile dome can be seen from all points in the city. It has been declared a National Historic Landmark and draws many visitors from all over the country.

Dr. Samuel Stahl served as rabbi since 1976.

Sources:
1. Frances Kallison, thesis material on the founding of Temple Beth-El.
2. Mrs. Sue Wiseman, executive director of Temple Beth-El.
3. Marcus Wells, resident of Round Rock and friend of Rabbi Stahl.


## THE MEXICAN PROTESTANTS

Most of the two million Hispanics who live in Texas are descendants of the colonists who settled New Spain. In 1519 Hernán Cortes landed on the coast of Mexico with 500 soldiers to conquer the land occupied by native tribes of Indians numbering between ten and twenty million people. Under Spanish rule, the only religion allowed by law was Catholicism. Later, when Mexico became an independent nation in 1821, the law prevailed, even though it was not always enforced. This was especially true in the area along the Red River and the Sabine River in northeast Texas.

Because of their early heritage, a majority of the people of Mexican ancestry were Catholics. In the beginning, there was little effort among Protestant groups to try to establish Spanish-language churches. Most of their activity was in areas with few people of Mexican descent.

Little evangelical work was done in South Texas by the Protestants until after the Civil War, when Methodists began to supply preachers. After World War I, other Protestant activity, especially in San Antonio, became noticeable. At first, some of it was on an individual basis. But efforts were later coordinated with established church groups.

266

*LA TRINIDAD UNITED METHODIST CHURCH,*
*built about 1886.*

A Baptist layman in San Antonio, R. A. Mathews, concentrated his time and money in building small neighborhood missions. By 1940, the First Baptist Church in San Antonio decided to lend financial support. Later, the church took over the entire effort.

There are now many Spanish-language Protestant churches throughout south and southwest Texas, including La Trinidad United Methodist Church in San Antonio, founded in 1876.

Sources:
1. Institute of Texan Cultures, San Antonio, Texas.
2. Interview with R. A. Mathews.

*LA TRINIDAD Methodist Church, built in 1967, San Antonio.*

*LA TRINIDAD Methodist Church, built in 1921, San Antonio.*

# LA TRINIDAD UNITED METHODIST CHURCH
## San Antonio – 1876

The churches in the Rio Grande Conference of the Methodist Church in Texas include at least a dozen that are over a hundred years old. La Trinidad Church in San Antonio is perhaps the most remarkable.

La Trinidad United Methodist Church is one of the oldest Spanish-language Methodist churches in the United States. It was organized through pressure from local ministers and members of their congregations to create a Spanish-speaking district within the geographical boundaries of the West Texas Conference, which is now the Southwest Texas Conference.

At a meeting of the West Texas Conference, held in Gonzales in December of 1874, the movement got under way, with Bishop J. C. Keener presiding.

Alexander H. Sutherland was named the presiding elder of the new district. Prior to that, he had been sent to Rockport and to Corpus Christi to study the Spanish language.

Since San Antonio was the heart of the Spanish-speaking population in the state, Sutherland visited the Alamo City soon after his appointment had been made. He then investigated the possibility of opening a Methodist center in the city. His efforts were so successful that at the annual conference the following year, a new minister from Corpus Christi, Jose Maria Casanova, was appointed as the first pastor.

The Mexican mission, now known as La Trinidad United Methodist Church, was organized in 1876 with seven members. At first, they met in private homes. As the membership grew, they used rented rooms across the street from the Farmer's Market at Plaza del Zacate. Ten years later, in 1886, the congregation moved to the corner of Pacos and San Fernando, where the first building was erected. Ignacio Z. Rivera was the pastor at the time.

In 1921 the second building was erected, with financial assistance from the Laural Heights Methodist Church in

269

San Antonio, where Frank Smith, who later became a bishop, was pastor. At the time, Julian Castro was pastor at La Trinidad and Dr. Frank S. Onderdonk was the presiding elder.

By 1967, the church was able, through its own leadership and resources, to construct the third building, which is now located at the corner of Pacos and San Fernando streets. Oscar F. Garza was then the pastor.

During the Mexican Revolution, La Trinidad was the spiritual refuge for many of the leaders involved in the movement. For many years, it was the only Spanish-language Methodist church in San Antonio and has been the mother church of many of the churches in the city. Because of this background over the past hundred years, La Trinidad has become the largest self-supported Spanish-language Methodist church in the United States. In 1980 the church had a membership of 1,308 and today continues to grow.

Through the years the church has been known as Mission Mexicana, La Iglesia Metodista Mexicana, La Iglesia Metodista La Trinidad, and currently, La Trinidad Iglesia Metodista Unida.

By 1980, La Trinidad had been served by thirty-five pastors during its history of more than 100 years. A number of them have been outstanding members of the conference and two of them, Juan N. Pascoe and Eleazar Guerra, were elected bishops of the Methodist church in Mexico. La Trinidad is recognized as one of the outstanding churches in San Antonio. The pastor, Alfred T. Grout, has been serving since the mid-1970s.

Sources:
1. *Servicio de Inauguracion — Del Nuevo Templo.*
2. La Trinidad — La Iglesia Methodista.
3. The Reverend Dr. A. Nanez, Edinburg, Texas.
4. Mrs. Minerva N. Garza, San Antonio, Texas.
5. Rev. Alfred Grout, pastor, La Trinidad United Methodist Church, San Antonio, Texas.

*MACEDONIA FIRST BAPTIST CHURCH, Bastrop.*

*BELL OF MACEDONIA FIRST BAPTIST.*

271

# THE AFRICAN-AMERICANS

Unlike other ethnic groups, African-Americans had no choice about coming to Texas. They came as slaves, and their descendants form the largest minority group in the state.

The establishment of black churches began about ten years after the Civil War. Prior to the Emancipation Proclamation, slaves attended the same church as did their owners. During the war, slave groups, frequently with help from the Freedman's Bureau, organized and held their own services.

There are too many black churches in Texas to select a single group for a representative sampling. Many of them started about the same time, and it is difficult to determine age, other than when a church building was constructed. In many cases the records are not available to verify stories that have been handed down from one generation to another.

The authors have selected a representative church in a community with a large black population to give an idea of what has developed since 1865. Also selected is a church with a different origin in a town where the black population is more limited.

## MACEDONIA FIRST BAPTIST CHURCH
### Bastrop — 1875

The Macedonia First Baptist Church is located in Bastrop, a Central Texas town with a large black population.

The church was chartered in 1875 and the first building, located where the M.K.T. railroad station later stood, was purchased from Mr. and Mrs. John P. Lake. The trustees at the time were Fred Atchinson, Friday Mathews, and Alex White. The bell located in front of the present building was purchased along with the building. It came from an out-of-service ferry boat that had been used on the Colorado River.

*ST. PAUL'S AFRICAN METHODIST EPISCOPAL CHURCH,*
*La Grange.*

The present church, built in 1974, is located on the corner of Pine and Chamber streets. It is modern in every respect, with a large and attractive sanctuary, offices for the minister and the associate minister, Sunday school rooms, a parlor for social events, and a kitchen with full equipment.

C. A. Williams has been the pastor since the new church was built, while B. A. Jackson has been the associate minister. Deacons (in 1980) were Clyde Hall, Lamore Wilson, Henry Calton, Oliver Clark, Wilson W. Williams, Charlie Barnet, Watson Hayes, and Walter Parker.

Macedonia Baptist Church has had nineteen pastors since it was chartered in 1875. Williams came in 1955. A complete list of those who have served included Father Joshua, Tom Pendergraph, Lofton, Gilmore, J. Johnson, Southern, Washington, Dr. T. S. Floyd, Dr. Jimmy Johnson, W. M. James, A. H. Brown, W. L. Green, S. L. Davis, N. S. Brown, H. L. Price, John Clark, Jerry Hemphill, and W. L. Tabor.

Much of the progress made by the Macedonia Church is traceable to the work of its women. Mrs. Mellie Williams, the wife of Deacon Wilson W. Williams, headed several organizations that planned fund-raising events and contributed to the social well-being of the congregation.

For a part of the African-American community in Bastrop, the Macedonia First Baptist Church is the core of activity that reaches out into other areas that contribute to the growth of the little Central Texas town.

Sources:
    1. Church history recorded at the church.
    2. Interviews with Deacon Wilson W. Williams and Mellie Williams.


## ST. PAUL'S AFRICAN METHODIST EPISCOPAL
## La Grange—(Building date 1852 or 1853)

After serving the Presbyterians of La Grange for a century, the oldest church building in La Grange, and one of the oldest in Texas, was sold to St. Paul's African Methodist Episcopal Church.

St. Paul's had its beginning as a religious denomination when black members of the Methodist Society of Philadelphia separated themselves. A similar move took place in Baltimore, after which the two groups allied and called a general conference in April 1816. Under the leadership of Richard Allen, first bishop of the African Methodist Episcopal Church, this denomination spread throughout

*THE ROCK CHURCH, Norse.*

*ST. OLAF LUTHERAN CHURCH, Cranfills Gap*

275

the United States, Canada, the West Indies, South America, Africa, and India.

A part of this movement, St. Paul's of La Grange is a member of the West Texas Conference and Greater Bay City District, whose presiding elder in 1980 was J. H. Phillips. Texas is a member of the 10th District of the African Methodist Episcopal Church, whose leader as of 1980 was Bishop John Hurst Adam.

The pastor of St. Paul's of La Grange in 1980 was P. A. Pittman who, together with the congregation, proudly carried on religious activities as part of a 128-year tradition.

Sources:
1. *The Fayette County Record,* May 25, 1979.
2. Conference with Richard L. Barton, Sr., publisher.

## THE NORWEGIANS

Although Bosque County was not the first Norwegian settlement in Texas, it is the largest and has retained its identity.

In February of 1854, the Texas legislature created Bosque County and offered 320 acres of free land to those who would homestead. Two of the Norwegian leaders in the Texas movement, Cleng Peerson and Ole Canuteson, urged their friends to settle in the area which was similar to their native land. It offered good soil, plenty of wood, and good water. The gentle, rolling prairie, located in the south central part of the county, with spring-fed streams and widely separated woodlands, brought many of the original settlers from Brownsboro, where an earlier settlement had been made.

Brownsboro, in Henderson County, was the first Norwegian settlement. At the suggestion of the Texas consul in New Orleans, Johan R. Reierson, who was interested in improving the plight of Norwegian laborers through immigration, came to Texas to look at the unoccupied land of the Republic that was being offered free to those who would settle it. He liked what he saw, and in Austin he visited with Gen. Sam Houston, who expressed a desire to have Norwegian immigrants help settle the new land.

In the spring of 1845, Reierson returned to New Orleans with his family and his parents. Later in the year, when Texas was admitted to the Union, his father, Ole, bought a land certificate of 1,476 acres of unclaimed Texas land. The next year, two of Reierson's brothers, Christian and George, arrived with fifty more settlers. The first settlement was called Normandy, but its name was later changed to Brownsboro.

When admitted to the Union in 1845 by treaty, Texas was allowed to keep its public land but also had to assume the responsibility for a $10 million debt. With no money to pay the debt, and with little credit, it became necessary for the state to use land scrip as money to conduct routine business. This eliminated some offers of free land that had existed during the days of the Republic, but it did not stop the Norwegians and other ethnic groups from coming to Texas to find new homes.

Records in the Land Office show that in 1854, Karl Questad, who had been in the advance party of Norwegian immigrants who had explored the regions along the Bosque River the year before, was the first to take out a deed for farm land in the newly created county. The country was so wild that roving Indians frequently raided the outlying farm houses. In 1867 Questad was attacked by the Comanches and escaped only by jumping off a cliff.

The first settlement in Bosque County by Norwegians was called Norse. A post office was established, and T. Theo Colwick became the postmaster. Later, the communities of Clifton and Cranfills Gap joined the first settlement to build a solid pocket of Norwegians who still maintain their identity.

The Norwegian colonists were for the most part Lutheran, and each family had a Bible, as well as Luther's "Catechism and Explanation." Worship services were initially held in private homes.

The Civil War brought a division in the ranks of the

Norwegians in Henderson and Bosque counties. For the most part they opposed slavery, but the records show that at least fifty Texans of Norwegian descent served in the Army of the Confederacy.

The 1860 census listed 326 Norwegians in the state. Even under the difficult conditions of Reconstruction days, the sons and daughters of Norway held together and moved forward through their pride and determination.

Ole Olsen Estrem was the first resident pastor to the Norwegians in Bosque County after the Civil War. During the years of his service, from 1869 to 1877, the first church was built at Norse — Our Savior's Lutheran Church. Estrem was succeeded by John K. Rystad, who served the Norse church for the next forty-eight years.

Rystad was responsible for founding an academy in Clifton in 1896. He also served as its first president. Then Clifton Junior College was established as the upper branch of the academy in 1922. The academy closed in 1936, and in 1953 the junior college merged with Texas Lutheran College at Seguin.

In 1886 the "Rock Church" was built in Norse. This building was constructed of native stone and originally had a dirt floor. Planks were laid on wooden kegs to serve as pews. The bell was acquired in 1897.

The church served Norwegian settlers of the area, which included the members of Our Savior's Lutheran Church of Norse until 1902, when the growth of the community necessitated the separation from the Norse church. It was then that St. Olaf congregation was formed. A new building was erected in Cranfills Gap in 1917 and is still in service today. The Rock Church is now used only in a limited capacity, for weddings and other special events.

The Norwegian settlers in Bosque County were a proud people, and their descendants have lost none of that feeling. Their Viking heritage remains in the old world language, customs, and traditions which were retained. Even today, many of these traditions are practiced to hold the people together. Each year an annual festival features the food, the songs, and the dances of their heritage. In part, this makes up for the decline of the Norse influence, which

278

is all but gone in Prairiesville and Brownsboro, in Henderson County.

Religious faith was strong among the settlers, and many of their sons have become ministers.

In an era of movement toward the cities, the Norwegians have remained on their land. Rural roads in the south-central part of Bosque County attest to this fact. Time and weather have tarnished the mailboxes along the way, but the Norwegian names on them are still quite clear. They have been repainted regularly, so there can be no mistake about who lives there.

Sources:
1. *The Norwegian Texans,* Institute of Texan Cultures, San Antonio, Texas.
2. Visits to Clifton and Cranfills Gap.
3. Conference with Mrs. Leonard Kiely and School Superintendent Richard Lairdon.

## THE POLES

The first Polish colony in America was established in Karnes County, Texas, about fifty miles southeast of San Antonio. Leopold Moczygembo, a missionary priest, was working in New Braunfels and wrote glowing letters to his family in Poland about the opportunities to be found in the new land. About a hundred families responded, sold their possessions, and sailed to find a place where they could realize their dreams.

The voyage took nine weeks. On December 3, 1884, the sailing ship, *The Veser,* landed in Galveston and the people started out by foot and by ox-cart to find the land Father Leopold had purchased from John Twohig, an Irish merchant from San Antonio.

The inland journey lasted three weeks. The women wore wooden shoes, and walking was difficult. They also wore ankle-length dresses and wide-brim hats with low, flat crowns. Some had to turn back even before they reached the spot where the San Antonio River is joined by Cibolo

279

*POLISH CATHOLIC CHURCH, Panna Maria.*

Creek, the spot where the village of Panna Maria was to be established.

On Christmas Eve, Father Leopold celebrated the traditional mass at midnight under a large oak tree and offered a prayer of thanksgiving for the survival of his people. It was behind this oak tree that he established the first Polish church in America. Father Leopold would serve as the pastor until 1856. He then returned to a broader area of religious activity until his death on February 23, 1891.

The members who turned back helped settle some of the new towns that were beginning to spring up, such as Victoria, Yorktown, and Mayersville (the only one that did not survive).

The following year 700 new families moved to Panna Maria, and in 1856 still a third group was added. The bell they brought from a church in Poland is still being used to call the faithful to worship.

As the Polish people continued to arrive, many of them spread out over the land that joined Panna Maria. The little village became the mother colony for such places as Bandera, St. Hedwig, Czestochowa, Kosciusko, Pawelekville, and Falls City. Since then, Poles have settled all over the state, but their roots remain in Karnes County and in the Church of the Immaculate Conception, which for more than 125 years has been their spiritual home.

## THE IMMACULATE CONCEPTION
## CATHOLIC CHURCH
### Panna Maria – 1854

The first Polish church in America was organized by Father Leopold Moczygembo in 1854. The building, constructed of stone and lime, was erected in 1856. It was destroyed by lightning in 1877 and was replaced by a new structure the next year. This building is still in use, having been remodeled in 1937 and dedicated to the Immaculate Conception of the Blessed Virgin Mary.

At first, Leopold was the only person involved who

*CROSS IN FRONT OF CHURCH OF NATIVITY*
*of Blessed Virgin Mary, Czestochowa.*

*NATIVITY OF BLESSED VIRGIN MARY, Czestochowa.*

283

could speak English. The children were taught to read and write, and in 1868 St. Joseph's school was established. It became the first Polish school in America. Today the building serves as the historical museum at Panna Maria and is filled with material that paints a picture of these brave people who suffered many hardships in trying to fulfill their dreams.

Leopold died in 1891 and was buried in the Mount Elliot Cemetery in Detroit, Michigan. In 1974, the centennial year of the Archdiocese of San Antonio, Bernard Goebel, pastor of Immaculate Conception of the Blessed Virgin Mary at Panna Maria, worked with Francis J. Furey, archbishop of San Antonio, and together they were able to bring Father Leopold's remains back home to Panna Maria. It seemed fitting that he should finally rest under the old oak tree where he held midnight mass on Christmas Eve in 1854.

Sources:
1. Personal interview, Father Bernard Goebel, pastor.
2. Edward Dworaczyk, *The First Polish Colonies of America in Texas.*


## THE CHURCH OF THE NATIVITY
## OF THE BLESSED VIRGIN MARY
Czestochowa — 1873

There are several Polish communities in Texas older than Czestochowa, but because of the close ties with Panna Maria during the founding days and the geographical location, it seems proper to treat it as part of the total picture.

As the population of Panna Maria continued to grow, many of the residents became restless. By keeping the parent community as a hub, the people would fan out in clusters, like spokes on a wagon wheel. One group of forty families settled about five miles from Panna Maria and in 1873 started a new community named Czestochowa (frequently called Cestochowa). The word means "Our Lady Often Saves" and is derived from the notable village in Poland which enshrines the famous painting of Our Lady of Czestochowa, the patroness of the Polish people.

In 1873 a small school was built which also served as a chapel. For a few years, the Panna Maria parish priest came once a month to say Mass, but in 1877 the people decided to become independent and made plans for a new church. The land was donated by Alton Jarzombek, Frank Mutz, and Jacob Lyssy. The stone was quarried from their fields, with some of it coming from Anton Skloss. The hauling was without cost and the lime was prepared by the settlers themselves.

When controversy arose over a possible division of the parish, Father Felix of Panna Maria sought help from Bishop Pellicer in San Antonio. After some negotiations, the new church was finally constructed and was blessed on February 10, 1878, placed under the patronage of the Nativity of the Blessed Virgin Mary.

In September of 1878, W. Pelezar was ordained to the priesthood and received his first appointment as the residential pastor of the new church. He remained until 1881 and then was replaced, after a series of moves in several of the churches, by W. Tyszkiewicz.

The church was remodeled in 1931 and some additions in height were made. An old cross from a church in the old country was added in front. Things remained as they were until 1973, when it was repaired and repainted a soft gray color with white trim. The church has a tall steeple that can be seen for miles.

The pastor in 1980 was Monsignor Erwin A. Juraschek, a noted historian and civic leader. Little-known information was obtained from him concerning the part Texas played in the American Revolution, over a hundred years before Czestochowa became a Polish settlement.

According to Juraschek, the area was called "New Spain" during those early days and there were many private ranches from land grants from the mother country. On these ranches were thousands of head of cattle, horses, sheep, and goats. Prior to the revolution, many of the horses were rounded up and driven east to supply the

285

*ST. STANISLAUS CHURCH, Bandera.*

colonists. Some of the cattle were also sent east, but over 13,000 head were shipped to Louisiana after the revolution began in order to supply the army of Gen. Bernardo de Galvez, after whom Galveston was named. He led the Spanish forces along the Gulf Coast against the British. After the battle of Saratoga, France, Spain and Holland declared war against the British when it began to appear that the American forces could win.

Not only did Texas cattle play a part in winning the war of independence, but according to Juraschek, it was a Texas horse that set off the alarm. "All of us have heard of Paul Revere and his midnight journey alerting the colonists that the British were coming," he said. "What is little known and seldom mentioned is that the horse he used came from the land where Czestochowa, Texas, now sits."

Sources:
   1. Interview, Rev. Msgr. Erwin A. Juraschek, pastor.
   2. *Centennial History – Czestochowa, Texas – 1873-1973.*
   3. *The Founding of Nativity of the Blessed Virgin Mary Parish.*
   4. *The Cestohowa-Pawelerville Chamber of Commerce Booklet,* Cestohowa, Texas.
   5. Edward Dworaczyk, *The First Polish Colonies of America in Texas.*

## ST. STANISLAUS CHURCH
### Bandera – 1855

The St. Stanislaus Church in Bandera was founded in 1855, one year after Panna Maria was settled, and is the second oldest Polish settlement in America. Settlers from Panna Maria had moved out, looking for a new place to establish themselves, and they liked what they saw along the Bandera River.

The first little church was built in 1858. Since no priest was available, the people congregated regularly for prayer and Polish congregational singing. Later on, a priest from Panna Maria would come once or twice a month to say Mass.

The second church, which is the present building, was built in 1876 and was constructed from stone provided by the parishioners, along with the labor required to complete it.

The first pastor, Clements Kucharczyk, arrived in Texas in 1866 with the Resurrectionist Fathers. He remained through the formative years until 1870, attending thirty families who tilled the soil and made cypress shingles that were in great demand in San Antonio.

The pastor in 1980, Monsignor Ralph J. Smith, presided over a congregation of about 300 people from Bandera, Medina, Pipe Creek, Tarply, and Center Point. About 350 people in the parish of 1980 had Polish names, but the native tongue was no longer spoken there. The Pol-

*CATHOLIC CHURCH, St. Hedwig.*

ish pride and the heritage that was brought from Panna Maria in 1855 are about all that remains to identify the origin of the church.

Sources:
1. Rev. Edward J. Dworaczyk, *The First Polish Colonies of America in Texas,* 101.
2. Personal interview with the Right Reverend Ralph J. Smith, pastor.

## THE CHURCH OF ST. HEDWIG
### St. Hedwig Parish — 1855

St. Hedwig in Bexar County, about eighteen miles southeast of San Antonio, has a different background from most of the other Polish settlements. The immigrants came prepared to work and brought the equipment they needed. They did not experience as many hardships as descended on the others who answered Father Leopold's call.

The first Polish settler was John Demmer, who owned a large amount of land by the time the immigrants arrived. He had been an army captain in the 1830 Polish Revolution and arrived in Texas in 1835. Settling in the St. Hedwig area in 1852, he married into an American family and changed his name to Dorstyn.

The immigrants of 1855 spent sixteen weeks at sea before they landed in Galveston. They then proceeded to San Antonio, where they met Demmer. He recommended the area of Cibolo, and when the committee that was appointed to investigate the possibilities reported favorably, arrangements were made to settle on one-half a section of land near Martinez Creek. The land was distributed in tracts of thirty and forty acres, with easy payment terms provided.

Little farming was done in the area until the Polish people came. Few of the Americans cared to work the soil. And when the slaves were freed in 1865, many joined the Polish colony and brought with them new methods that the Polish people readily accepted.

St. Hedwig soon became an established settlement, confident and self-supporting. The people brought with them farm implements — even wagons that had been taken apart and shipped on the boat. They built their homes from logs and completed them with thatched roofs of mud and prairie grass.

The first church was built in 1857 on the property of Ludwig Zaiontz. Father Rossadowski was the first pastor to attend the colony. A series of pastors followed, including A. Przyborowski, who came from Yorktown in 1914 and remained for nineteen years.

The church was built with logs and then was replaced by a stone building in 1868. It was enlarged in 1900 and again in 1924. In that year, there were 250 families, with 65 children in school.

Today, St. Hedwig Parish is situated on the red sand of Bexar County, where field crops and orchards do well and facilities are more accessible. Theo Leonard was pastor at St. Hedwig as of 1980.

Source:
1. Edward Dworaczyk, *The First Polish Colonies of America in Texas.*

## OTHER POLISH SETTLEMENTS IN TEXAS

St. Michael's Parish in San Antonio is one of the older Polish settlements in Texas, having been established in 1855. It is the only Polish church in the city. Because it is in the city, the membership has been diluted and it has been more difficult to maintain any semblance of the Polish language and customs. Even so, the Polish influence remains.

Other Polish communities in the state are more recent and are consolidations rather than true Polish settlements. The church in Yorktown shows a founding date of 1855, the same as Bandera, St. Michael's, and St. Hedwig; however, the early members were Germans who were joined by several Polish families who had turned back from Panna Maria.

Other Polish settlements that are outgrowths from the original settlers at Panna Maria are Kosciusko, Falls City, Polonia, New Waverly, Brenham, Marlin, Bremond, Anderson, Bryan, Chapel Hill, Bellville, Rosenberg, and Richmond. From a few families who were willing to face the hardships of a new land have come a people who have survived and blended well in the cosmopolitan atmosphere of Texas.

Source:
1. Edward Dworaczyk, *The First Polish Colonies of America in Texas*.

## THE SWEDES

Immigrant Swedes, intent on escaping from the autocratic rule of their homeland, began coming to America toward the end of the nineteenth century. Although Sweden was an agricultural nation, the good land was held only by aristocratic families. The remaining land would not support a farmer and his family.

The man generally recognized as the father of the Swedish movement in Texas was S. M. Swenson, one of the first to break away from the old country. He landed in New York in 1836 and two years later arrived in Houston. At the age of twenty-five, he became the overseer of a large plantation near Richmond, owned by Dr. Edmund Long.

After Dr. Long's death, Swenson was joined by his uncle, Svante Palm, and in 1844 they went into the mercantile business in La Grange, in Fayette County. Then, in 1848, Swenson married Dr. Long's widow and was involved in a number of business enterprises, one of which was Swedish immigration.

He went back to Sweden in 1847 to recruit immigrants, and the following year twenty-five more arrived. Most of them came under the indenture system; Swenson paid their passage and they worked for him until the debt was paid.

By then Swenson had become an outstanding merchant in Austin. He remained there until it became necessary to flee because of his stand on the slavery question, which was sympathetic to the North. When he returned after the war, he took his family to New Orleans and then to New York. Although he never relinquished his Texas holdings, he never again lived in the state. His influence and financial position were felt in Texas until his death in 1896.

Between 1838 and 1890, more than 7,000 Swedes came to Texas from Sweden. There was also a new kind of immigration that developed, largely due to Swenson's influence. More than 8,000 people of Swedish ancestry, who had settled in the North, the East, and in Canada, came to Texas because of the availability of new farm land, much of it owned by S. M. Swenson and his sons. They had picked it up by purchasing from the government of the Republic land certificates that were being used in place of money. The movement of Swedes from those areas lasted for two decades.

The Swedish people in Central Texas today have mixed emotions about S. M. Swenson. Some of them feel he was motivated by the pride of his race and the desire to help his people. There are others who do not feel so kindly. In any event, it can be noted that while S. M. Swenson gave land to help establish Swedish Lutheran churches, he was a charter member of the historic St. David's Episcopal Church and was its greatest benefactor during the early years of growth. In 1852 he gave a melodean to the church that was originally called the Church of the Epiphany. Later, he gave a house and lot to the rector. He was named senior warden in 1859, when the church was reorganized and named St. David's.

Central Texas is considered the center of the Swedish movement in the state. By 1968, the Swedes made up twenty-five percent of the population in Travis County. As time passed, Williamson County also became a Swedish stronghold.

The early settlers generally favored elementary education but opposed anything beyond that because they associated higher education with the aristocracy of the old country they had left behind. Even so, two Swedish colleges

292

*PALM VALLEY LUTHERAN CHURCH, Round Rock.*

293

were opened in Texas: Trinity Lutheran College in Round Rock in 1906 and Texas Wesleyan Academy in Austin in 1912. The latter survived a quarter of a century, but then failed due to lack of support.

Religious institutions played a prominent part in developing Swedish communities in Texas. Until the late 1930s, each community of Swedes had a Swedish-language church. The practice of conducting services in the native tongue began to fade, and by the 1940s there were about thirty Lutheran, fifteen Methodist, and several Evangelican Free and Swedish Baptist churches that had assumed the roles of leadership.

Swedish names in the Central Texas area that still exist are Lind, Manda, Govalle, New Sweden, Hutto, and Swenson. Austin's Bergstrom Air Force Base was named after the son of a Swedish settler, Capt. J. A. E. Bergstrom, who was the first World War II casualty from the capital city.

Even though the concentration of Swedes is still found in Travis and Williamson counties, there are pockets near Stamford, Lyford, Melvin, Brady, Fort Worth, Dallas, and Waco. For the most part, they are second- to third-generation Texans. From the beginning, the Swedes have played such a vital part in the economy and the Texas way of life until it is almost impossible to find characteristics that mark them as a distinctive group.

## THE PALM VALLEY LUTHERAN CHURCH
### Round Rock – 1870

The Palm Valley Lutheran Church, first known as the Brushy Church, had a modest beginning and was closely associated with the first settlement in the Central Texas area, Kenny's Fort. The settlement was established in 1838, the same year that S. M. Swenson came to Texas, where he soon became the leader of the Swedish movement in the new Republic.

In 1861, Andrew J. Nelson, who was aware of the spiritual needs of the community, used three of his workers to build a log church. It was also used as a school system. The first Swedish religious service in Texas was held later that year.

Among the early immigrants who settled in the tranquil Oak Valley were Mrs. Anna Palm and her six sons. In 1863, the same year that S. M. Swenson made his escape to Mexico, Anna Palm's youngest son, Henning Palm, died from exposure and pneumonia. When asked where he should be buried, she responded, "Under the tallest tree there."

This was the beginning of the Palm Valley Lutheran Cemetery, just south of the spot where the present-day church was built in 1894. The name was selected because of the contributions made by the Palm family and the influence they had in developing the area.

Anna Palm was an aunt of S. M. Swenson. After the Civil War ended and he had returned to live in New Orleans, she wrote him and requested that the land where Henning was buried be designated as a cemetery. She also asked for enough land for a church and a school. Swenson granted her request and deeded 21⅖ acres to be used for a church, the cemetery, and a school. He named Arvid Nelson, Daniel Hurd, Andrew Palm, and C. A. Engstrand as trustees.

The first pastor, D. N. Tillman, who was of Finnish descent, organized the first congregation on November 27, 1870. It was made up of sixty men, thirty-three women, and sixty-one children. This is considered to be the official beginning of the Palm Valley Lutheran congregation, just outside of Round Rock. The name of the settlement had been changed from Brushy to Round Rock in 1854.

In 1872 a second church was built to replace the log building. At that time, A. J. Nelson contacted the Swedish Lutheran Augustana Church of North America and asked that a pastor be sent to the congregation. Pastor Hokson visited Round Rock in 1875, and at that time the Palm Valley congregation joined the Augustana Lutheran Synod. The Mission Board sent Pastor J. O. Cavallin on a temporary basis.

In 1876, Pastor Martin Noyd was called to Palm Valley

*GETHSEMANE LUTHERAN CHURCH, first building, Austin.*

296

as the first resident pastor under the new affiliation with the Augustana Lutheran Synod. Other pastors include A. W. Stark, Gustaf Berglund, R. P. Ascell, Oscar Nelson, C. E. Carlston, O. M. Bloom, A. L. Scott, Emerson Urelius, and Oliver M. Berglund. It is interesting to note that O. M. Bloom served the congregation under the two calls for a total of thirty-five years.

Under the leadership of Gustaf Berglund, the final decision was made in April 1894 to construct a new church building. The cornerstone was laid in June of that year for a Gothic-style building, seventy feet long and forty feet wide, with a tall tower that makes an impressive sight from a distance. The cost of the structure was approximately $10,000 and was free from all debt when it was dedicated on April 12, 1896.

Berglund died in 1899 and is buried in the Palm Valley Cemetery, near the church he served so well.

Oliver M. Berglund, who assumed the pastorate in August of 1969, is the grandson of Gustaf Berglund. Under the leadership of the grandfather, the new structure became a reality. Under the grandson, the stately building has come to house one of the largest congregations of Augustana Lutherans in the state.

It was the desire of the founding fathers to have the picturesque white steeple that graces the Palm Valley Church stand as a beacon of comfort for all who came that way. The original Swedish minutes stated that the church "must have a steeple that can be seen from far and wide."

The request has been more than fulfilled. Hardly a day goes by without visitors and travelers who pass by to "just see the steeple." Some of those who have stopped have included pilots from World War II who wanted to get a closer view of the steeple they used as a landmark when they were flying training missions.

Sources:
1. Teddy Behrens, *History of the Palm Valley Lutheran Church.*
2. Newsletter, Institute of Texan Cultures, San Antonio, Texas.
3. *A Brief History of the Palm Valley Lutheran Congregation 1870–1970.*

*GETHSEMANE LUTHERAN CHURCH, Austin, present building.*

4. Personal interviews with Pastor Oliver M. Berglund, Round Rock, Texas.

5. *The Round Rock Leader,* February 10, 1977.

6. The Swenson Story — A News Report.

# THE GETHSEMANE LUTHERAN CHURCH
## Austin – 1874

By 1868, people of Swedish extraction made up about twenty-five percent of the population in Travis County. As they ventured into a new land to find homes, they brought with them their faith.

After the first Swedish-Lutheran liturgy occurred on December 12, 1868, those participating decided to organize a Lutheran congregation. This they did and named Svante Palm as the chairman. It was their desire to become united with the Lutheran church in Sweden, so in January of 1869 they sent a letter to the Lutheran archbishop of Sweden, requesting that Pastor K. Karlen be appointed to lead the new Austin congregation.

The Lutheran church in Sweden referred the request to the newly founded Augustana Synod in the United States, but there the request was denied because the young organization was having problems meeting the needs of its own congregations.

The Swedish people, determined to build a church in Austin, proceeded without Synod help to erect a building that was dedicated on March 10, 1874. It was one of the first public facilities for Lutheran worship in Texas. (The building was where the Austin Central Library now stands, at 800 Guadalupe.)

In the fall of 1874, the Augustana Synod called Dr. P. S. A. Lindahl to the Austin congregation. He was the first pastor from the Synod to preach in Texas. His time of service was short, but because of his recommendation, the Synod assigned pastors for the congregation. With the assignment of L. A. Hoganzon, the congregation was ready to accept official membership in the Augustana Synod. Official membership was confirmed on February 18, 1875. Thus the year 1975 marked the centennial anniversary of Gethsemane's in the national Lutheran body.

There were eighty-eight confirmed members when Gethsemane joined the Augustana Synod. Despite their national support, the congregation decreased to thirty con-

*NEW SWEDEN LUTHERAN CHURCH,*
*New Sweden (near Manor).*

300

firmed members during the period between 1875 and 1882. The leaders in the church nevertheless refused to give up. They erected a new building to better serve the needs of the congregation.

In November of 1883, the new church was dedicated. It was built on North Congress Avenue and 16th Street and was constructed from stone from the old state capitol that had burned in 1881. Its style reflected the Gothic architecture of the Swedish churches the immigrants had known and loved.

Gethsemane moved into the twentieth century with the hope of continued growth and service, but there were difficult days ahead. Vacancies occurred in pastoral leadership, and members drifted away. However, with the help of the Augustana Synod, the congregation started moving forward again. A parsonage was built and an educational building added.

By 1950, it was evident that the state government complex would soon move beyond the church boundaries, so the Gethsemane leaders decided to purchase property at 200 West Anderson to build the third church so that expansion would not be limited.

The stately old Gothic building on Congress Avenue is still standing, the state buildings having had to move beyond it. In 1965 the Texas legislature passed a bill signed by Governor John Connally that has prevented the demolition of the landmark.

On Anderson Lane, a church building and educational facility was dedicated on March 3, 1963. In January of 1978, work began on a new section of the building, which was dedicated in November of 1979.

The pastor in 1980 was Karl A. Gronberg.

Sources:
1. *The Centennial Booklet 1869–1969.*
2. *A Festival of Dedication 1978–1979, New Edition.*
3. Gethsemane Lutheran Church.
4. Interviews with Pastor Oliver M. Berglund of the Palm Valley Lutheran Church in Round Rock on Swedish history in Texas.

301

# THE NEW SWEDEN LUTHERAN CHURCH
## Travis County—1876

A pilot who flies over Central Texas and depends on landmarks as checkpoints should know the churches. The rolling hills and wide fertile valleys are dotted with structures that look very much alike. Their tall steeples lend dignity to the countryside, but add confusion for those who are looking down on the broad area with a hope of finding a familiar sight.

The tallest steeple is on the New Sweden Lutheran Church, located near the little town of Manor in east Travis County. The church is about all that has survived in the Swedish settlement developed by a group of young men who had been sponsored by S. M. Swenson.

Two young men in the group, Adolf Fredrik and Anders J. Anderson, became the founders of New Sweden and charter members of the first church. Their efforts were felt immediately, almost before the settlers could become established in their new homes.

An announcement was made that all persons of the Lutheran faith who were interested in forming a congregation should meet on February 23, 1876, at one of the American churches in Manor. J. O. Cavallin, who was serving as the missionary pastor for the area, was in charge of the meeting. He was elected permanent chairman and G. J. Ax was named the secretary. Deacons and trustees were elected, and efforts were made immediately to have the congregation incorporated. It was then necessary to request membership at the next meeting of the Augustana Synod, which would be in Jamestown, New York, later in the year. Pastor Cavallin was selected to handle the necessary details.

The congregation was first known as the Swedish Evangelical Lutheran Congregation of Manor. The name was changed in 1887 to the New Sweden Swedish Evangelical Lutheran Congregation. It retained that name until 1957, when it became a dual parish with Lund because of the declining memberships in rural churches.

Martin Noyd was called by the Mission Board to preach during the Christmas holidays. With the assistance of Pastor Cavallin, Noyd helped to hold services every day, but some of the meetings had to be postponed or canceled because of weather and poor road conditions.

The first communion service was held in the home of Carl P. Peterson. It was then that the location for a new church was discussed. Brushy Knowb, which was a German community, and Knight Ranch, which had cheap land, were the two locations in question. Because most of the people were buying land to the east, Knight Ranch, which later became New Sweden, was finally selected.

The new church was completed in 1879, free of debt. All of the necessary funds had been provided by the forty-three members, except for forty dollars given by landowners in the vicinity. Much of the labor was donated.

Martin Noyd, who served from 1876 to 1882, was the first pastor of the congregation. He was also the first Texas pastor of the Augustana Lutheran Church to hold a regular pastorate. All of the others were on a circuit.

Noyd came to Texas from Illinois and was in and out of the state on several occasions. He left New Sweden to become president of Luther College at Wahoo, Nebraska. Returning to Texas in 1887, he served at Palm Valley, near Round Rock, in Williamson County, until 1892.

J. A. Stamline filled the pulpit in New Sweden as a student minister in 1878. He served again after he returned from a synodical meeting in Altona, Illinois, where he was ordained in 1882. He served congregations in Texas for forty years and became the first president of Trinity College in Round Rock. He died in 1928 and was buried in the New Sweden Cemetery.

Another student minister, Gustaf Berglund, was called as pastor in 1885. He was ordained at a synodical meeting in Minneapolis, Minnesota, in 1886. Berglund remained at New Sweden for three years before he moved to Austin. After three years there, he moved to Brushy (Palm Valley), where he remained until his death in 1889.

Pastor Berglund was the grandfather of Oliver M.

Berglund, who occupied the pulpit at New Sweden as a student minister before he was ordained and ultimately became the pastor at Palm Valley, near Round Rock, where he began service in 1969.

J. A. Stamline returned to New Sweden for the second time as pastor in 1889. During his service, the Kansas Conference met there in 1891. This event breathed new life into the church that reached out to congregations across the state.

L. G. Gillstrom moved to New Sweden from Georgetown in 1894 and remained until 1899. By then, many of the families were buying land farther east and moving away from the church. A chapel was built in 1896 to accommodate them, and services were held in the church on alternate Sundays.

A new pipe organ was installed in the church, a gift of the newly organized society of young people. At the same time, needed repairs were taken care of and thirty new benches were purchased (which are still in use at the present sanctuary). As usual, the necessary money for repairs was raised by subscription.

Services were handled by a student minister and Pastor Stamlin until Dr. A. L. Scott arrived in 1904. Pastor Rydholm had served briefly, but he died after only two years.

Dr. Scott remained at New Sweden until 1935, with the exception of one year that he spent in Fort Stockton. He was known and well received throughout the state and had the honor of being the first president of the Texas Conference, which was organized at Palm Valley in 1923. The Scott Memorial Chapel at the Trinity Lutheran Home in Round Rock was dedicated to him.

In 1921 and 1922 a new church and parsonage were built at New Sweden. The building, as it stands today, has a 104-foot, copper-covered spire that can be seen for miles. It has drawn thousands of visitors who come to take pictures and admire the imposing interior of the sanctuary.

Until 1923, the Swedish language was used for all services. The change to English began with the evening services and was gradual because many of the older members preferred their native tongue. The first confirmation class conducted in English was in 1927, when about half the class voted to make the change.

Like other Swedish churches, New Sweden has a well-kept cemetery as part of the complex. It is located on the site of the original church, about two miles west of the present structure. A tradition is to hold early morning Easter services at the cemetery, where members can place flowers on the graves of their loved ones. The maintenance of the cemetery is provided by an endowment fund that is self-sustaining.

In 1935, Fred G. Olson arrived in Texas to follow Dr. Scott, and he remained until June 1, 1943. A. W. Almquist came to New Sweden in April of 1946. While he served as pastor, the seventieth and seventy-fifth anniversaries of the church were celebrated. After the seventy-fifth anniversary was held in 1951, the interior of the church was renovated.

With the resignation of Almquist, Carl A. A. Larson of Bethlehem-Lund was called to serve as vice-pastor. Student Oliver M. Berglund received a license as a lay minister and served his home church until the arrival of Fred G. Hedberg and his family in 1954. Hedberg's service was short, as he was called to develop a mission in Gos City, Indiana. From there, he went to Millersburg, Ohio, and to Newell, Iowa, where he served until his death in April of 1976.

A dual parish with Lund was created with a membership of about 300. Carl Larson was called to serve the dual congregations, and remained until Pastor Messer, who later served on the Navajo Reservation in Arizona, came in 1966. He served until 1971.

Alfred O. Hoerig came with his wife, Patty, and their two children to accept the challenges of the dual parish. They were the first to occupy the new four-bedroom brick home that had been built in 1973 to serve as the parsonage.

Hoerig was born November 3, 1939, in Shiner, Texas. His formal education began in a two-room school and then the family moved to Yoakum, where he graduated from high school. He finished Texas Lutheran College at Seguin,

*BETHEL LUTHERAN CHURCH, Jones County, early building.*

married Patricia Lee Mitchell, and went to the Central
Lutheran Seminary in Fremont, Nebraska.

After graduating, he accepted a post in Corpus Christi
in June of 1966. From there, he went to San Antonio. Since
a year of internship had been served in Buffalo, New York,
the Hoerigs welcomed the call from Bethlehem-New
Sweden.

Sources:
1. Mrs. Luther G. Lundgren, *A Century on the New Sweden Prairie.*
2. Interview with Oliver M. Berglund, pastor of Palm Valley
Lutheran Church, Round Rock, Texas.

# BETHEL LUTHERAN CHURCH
## Ericksdahl—1905

The little Swedish community of Ericksdahl, near Avoca, in Jones County, is one of thirty-five settlements that can be traced to the efforts of S. M. Swenson, the recognized leader of the Swedish movement in Texas.

In 1854 land certificates were issued by the state to those who were willing to build railroads. S. M. Swenson secured scrip for 100,000 acres of government land, part of which was in Jones County.

The Jones County land was used for ranching until after the turn of the century. It was then that Swenson authorized his two sons, who operated under the name of the S. M. Swenson Land and Cattle Company, to sell the land to settlers of Scandinavian descent. When Swedish families in Travis County heard about the possibility of owning good land in the new country, they took the train to Avoca. Ericksdahl then came into being.

Two Swedish ministers from Travis County, L. J. Sundquist and Dr. J. A. Stamline, went to the new settlement near Stamford in 1905 and began making plans to establish a Swedish congregation. The first services were held at the home of N. M. Segerstrom in February of 1905. Both Stamline and Sundquist participated, and the infant son of the S. P. Bergtson family was baptized. Those who attended the meeting were the families of S. P. Bergtson, J. P. Hokanson, John Lunn, Bud Swenson, A. J. Swenson, and N. M. Segerstrom.

A second meeting was held at Flag Creek by Dr. Stamline in May of 1905 and included all of the Swedish settlers living on farms and ranches in the area, as well as visitors from Austin who were looking at land that was still available from Swenson's company.

On January 25, 1906, the congregation was formally organized by Dr. Stamline. Charter members were C. G. Seth and his family, the A. J. Swenson family, the N. M. Segerstrom family, Mr. and Mrs. Bud Swenson, Mr. and Mrs. John Lunn and their son, Linus, the J. P. Hokanson

*BETHEL LUTHERAN CHURCH, Jones County, present building.*

308

family, John Peterson, Algot Johnson, Elias Bjorn, Theodore Pearson, Eric Seth, and Oscar Magnuson.

The church, named the Bethel Lutheran, began as a Swedish Lutheran Church. The Swedish language was used and Swedish customs were followed. With a few exceptions, all of the members were Swedish and spoke the language fluently. Only the Willing Workers, a women's organization, was English-oriented.

The first Sunday school was organized in March of 1906, with J. P. Nelson elected superintendent. Mrs. Edwin Valentine and Mrs. Fritz Olson were the first Sunday school teachers. Mrs. Valentine also served as secretary and organist. Sunday school and morning services were held in private homes until the church was built in 1907.

With L. J. Sundquist as chairman of a committee made up of C. G. Seth, Edwin Valentine and Martin J. Olson, a site was selected from land offered by the Swenson Ranch. The "Little White Church on the Hill" was completed in the fall of 1907 at a cost of $2,520. The first pastor was Theodore Seashore, who did not arrive until February of 1908.

In the early days of Texas, a school was second only to a church, so in 1908, after the church had been completed, a one-room schoolhouse was erected on the C. J. Oman farm, less than half a mile from the church.

The present Bethel Church was begun in November of 1939. The cornerstone was laid about a year later, in October of 1940. Construction took two years, because most of the labor was donated by members of the congregation and the rock used had to be taken from the church site, which was the location of the original structure. The building is over one hundred feet long and sixty feet wide. It has a seating capacity of between 450 and 600 people, when the balcony is used and a back room opened.

Hugo B. Haterius was the minister at Bethel Lutheran when the new church was built. He had come in 1919 and served until his retirement in 1968.

The officials involved in the planning and construction of the new church were F. E. Olson, Okey Richards, Martin

Reed, A. J. Swenson, Ed Newquist, Carl Hedburg, E. O. Soderberg, Harry E. Gustafson, and E. W. Carlson, who were deacons. The trustees involved were O. F. Seth, Gust Nelson, Harry Nelson, E. P. Armstrong, M. O. Johnson, R. C. Richards, Sam Baseland, and A. H. Lundgreen.

Bethel Lutheran Church has had two resident ministers since the retirement of Dr. Haterius. Stan Jourgenson served from 1968 to 1971 and the current minister, Stan Leaf, has served since then. By 1980, Bethel Lutheran had had six resident ministers during the seventy-three years of its existence.

As the years have passed, the economy in Jones County has changed and the membership of Bethel Lutheran has also changed. It is no longer predominantly Scandinavian.

At one time, membership of Bethel Lutheran was approaching 400, but since then there has been a decline that can be traced to changes in the economy and the disappearance of the small farmer.

Sources:
1. Hutto and Shelton, *The First 100 Years of Jones County*.
2. The Ericksdahl Community.
3. The Bethel Lutheran Church.
4. *70th Anniversary, 1906–1976*.
5. Personal interview with Arnold Peterson, Round Rock, Texas, former member.

## EVANGELICAL FREE CHURCH
### Georgetown – 1884

With the organization of this congregation came the beginning of the Evangelical Free Church in Texas. A group of young people from Sweden began meeting for the purpose of prayer and study. From this beginning, a permanent organization was finalized in 1891 with twenty-one charter members.

The first church building was constructed in 1892, four and one-half miles southeast of Georgetown on the Hutto Road. In 1924 a larger building was erected on the

310

*EVANGELICAL FREE CHURCH, Georgetown.*

same site. The church moved into Georgetown in 1963, when a modern building was completed.

Among the young men from Sweden who began the meetings for prayer and group study were C. O. Young-bloom, Oscar Johnson, Ed Frizen, and Kristin Forsvall. Itinerant Free Church preachers to visit Central Texas and this church in its early years of existence were C. V. Peterson, Edward Thorell, and Nels Saabye. C. O. Shalstrom, a man of zeal and charisma, stayed for some time in 1891–92 and conducted a very successful revival. Later in the decade came revivals by Gust F. Johnson and John Herner.

Charter members of the church were C. O. Young-bloom, J. J. Lawson, John Grogren, C. H. Gustafson, Gust F. Johnson, Mr. and Mrs. Carl Anderson, Mr. and Mrs. C. E. Anderson, Mr. and Mrs. Carl Bjork, Mr. and Mrs. Hans Bostrom, Mr. and Mrs. S. A. Johnson, Mr. and Mrs. Sven Peterson, Mr. and Mrs. John Lax, and Mr. and Mrs. J. A. Sandberg.

Those contributing to success and growth of the church include, among others, Hubert Ekvall, Lyndon Rosenblad, Tom Anderson, P. A. Carlson, Carvin Young-bloom, Irene Lindquist, Oscar Ekdahl, Gus Johnson,

ST. PAUL LUTHERAN CHURCH, Serbin.

Tillman Johnson, Wesley Nord, Weldon Lindquist, and Carl Johnson.

Source:
1. Carvin Youngbloom supplied church bulletins and pictures.

## THE WENDS

## ST. PAUL LUTHERAN CHURCH
### Serbin — 1854

The only known congregation in Texas to organize and select a minister before they came to this country was a group of Wends from Preussa (Prussia) and Saxony, Germany. On May 23, 1854, they extended a call to Johann Kilian to lead their group to a new land.

According to church records, the goal of the newly organized congregation was: "The immigration to the State of Texas in North America with the intention of establishing a Colony in which an Evangelistic Lutheran Church, a church of pure Biblical confession, could find a place [to worship]."

In September of 1854, more than 500 immigrants left Hamburg, Germany, for England and then to Galveston after they had come by Cuba. During the trip, seventy-three of the members died of cholera and survivors were quarantined in Queenstown from September 30 to October 22. After a very difficult crossing, filled with many hardships, the immigrant ship, the *Ben Nevis*, landed at Galveston on December 14, 1854.

From Galveston, the immigrants traveled 200 miles inland to establish a colony in which they would be free to continue their faith and confession. Some of the members who began running out of money found it necessary to stop in Industry, New Ulm, and similar small settlements along the way to find work.

The little community of Serbin, in Lee County, finally became the home of the Wends. Many things had to be considered and a series of hardships overcome before the proper land was found and purchased for the colony. The people were beset by sickness and also the drought of 1856 and 1857. They had settled in a savage land, were unfamiliar with the language and the customs of those already there, and were separated from those who had chosen the same fellowship and faith that they were fighting so hard to retain.

Besides having to construct the required dwellings during the first year, it was necessary to build a parsonage for Pastor Kilian. The parsonage was started during the summer months of 1855 but had to be delayed because of the illness of many of the members. It was not until October 17, 1855, that the pastor was able to move into his new home, which also served as a place of worship and a school. The frame church, which was later used as a school, was not built until 1859. The dedication service was conducted by Kilian on Christmas Day, 1859, in Wendish, German, and English.

In the early years, the congregation consisted only of

Wends and the services were held only in the Wendish language, as were the congregational meetings. Then, at the beginning of the Civil War in 1861, the first German Lutherans were accepted into the congregation. From that time, the services were conducted in both Wendish and German. According to the records in 1869, there were 128 families in the group, with a total membership of 581. Of these, 363 were adults and 218 were children. The racial division was 493 Wends and 88 Germans.

Besides the St. Paul congregation in Serbin, Johann Kilian served New Ulm in Austin County, a sister community of about twenty families. He also preached in the Louis Settlement and in Swiss Alp, in nearby Fayette County. He went to Roeders Mill at Shelby in Austin County and to Bastrop in Bastrop County, all in Central Texas. With so many German Lutheran families coming to Texas, most of them without spiritual affiliation, it was unfortunate that the request by Kilian for a traveling missionary was turned down. As it was, he was the only Missouri Synod pastor in Texas from 1854 to the fall of 1868, when Pastor Zimmermann was ordained and installed at Rose Hill in Harris County.

The cornerstone for a new cutstone church was laid, along with the foundation, in 1867. The building continued through 1868 and until the middle of 1869, when progress was completely halted until toward the end of 1870. Work began again in 1871, and the new church was dedicated on December 3, 1871.

From the beginning, the instruction of the youth of the congregation was one of the primary objectives. At first the pastor was the teacher. He was followed shortly by Pastor Lehnigf, who in turn was replaced by Ernst Leubner, who served until 1870. Kilian again served until 1872 when his son, G. A. Kilian, took over and served for forty-four years. A number of teachers served as the years passed until the current leader, Eldon Heinze, took over in 1971. During those years, Daniel Weise was installed as the lower grade teacher.

In March of 1978, plans for a new school were accepted

314

by the congregation, and the attractive new building was dedicated on January 7, 1979. The old building, which remains on church property, was donated to the Wendish Heritage Society to be used as a museum.

One of the unusual features of the St. Paul Lutheran Church is the pipe organ. It was built in Austin in 1904, which also was the church's fiftieth anniversary. The builder, Ed Pfeifer, came to New York from Germany in 1865. He opened a music store in Austin in 1875 and built a total of only five organs. He made his own wooden pipes but bought the metal pipes and chests from manufacturers in the East. One of the organs went to Baylor University in Waco. Another went to the First Protestant Church in New Braunfels in 1898, and in 1900 he built one for the Zion Lutheran Church in Walburg, in Williamson County, near Georgetown. The last of the large organs was the one in Serbin. After that he built one more, small, two-rank house organ. The seventy-fifth anniversary of the installation of the organ was held September 30, 1979. It had been completely restored in 1972 by Otto Hofman of Austin.

In 1915 the congregation at St. Paul decided to purchase a new bell for the church. The old bell, which was brought from Germany in 1854, stood for many years in the entrance of Kilian Hall at Concordia College in Austin. It was later placed in a pedestal in front of Birkman Chapel, also on the Concordia campus, where it still stands.

Paul W. Hartfield was installed as pastor of St. Paul Lutheran Church in Serbin on May 1, 1977. Daniel Weise was released as teacher so he could enter Concordia Seminary in St. Louis. Daniel Engler was then installed as the lower grade teacher.

Also in 1977, the Winsor Oil Company drilled a well on church property that turned out to be a medium-sized producer. It came at the time the building committee was working on plans for the new school.

Sources:
1. Interview with Pastor Paul W. Hartfield, St. Paul Lutheran Church.
2. *St. Paul Lutheran Church, 125th Anniversary 1854–1979*, Serbin, Texas.

315

# IX

## HISTORIC CHURCHES WITH UNUSUAL FEATURES

### MISSION SAN FRANCISCO DE LOS TEJAS
### Crockett — 1690

Located in the Davy Crockett National Forest, this mission was the first Spanish effort in the province of Texas to bring Christianity to the Tejas Indians. The old mission, second in age only to Ysleta, is located near Crockett on the famed Old San Antonio Road (El Camino Real).

Spanish Franciscan priests led by Fray Damian Massanet founded Mission San Francisco de los Tejas in 1690. Three years after the mission was founded, hostilities with the once friendly Indians forced the missionaries to flee, burning the mission as they departed.

In 1716, Domingo Ramon led a Spanish expedition back to the east bank of the Neches River, a few miles from the original location, and reestablished the mission. This mission was abandoned in 1719, reestablished in 1721, and eventually was removed to San Antonio in 1731 after Spain withdrew her military support from the East Texas mission. The mission was renamed in its new home in San Antonio as San Francisco de la Espada.

Mission Tejas State Park was founded in 1935 on the site which was regarded as the authentic location when an old cannon was found buried there. The cannon was believed to have been placed in the earth by the Spaniards when they abandoned the mission in 1693.

316

*MISSION SAN FRANCISCO DE LOS TEJAS – first Spanish effort to bring Christianity to the Tejas Indians, located in the area that is now Texas.*

317

Source:
1. *Mission Tejas State Historical Park* (Texas Parks and Wildlife).

## PILGRIM BAPTIST CHURCH
(First known as Pilgrim, Predestinarian Regular
Baptist Church of Christ)
Elkhart (Anderson County) – 1834

The church, generally recognized as one of two or three of the oldest Protestant churches in Texas, is located two and one-half miles southwest of Elkhart, in Anderson County. Another distinguishing feature of this church is that it is probably the only one in ecclesiastical history to have migrated.

In the summer of 1832, a man from Crawford County, Illinois, entered Texas hoping that he might obtain permission from the Mexican government to establish churches in Texas. In a vision, Elder Parker claims to have seen a map showing him the way to Texas.

In San Antonio, Parker, knowing that the Roman Catholic church was the only religion legally permitted in the state of Texas-Coahuila, made his plea before the Mexican governor. This shows that laws regulating religion in Texas were not always strictly enforced. Although the governor supported the law which stated that no church except Catholic could be established, he did give Parker a brilliant idea. The governor assured Parker that the Mexican government had "no intention of molesting churches already established."

Parker returned to Illinois to lay his plans before the Pilgrim Church. The organizational meeting took place on July 28, 1833. He and the other six members, together with all their possessions, took the long trail to Texas. This "already established church" held its first service in Texas on January 12, 1834, near the site of the present town of Anderson.

After a short stay, the original group divided. The original church removed to Fort Brown, on San Pedro

318

*THE PILGRIM BAPTIST CHURCH near Elkhart, Texas –*
*probably the only church to have migrated.*

Creek in Houston County, a few miles east of the present town of Grapeland.

The "arm" group of the church went up the Navasota River to find ill-fated Fort Parker. It was at this fort that the Comanche Indians took captive Cynthia Ann Parker, who later became the mother of Comanche Chief Quanah Parker.

When the original church left Fort Brown and went to the Elkhart area, Shiloh remained as the "arm" church. It still remains active.

The first structure for the Pilgrim Church was a twenty-foot-square log cabin. The people sat on logs hewn on one side and supported on pegs. A mud-and-rock chimney provided a fireplace for heating. The floor was made of hard, pounded clay, and the doors and windows were closed by battened shutters.

Three other buildings have supplanted the first log house. A frame house was built in 1857; a larger one of the same kind in 1890; and the present red brick building erected in 1929.

An exact replica of the original church was made in 1948, and it is now listed as a historic and scenic spot along the Dogwood Trail.

Source:
1. Mary Kyle Tucker, *Oldest Protestant Church* (Archives, Texas Baptist Convention, Southwestern Baptist Theological Seminary, Fort Worth.)

## THE CHRISTIAN METHODIST EPISCOPAL CHURCH
Fredericksburg — 1877

Although the black community in Fredericksburg has been virtually nonexistent for many years, there is still a black church in the community. It goes back to the days following the Civil War, when a few black families tried to remain in the German community.

A black schoolhouse was built in 1877 on property that was adjacent to the church site. It is thought that religious services were conducted there until the church was completed ten years later.

When the black community disappeared, the use of the church building decreased and it deteriorated. Cora Phillips, widow of a well-known Gillespie County veterinarian and church trustee, suggested that the church be restored for use by a youth organization of several faiths. In 1974 the work was done and gained national recognition. Dr. Robert Mosby, the son of the third black minister for the congregation, and William H. Mosby preached at the ceremonies in February of 1976, when the restored building was dedicated as the Christian Methodist Episcopal Church.

## ST. DOMINIC CATHOLIC CHURCH
D'Hanis — 1847

The ruins of this famous old church stand as evidence of the French influence that came to Texas with the settlers from Alsace, France. The unusual feature is the adjoining

320

*THE RUINS OF ST. DOMINIC CHURCH and Cemetery, D'Hanis.*

321

*TEXAS A&M CHAPEL – Texas A&M University's All Faiths Chapel, constructed in 1957 for $257,000, is used for weddings and various special programs, as well as for meditation. It was paid for by the Former Students Association.*

cemetery that has the same shaped and designed tombstones as those found in French cemeteries in New Orleans.

The congregation was formed in 1847, and in 1853, when D'Hanis became a mission parish, a limestone church was built. The timber used was brought by ox-wagon from the Medina River. The church was expanded in 1868 and used until 1914, when a new town and a new church was built a few miles away.

The cemetery originated with the burial of a child in 1847 and was used until 1893, when a new cemetery was started.

## ST. MARTIN'S CATHOLIC CHURCH
### Round Top

St. Martin's is one of the smallest Catholic churches in the world that is actually used as a church. It is not a replica or a model to attract attention.

*ST. MARTIN'S CATHOLIC CHURCH, Round Top*

With a seating capacity of approximately twenty people, there is a complete altar area with room for the priest. An adjacent cemetery has thirty to forty headstones.

The reputation of the little church is nationwide, and hundreds of tourists stop in Round Top to visit.

## VEREINS KIRCHE
### Fredericksburg — 1847

The replica of *Vereins Kirche* "community church," in use in Fredericksburg today, recalls the history of the first public building in the German community to serve as a church for all denominations, a school, and a community building for political purposes.

Built in the summer of 1847 after John O. Meusebach,

*VEREINS KIRCHE, Fredericksburg*

324

the commissioner of the German Migrant Company, had made a peace treaty with the Comanche Indians, it was the center of activity.

After the celebration of the fiftieth anniversary of the arrival of the first settlers, it was torn down. The replica was first used as a museum and library, and later was converted to the office for the Chamber of Commerce. The latest function of the building was to serve as headquarters for the local Historical Society.

## ST. JOSEPH'S CATHOLIC CHURCH
San Antonio – 1868

The cornerstone of this historic church was laid in 1868 by a group of San Antonio's many German Catholic immigrants who wanted a place to worship in their own language.

In 1891 four bells with matched tones were purchased and consecrated. The bells weighed 3,000, 1,500, 700, and 300 pounds and were given the names of Joseph, Mary, Henry, and Joseph by their donors, as was the custom.

The Gothic-style church was without a steeple until 1898, when the spire was erected to complete the structure as it is today. The stained glass windows were brought from Germany and installed in 1902.

Joske's Department Store

wanted to purchase the church and rectory in 1945 for expansion purposes, but the parishioners voted unanimously not to sell. Today St. Joseph's stands as a jewel that is encircled by Joske's — a unique sight for natives and visitors alike.

St. Joseph's was designated as a historic building by the Texas Historical Survey Commission in 1955.

## IGLESIA BAUTISTIA FREDONIA HILL
Nacogdoches

With the exception of Nacogdoches, Texas, where a Mexican garrison was located prior to Texas independence, there are no people of Mexican descent in East Texas in sufficient numbers to establish many churches. Those who support Iglesia Bautista Fredonia Hill are descendants of those people who occupied the garrison over 150 years ago.

*THE CHURCH WITH THE MOST BEAUTIFUL VIEW – St. Luke's Episcopal Church, located at Lake Travis in Austin, has the most beautiful setting of any church in the state. It is in constant demand for weddings and other events.*

*SAINT MARTIN'S EVANGELICAL LUTHERAN CHURCH New Braunfels – 1860. Saint Martin's Evangelical Lutheran Church in New Braunfels is the earliest remaining Lutheran church building in Texas. It was built in 1860 and has been moved to the loop outside the city, where it is accessible to visitors.*

328

*CORN HILL CATHOLIC CHURCH, Williamson County. Corn Hill
Catholic Church, near Schwertner, Williamson County, shows the twin
tower architecture of German churches usually found in the old country
but seldom used in the United States. At one time Corn Hill was a
thriving town with a population of 4,000, including eleven doctors.*

*THE CHURCH with the tallest ceiling – the First United Methodist Church in Paris, Texas, has a ceiling seventy-five feet high, which is three feet higher than the Jewish synagogue in Dallas.*

*THE CHURCH with the most unusual archictectural design – First Baptist Church in Austin.*

THE FIRST CHURCH in Shackelford County, First United Methodist
Church of Albany. It is the oldest congregation in the Northwest Conference of the Methodist Church.

BROADWAY CHURCH OF CHRIST, Lubbock – believed to be the
place of the first Christian worship on the Texas High Plains. Two
former ministers became presidents of major universities.

331

*SWEDISH METHODIST CHURCH, Hutto – believed to be the only Swedish Methodist church left in the area.*

*FIRST METHODIST CHURCH, Leonard – provided a setting for the award-winning book* Papa Was a Preacher. *The story of "Pastor Porter," written by his daughter, was also a best-seller.*

332

# Bibliography

Baptist General Convention of Texas. *Centennial Story of Texas Baptists*. Dallas: Burt Building, 1936.

Boren, Carter E. *Religion on the Texas Frontier*. San Antonio: Naylor Company, 1968.

Brooks, A. D. *History of Ellis County Baptist Association*. Hillsboro: 1907.

Brown, Lawrence L. *The Episcopal Church in Texas 1838–1874*. Austin: Church Historical Society, 1963.

Cohen, Ann Nathan. *The Centenary History of Congregation Beth Israel of Houston*. Houston: 1954.

Curl, R. E. *Southwest Texas Methodism*. InterBoard S.W. Conf.: 1937.

*Czech Texans, The*. Institute of Texan Cultures, San Antonio.

Dworaczyk, Edward. *The First Polish Colonies of America in Texas*. San Antonio: Naylor Company, 1936.

Eckstein, Stephen D., Jr. *History of Churches of Christ in Texas*. Austin: Firm Foundation, 1963.

*French Texans, The*. Institute of Texan Cultures, San Antonio.

Fuller, B. F. *History of Texas Baptists*. Louisville, KY: Baptist Book Concern, 1900.

*German Texans, The*. Institute of Texan Cultures, San Antonio.

Gittinger, Ted, et al. *The St. Louis Church*. San Antonio: Graphic Arts, 1973.

*Greek Texans, The*. Institute of Texan Cultures, San Antonio.

*Handbook of Texas*. Ed. by Walter P. Webb, et. al. Austin: Texas State Historical Association, 1952.

*History of Palo Pinto County*. Dallas: Taylor Publishing Co.

Hutto and Shelton. *The First 100 Years of Jones County*. Anson: n.d.

*Jewish Texans, The*. Institute of Texan Cultures, San Antonio.

Johnson, T. H. *Plum Grove Baptist Church*. Privately published.

Kowert, Elsie. *Old Homes and Buildings of Fredericksburg*. Fredericksburg Publishing Co.: 1977.

*Mexican Texans, The*. Institute of Texan Cultures, San Antonio.

Morgan, William M. *Trinity Protestant Episcopal Church, 1841–1953*. Houston-Galveston: Anson Jones Press, 1954.

333

Morrell, Z. N. *Flowers and Fruits in the Wilderness.* St. Louis: Commercial Printing Co., 1872.

Nail, Olin W. *Texas Methodist Centennial Yearbook.* Privately published, 1934.

*Norwegian Texans, The.* Institute of Texan Cultures, San Antonio.

Phelan, Macum. *A History of Early Methodism in Texas.* Nashville: Cokesbury, 1924.

——. *History of Methodism in Texas 1867–1902.* Dallas: Mathes, Van Note and Co., n.d.

Spurlock, Virgie W. *The History of McMahan's Chapel.* Privately published, 1980.

Tanner, Barrett. *The History and Treasures of St. David's Church.* Austin: 1976.

*Texas Almanac.* Dallas: Dallas Morning News, 1980.

Thrall, Homer S. *A Brief History of Methodism in Texas.* Hasville: 1894.

*Union Baptist Association Centennial History, 1840–1940, The.* Brenham, TX: Banner Press, Inc., 1940.

Vernon, Walter H. *William Stevenson, Riding Preacher.* Dallas: SMU Press, 1964.

# Index

Andersen, Hans Christian, 225
  Mads, 224
Andersen family, 223
Anderson, A. J., 188
  Anders J., 302
  C. E., 311
  H. L., 237
  Jim, 70
  Mrs. C. E., 311
  Ruth, 3
  Sharon, 70
  Tom, 311
  Wiley B., 66
Andres, Vincent, 41
Andrews, S. P., 14
Angel Chapel, 88
Angelopulus, ——, 250
Anglo-Catholicism, 105
Anglo settlers, 36
Annual Conference in 1940, 159
Annual Conference of Methodist Ministers, 185
Annunciation Greek Orthodox Church, Houston, 250
Ansgar Evangelical Lutheran Church, Danevang, 222
Anthony, Mrs., 86
  Rhoddy, 84, 86
Antioch Church of Christ in San Augustine, 84–85
Apache Indians, 36
Archdiocese of San Antonio, 284
Argall, Homer, 166
Arkansas, 79, 177
Arkansas Territory, 146, 160, 167, 185
Armacost, Mrs. C. A., 70
Armstrong, E. P., 310
Army of the Confederacy, 278
Arnold, Matthew, 200
Arnold family, 102
Ascell, R. P., 297
Ashbel Smith Building, 46
Askew, Rev., 3
Assumption of the Blessed Virgin Mary, 218

Atchinson, Fred, 272
Aten, A. P., 78
  W. C., 70
Atterberry, Henry, 90
Augustana Lutheran Church, 303
Augustana Lutheran Synod, 295, 297
Augustana Synod, 299–302
Austin, D. B., 88
  Moses, family, 146
  Stephen F., 56, 136, 147, 169
Austin Central Library, 299
Austin College, 191
Austin Colony, 146–147
Austin County, 215, 243, 314
Austin Labor Temple Association, 159
Austin Lodge of Free and Accepted Masons, 125
Austin Presbyterian Theological Seminary, 191
Austin Statesman, The, 129
Austin Street Methodist Church, 235
Austin, Texas, 34, 44, 53, 54, 63, 68, 84, 94, 111, 119, 155
Austria, 215
Avery, Harris G., 196
Aves, Charles S., 121
  Henry D., 113
Awbrey, Urban, 95
Ax, G. J., 302

B
Bachman Creek, 152
Bacon, Summer, 148, 191
Bagby, W. H., 78
Baggett, Mrs. J. O., 70
Bailey, James, 196
  S. M., 179
  William Overton, 13, 16
Bailey, Texas, 102
Baker, Bill, 102
  Daniel, 199, 200
  Don, 95
  J. L., 211

336

338

Brazoria, Texas, 34, 44, 104,
  162, 195
Brazos Presbytery, 191
Brazos River, 92
Brenham, Texas, 10, 216
Brennan, Thomas F., 35, 59
Brent, James, 163
Brewer, G. C., 95
Brickley, H., 60
Brill, John F., 87
Brim, W. W., 206, 208
Briscoe, J. R., 22, 27
Bristol Baptist Church of Ennis,
  30
British Isles, 117
British West Indies, 259
Britton, Susan Taylor, 124
Broach, L. B. III, 167
Broadway of America, 36
Broadway Church of Christ,
  Lubbock, 331
Brochstein, I. S., 257
Brooks, A. D., 29
  N. S., 205
Brothers of Holy Cross, 54
Brown, ——, 78
  A. H., 274
  Minor, 78
  N. S., 274
Browne, John T., 57
Brown family, 79
Browning, Mirian, 256
Brownsboro, Texas, 276, 277
Brownsville, Texas, 35, 42, 215
Brushy Church, 294
Brushy Knowb, 303
Bryant, Choice, 94
  George, 94
Bryan, Texas, 63
Brymer family, 79
Buchanan, C. C., 101, 102
  J. L., 206
  Logan, 94
  William, 213
Buchanan family, 213
Buck, Johnny, 96
Buckner, H. F., 8

Buckner Orphans' Home, 2
Buddin, F. A., 154
Buffalo Bayou, 16, 90
Bullock, ——, 78
Bunting, Robert F., 200
Burdett, Charles, 29
Burke, James, 196
Burks, N. T., 166
Burleson, Rufus C., 1, 6, 8, 10,
  14, 28, 30
Burleson County, 215
Burnet, David G., 195
  Mrs. Sarah A., 13
Burnett, F. R., 66
  T. R., 100
Burns, W. C., 103
Burts, Mrs. W. P., 207
Busby, Horace, 93
Bush, ——, 78
  George L., 78
Butler, G. W., 3
  Michael, 54
Byars, Noah T., 1
Byrne, Christopher E., 35, 47, 54
Byzantine-style, 252

C
Cabe, Ernest, 95
Cachand-Ervendberg, Louis,
  242–245
Caddo Indians, 202
Cain, Sam Houston, 18
Caine, T. W., 74
Caldwell, Oliver B., 200
  Orville H., 206
  William, 209
Caldwell, Texas, 216
Calhoon, Florence, 188
  T. F., 189
Calton, Henry, 274
Cambridge, Massachusetts, 262
Campbell, Alexander, 11, 62, 75,
  77, 83, 92, 98
  Thomas, 62, 83
Campbell family, 79
Canary Islands, 39
Caney Creek camp meeting, 179

Christian Methodist Episcopal
    Church, Fredericksburg,
    320
Christian Services Center, 96
Christian Women's Board of
    Missions, 80
Christian Youth Fellowship, 81
Christinsen family, 223
"Christus" statue, 241
Chromick, Joseph, 217
Church of the Annunciation, 56
Church of Christ, 62, 63
Church of Christ in Dallas, 78
Church of Christ at Gober, 88
Church Council, 236
Church of the Epiphany, 111,
    122, 124, 125, 292
Churches of Christ, 83–103, 105
Church of the Good Shepherd
    at Jacksonville, Florida, 129
Church of the Immaculate
    Conception, 281
Church Square, 185
Cibolo, 289
Cibolo Creek, 279
Cilly, Roger H., 121
Cincinnati, Ohio, 172
"Cinderella," 68
Circleville, 78
Cistern parish, 221
Ciudad Juárez, Mexico, 36
Civil War, 13, 16, 18, 48, 67, 84,
    94, 98, 100, 105, 108, 125,
    133, 141, 157, 175, 179, 188,
    191, 197, 202, 254, 264, 266,
    272, 277, 295, 314, 320
Claretian fathers, 39
Clark, Addison, 62, 67, 68, 72,
    78, 100
  Daniel C., 166
  Gov. Edward, 125
  Exa, 87
  Gertrude, 70
  John, 274
  Joseph Addison, 62
  Lee, 72
  Oliver, 274

  Randolph, 62, 66, 67, 72, 100
Clarksville, Texas, 62, 84, 146,
    180
Claw, J., 6
Clayton, Nicholas J., 46, 53
Clear Creek Baptist Church, 10
Cleaver, Tony M., 29
Cleburne, Texas, 84
Clemens, A. E., 27
  J. J., 111–112
Cleveland, D. B., 71–72
  Sess, 115
  Will, 115
Cleveland family, 73
Clifton Junior College, 278
Clifton, Texas, 277
Cline, Mrs. Vivian, 102
Cloud, John Wurts, 104
Coahuila, 39
Cobb, Nicholas Hamner, 104
Cochina Creek, 162
Cochran, J. H., 153
  Mrs. Nancy Jane, 152, 153
  W. P., 153
  William M., 152
Cochran Chapel, 152–155
Cochran Chapel United Metho-
    dist Church, Dallas, 152
Cockrell, ——, 73
Codge family, 79
Cohen, Henry, 259
Colby, Anna, 213
Cold Springs Church of Christ,
    Lancaster, 89–92
Cold Springs congregation, 65
Cole, C. L., 91
  J. B., 67
Coleman, Clyde, 29
Collard, James H., 166
College Station, Texas, 144
Colley, A. O., 98
Collie, Jim, 206
Collin County, 62, 83, 201
Collins, Mrs. Bryant, 70
  Mrs. N. E., 32
  W. C., 166
Colorado County, 243

341

Colorado River, 8, 10, 74, 124, 136, 155, 173, 272
Colorado River Valley, 106
Columbia, Texas, 195
Columbus, Texas, 10
Colwck, T. Theo, 277
Comal Valley, 49
Comanche Indians, 36, 277, 319, 325
Committee on New Parishes, 133
Community of Benedictine Fathers, 48
Comonero, Chief Mariano, 37
Compton, H. O., 188, 189
Concord Baptist Church, 6
Concordia College, 315
Confederacy, 39, 46
Confederate army, 100, 124
Confederate Congress, 126
Congregation Adath Yeshurum, 256
Congregation of the Mission, 43
Connally, John, 301
Connecticut, 13, 111
Connelly, J. W., 28
Conner, Rev., 3
Continuing Medical Education, 252
Cook, R. G., 89
Coombs Creek, 98
Cooper County, Missouri, 3
Copeland, Kenneth W., 171
Copes, J. Wilson, 196
Corbin, C. C., 72
Cornelius, Raymond, 165
    Vernon, 167
Corn Hill Catholic Church, Williamson County, 329
Corpus Christi, Texas, 35, 44, 141
Corsicana, Texas, 190
Cortes, Hernán, 266
Cottage Prayer Meeting group, 80
cotton, 37
Cotton Exchange, 119
Council, ——, 78
county seat of McKinney, 62

Covey, J. V. E., 21
Cowan, S. A., 28
Coward, David, 22
Cox, Burwell, 206
    F. L., 95
    T. W., 6, 8, 10
Cox family, 79
Craig, W. R., 100
Crain, Mary, 3
Crane, William Carey, 8, 10, 16
Cranfills Gap, Texas, 277, 278
Crank, Edwin, 29
Crawford, E. L., 167
    Jacob, 166
    Mattie Hoard, 100
Crawford County, Illinois, 318
Creath, J. W. D., 8
Criswell, W. A., 32, 33
Criswell Center for Biblical Studies, 33
Crockett, Texas, 160, 173
Crum, Mrs. P. G., 70
    Rolfe P., 135
Crutchfield, D. M., 202
Cuero, Texas, 34
Cullen, C. P., 166
    D. P., 166
    Mattie Mae, 70
    Opal, 70
    Oscar, 70
Cumberland Church of Fort Worth, 208
Cumberland Presbyterian, 148, 191, 208, 212
Cumberland Presbyterian Church, 169, 190, 210
Cummins Creek community, 243
Curry, J. H., 32
Czech Catholics, 217
Czechs, 215
Czestochowa community, 284
Czestochowa, Texas, 281

**D**
Dabney, ——, 78
Daily, W. M., 29
Dallas, W. O., 78

342

344

F

First Christian Church of Palo
Pinto, 71
First Christian Church in Taylor,
78, 84, 100
First Christian Church of Van
Alstyne, 62, 64, 82
First Concord Baptist Church,
18
first Episcopal service, 138
First Evangelical Lutheran
Synod, 240
First Mantua Christian Church,
64
First Methodist Church, Hous-
ton, 174
Leonard, 332
First Methodist Church in
Austin, 159
First Methodist Episcopal
Church, South, 180
First Presbyterian Church, Fort
Worth, 207
Houston, 195
La Grange, 199
Tyler, 204
U.S.A., of Bonham, 206
First Presbyterian Church of
Fort Worth, 209
First Protestant Church, New
Braunfels, 241–247, 315
First United Methodist Church,
Crockett, 160
Houston, 172, 176
Liberty, 185
Nacogdoches, 167–171
First United Methodist Church
of Albany, 331
First United Methodist Church
of Austin, 155
First United Methodist Church
of Crockett, 166
First United Methodist Church
in Paris, Texas, 330
Fish, J. F., 108, 131
Fisher, Charles W., 189
Charles W., Jr., 189
Mrs. Charles W., Sr., 189

Fite, W. A., 81
Flag Creek, 307
Flake, Arthur, 32
Flannagan, Patrick, 48, 50
Flatonia parish, 221
Fleming, S. C., 91
William, 90
Fleury, L. J., 50
Flournoy, George M., 126
Floyd, ——, 87
C., 91
T. S., 274
Flusche, Anton, 59
August, 59
Emil, 59
Flusche Land Office, 59
Foley, Blanche, 58
Foltz, Clyde D., 79
Fontaine, Edward, 122, 124, 128,
174
Jake, 124–125
Foote, Wilma Sexton, 165
Forank, ——, 57
Ford, H. R., 81
Foreign Committee, 106
Foreign Committee of the
General Convention of the
Episcopal Church, 104
Foreign Mission Service, 106
Forest, John A., 218
Forsvall, Kristin, 311
Fort Bend County, 215
Fort Brown, 318
Fort Clark, 84
Fortner, M. F., 153
Mrs. M. F., 153
Fort Parker, 319
Fort Stockton, 304
Fort Sumter, 125
Fort Towson, Indian Territory,
180
Fort Worth, Texas, 16, 73, 84,
92, 130, 294
42nd Massachusetts Regiment,
46
Foster, Ray, 89
Fouse, T. M., 53

Fowler, L. M., 166
  Littleton, 162–163, 168, 173,
    174
  Mrs., 173
France, 109, 227, 253
Franciscan missions, 40
Franciscus, P. J., 54
Franke, Milburn, 237
*Frauenverein* (Women's Orga-
    nization), 247
Frederick, Loyd, 94
Fredericksburg, Texas, 51, 228,
    231, 238
Fredonia Hotel, 171
Fredrik, Adolf, 302
Freed, ——, 102
Freed-Hardeman College, 102
Freedman's Bureau, 272
Freedmen's Aid Society, 159
Freeman, E. R., 29
  George Washington, 107–108,
    111, 150
Frehner, John F., 236
French, John, 100
  Mrs. John, 213
French missions, 56
French River, 201
Friendship Church, 3
Frizen, Ed, 311
Frost, J. M., 32
Frydek community, 215
Fuller, B. F., 10, 22
  Clayson, 95
  Frank, 138
  J. A., 27–28
  W. H., 200
Fullerton, L. R., 102
Fullinwider, Peter, 191
Funstival, 252
Furey, Francis J., 284
Furr, Mrs. Norma, 203

**G**
Gaines, Inez, 70
  Jimmy, 70
  Nancy, 70
  Col. T. W., 181

  Taylor, 70
Gainesville, Texas, 60
Gallagan, James H., 54
Gallagher, Nicholas A., 35, 46,
    217
Galveston County, 225
Galveston Diocese, 186
Galveston district, 174
Galveston Harbor, 13, 46
Galveston Information Bureau,
    259
Galveston, Texas, 11, 30, 34, 44,
    46, 53, 65, 104, 108, 117,
    119–121, 195
Gano, John, 100
  John Allen, Jr., 77
  John Allen, Sr., 77–78, 98
  Gen. Richard M., 30, 77, 84, 98
Gardet, Augustine, 42
Garfield, James A., 83
Garland, John D., 94
Garland Road Church of Christ,
    Dallas, 30, 33, 97
Garner, Otis, 95
Garrard, A. T., 3
Garrett, C. B., 167
  Charles, 142–144
Garrison, ——, 70
Garza, Oscar F., 270
Gastry, C. J., 100
Gatewood, George S., 166
Gatlin, G. J., 95
Gay Hill, 195
Geiman, Abe E., 70
  Helen, 70
General Assembly, 209
General Conference, 174
General Conference of 1840,
    164
General Conference of 1902,
    165
General Conference of the
    Methodist Episcopal
    Church, 172
General Convention, 104, 135
General Convention of 1874,
    142

347

Grimm, Brothers, 225
Grisham, Noel, 102
Grogren, John, 311
Gronberg, Karl A., 301
Gross, J. L., 16
Gross Bank, 131
Grout, Alfred T., 270
Grundner, Theodor, 50
Grundtvig, F. L., 224
Gruntvig, N. T. S., 222
Guadalupe River, 41, 245
Guerra, Eleazar, 270
Gulf of Mexico, 13, 43
Gury, ——, 53
  Victor, 218
Gustafson, C. H., 311
  Harry E., 310
Guthein, I. K., 265
Guthrie presbytery, 211

**H**
Hackenberger, Mrs. Fred, 188
Hacker, R. H., 210
Hadley, L. B. T., 14
  Mrs. Piety, 14
Hal, Laurens Allen, 131
Halff, Mayer, 265
Hall, B. F., 65
  Clyde, 273
  Colby D., 81
  J. B., 166
  J. M., 95
  Minister, 68
  Peter, 66
  Robert M., 200
  W. E., 68
  W. W., 195
Hall of Congress, 125
Hall of Records, 140
Halpain, Richard T., 199
Hamblen family, 79
Hamburg, Germany, 313
Hamilton, A. J., 125
  G. W., 78
  James, 78
  R. V., 100
Hanks, R. T., 32

Hanna, John, 32
Hannach (slave), 193
Hansbrough, E., 95
  Mrs., 94
Hansen family, 223
"happy Danes," 222
Hardin, J. G., 189
  John Wesley, 190
Harding, "Weeping" Joe, 98, 100
Hargraves, Martin, 189
Hargrove, Mac, 28
Harkin family, 79
Harmony Lodge of Galveston,
  259
Harrel, Carla N., 198
Harris, Bent, 95
  Emmett, 70
  J. Ed., 169
  Mayme, 70
  W. W., 32
  William Mercer, 13
Harrisburg, Texas, 56
Harris County, 225, 314
Harris family, 79
Harrison, Lewis Carter, 129
Harrison schoolhouse, 88
Hartfield, Paul W., 315
Harvey, Thomas, 14
Haskell, Abigail, 13
  Barnabas, 13
Haskin family, 79
Haterius, Hugo B., 309
Hatley, James W., 28
Hawaii, 16
Hayden, S. A., 29
Hayes, Margaret, 70
  Watson, 274
Hayes River, 201
Haynie, John, 155
  Samuel G., 126, 127
Hazelwood, Cal, 72
  George, 72
  W. W., 169
Heacock, Jack D., 160
Head, E. D., 16, 17
Heard, Bill, 70
Heath, Jim, 95

*Houston Chronicle,* 14
Houston Circuit, 173
Houston County, 162
Houston Creek Baptist Church
  of Christ, 28
Houston Creek schoolhouse, 28
Houston Land and Trust Co.,
  115
Houston, Texas, 1, 2, 16, 17, 30,
  34, 44, 56, 57, 104, 108, 111,
  117, 119-120, 139, 162, 173,
  254, 256
Houston Weather Bureau, 195
Howard, Robert O., 100
  William, 13
Howell, Roy, 102
Hubertus, Gerald, 230
Huckins, James, 1, 10, 11, 13-14,
  30
Huddleston, Mrs. J. C., 188
Hudgins, W. Douglas, 16, 17
Hueber, F., 95
Hughes, C. W., 165, 167
  Howard, 78
  J. E., 28
  J. H., 78
Hugo, P., 60
Humphrey, R. M., 16
Hungary, 215
Hunt, ——, 17
  Miss Alma, 32
Hurd, Daniel, 295
Hurroughs, H. M., 21
Hutto, 294
Hutton, S. W., 73
Houston Area, Texas and Gulf
  Coast Conference of the
  United Methodist Church,
  171

**I**
I.G.N. Railroad, 77
Iglesia Bautista Fredonia Hill,
  Nacogdoches, 326
Illinois, 155
Immaculate Conception, Sealy,
  217

Immaculate Conception of the
  Blessed Virgin Mary at
  Panna Maria, 281, 284
Immaculate Conception Catho-
  lic Church, Panna Maria,
  281
Independence Baptist Church,
  8, 10, 18
Independence, Texas, 1, 6, 28, 30
Indiana, 89
Indians, 119
Industry, Texas, 243
Ingraham Building, 169
Inman Christian Center, 69
Institute for Biblical Studies, 96
Iowa, 90
Irahood, C. B., 79
Irvine family, 213
Isaac, Jake, 95
Italian style, 57
Italy, 85
Itinerant Free Church, 311
Ives, Caleb, 111
  Caleb Semper, 104, 106-108,
  117, 119

**J**
Jack (slave), 193
Jackson, B. A., 273
  Chester, 102
  Hulen, 89
  J. W., 95
  O. I., 88, 89
  Oliver, 95
  T. J., 6
Jackson, Mississippi, 124
Jackson School, 88
Jacobs, Rabbi, 258
  William States, 197
James, Sophia, 21
  W. M., 274
  William, 200
Jannsen, ——, 236
Japan, 16
Jarvis, H. Troy, 200
Jarvis Christian College for
  Negroes, 63

351

**K**

L

354

Poland, 215
Polish colony, 289
Polish communities, 290
Polish settlements, 290
Polk, ——, 120
  Amanda, 192–193
  John, 192
  Synta, 192
Polley, N. O. H., 91
Polly, J. H. O., 65
Pontifical Mass, 57
Pool, Bob L., 167
Pope, Kenneth, 159
Portman, Rev., 28
Portuguese Synagogue of New
  Orleans, 258
Postel, Karl, 215
Potts, T. S., 28
Powell, Ben H., 159
  J. T., 21
  John, 166
Power, James, 3
Prague, Czechoslovakia, 218
Praha community, 215
Praha, Czechoslovakia, 221
*Prazka Paut*, 221
Prendergast, Michael, 53
Presbyterian, 41
Presbyterian Church, 104, 173
  U.S. (Southern Presbyterian),
    190
  U.S.A., 191, 209, 211
  U.S.A. (Norhtern Presby-
    terian), 190
Presbyterian Historical Founda-
  tion, 193
Presbyterians, 28, 30, 72, 86, 119
Presbyterian U.S.A., 212
Pribble, Lucille, 70
Price, H. L., 274
  I. W., 72
  I. W., family, 73
  John A., 206
Pridal, Francis, 216
Primitive Baptist Church, 10
Primitive Baptist Church of
  Tioga, 23

Primitive Baptists, 3
Prison Reform Association, 127
Proffitt, Otis, 102
Prosper Presbyterian Church,
  210–212
Prosper Presbyterian Women's
  Association, 211
Prosper, Texas, 211
Protestant, 48, 56, 131, 149
Protestant Episcopal Church,
  105, 139, 144
Protestant Episcopal Church in
  Houston, 109
Protestant movement, 148, 185
Providence Baptist Church, 8
Przyborowski, A., 290
Pugh, Travis, 79
Pugh family, 11
Pullias, C. M., 98
Pummil, J. L., 100

**Q**
quarterly Conference, 171
Queen Anne architectural style,
  137
Querat, ——, 57
Questad, Karl, 277
Quick, Ernest, 28
Quillian Memorial Center, 176
Quin, Bishop, 114–115
  Clinton Simon, 105, 130
Quinlan, Michael A., 54
Quintana, Texas, 195

**R**
Rabb, John, 147, 179
Ragle, Sheridan, 94
Raines, F. M., 78
Rainey, Mrs. Mary, 22
  S. D., 22
Ramon, Domingo, 316
Ramsey, Billy, 95
  Frank A., 206
  Henry, 96
  P. T., 167
Rand, Joseph O., Jr., 198
Randall, Mark, 70
Randolph College, 67

361

**S**

Swedish movement, 125, 291–
292, 307
Sweeney, J. B., 78
Sweet, L. A., 100
L. J., 90
R. B., 95, 100
Swenson, 294
A. J., 307, 310
Bud, 307
Svante Magnus, 125, 291, 292,
294–295, 302, 307
Swindall, D. D., 29
Swisher, John G., 126
Synod of Texas, 191

**T**

T&P Railroad, 142
Tabor, W. L., 274
Tabor community, 215
Tackett, E. M., 100
Talen, Jan, 200
Taliaferro, Robert H., 13
Tally, ——, 78
Tarkington, ——, 78
Tarkington Prairie Junior High
School, 20
Tarrant County, 100
Taylor, Eleanor, 71
Stephen Slade, 71, 73
Taylor church, 78
Taylor St. Presbyterian Church,
U.S.A., 209
Taylorsville, 77
Taylor, Texas, 77, 216
Teddlie, Horace, 100
Tillit S., 100
Tefteller, T. S., 206
Tejas Indians, 316
Temperance Hall, 258
Temple Beth El in Corpus
Christi, 259
Temple Beth-El in San Antonio,
264–266
Temple Beth Israel in Houston,
254, 260
Temple B'nai Israel, Galveston,
258

Temple Emanu-El, Dallas, 260–
262
Temple Emanuel in New York
City, 259
Temple, Texas, 216
Templeton, George A., 193
Ten Mile Creek, 65, 89, 90
Tennessee, 98, 101, 102, 107,
149, 162
Tennessee Conference, 146, 173
Tennessee River, 201
Tenney, S. F., 205
William C., 200
10th District of the African
Methodist Episcopal
Church, 276
Terrell, Texas, 84
Terry, Brooks, 100
R. C., 189
Samuel L., 214
Teutonic people, 48
Teuto Settlement, 242
Texarkana, Texas, 62, 84
Texas A&M College, 144
Texas Annual Conference, 176
Texas-Arkansas border, 64
Texas Baptist, 1
Texas Baptist Convention, 16
*Texas Baptist Herald*, 16
Texas Baptist Historical Mu-
seum, 8
Texas Bible Chair at the Univer-
sity of Texas, 69
Texas Christian Missionary
Society, 68
Texas Christian University, 62,
63, 70, 73, 75, 79, 84, 92,
100
Texas-Coahuila, Mexico, 56, 318
Texas Conference, 164–165, 174,
178, 185, 189, 304
Texas Constitution, 84
Texas Declaration of Indepen-
dence, 1, 6, 64, 84, 133
Texas Greek communities, 252
Texas Hill Country, 231

Texas Historical Commission, 171
Texas Historical Landmark, 43, 179
Texas Historical Survey Commission, 326
Texas legislature, 100
Texas Lutheran College, 236, 237, 278, 305
Texas Medical Association, 157–159
*Texas Methodist Centennial Yearbook*, 163
*Texas Methodist Historical News*, 160
Texas Mission, 163, 172
Texas Missionary Society, 63, 84
Texas Mission District, 173
Texas Mission of the Methodist Church, 168
Texas Presbyterian Churches, 190
Texas State Historical Association, 154
Texas State Historical Survey Committee, 43
Texas State Military Board, 126
Texas State Teacher's College, 169
Texas Synod, 236
Texas Synod of the Lutheran Church, 235
Texas Synod of the Presbyterian Church, U.S., 191
Texas Wesleyan Academy, 294
"The Old Three Hundred," 56
Thom, Robert, 157
Thomas, David, 155
  Martin H., 200
  Mike H., Sr., 80
  O. S., 153
  Roy, 95
  S. A., 73
Thompson, Dora, 70
  James K., 209
  R. W., 29
  Samuel, 146

Thomsen family, 223
Thomson, John, 193
Thorell, Edward, 311
Thorpe, Jesse L., 90
Thorp Spring, 63, 92
Thrall, Homer S., 155
Thurman, J. H., 21
  James, 89
Tidwell, Amos, 146
  J. B., 16
Tigua Indians, 36, 37
Tillers, H. D., 206
Tillman, D. N., 295
  Dan, 96
Timmouth, Vermont, 107
Timon, John, 34, 43–44, 46, 56
Tipps, Sarah, 3
Tittsworth, J. Lem, 200
  Levi, 88
Tolson, John F., 198
Tomlinson, F. L., 29
Tonkawa Indians, 47
Tooley, L. B., 183
Tower, Joe T., 151
  Sen. John, 151
Townsend, Debra Hill, 198
Trader, T. R. B., 112
Trans-Pecos area, 105
Travis, William B., 39, 148, 160, 172
Travis Church, 10
Travis County, 126, 225, 292, 294, 299, 307
Travis County jail, 127
Travis Street United Methodist Church, La Grange, 177
Travis, Texas, 1
Treumen family, 223
Trigg, Mrs. Jones, 74
Trimble, ——, 67
  Mrs. T. M., 71
Trinity Church, 104, 108, 120, 121
Trinity Church in New York City, 134
Trinity College in Round Rock, 303

Virginia, 11, 62, 109, 119, 127, 130
Virginia Theological Seminary, 111
*Volksfest*, 238

**W**

Wack, J. M. J., 49, 50
Waco Indians, 47
Waco, Texas, 2, 28, 30, 84, 294
Waco University, 28
Wages, J. R., 166
Wagner, ——, 236
*Waisenhaus*, 245
Wakefield, Miss Audra, 28
Waldrep, Burnell, 70
  Cherry, 70
Waldrum, Ray, 102
Walker, E. H., 93
  Johnny, 93, 94
  Richard, 174
  W. H., 100
Wallace, Edna, 95
  Foy, Jr., 94
  Foy, Sr., 95
*Walnut Grove Banner, The*, 202
Walnut Grove Presbyterian
  Church, McKinney, 201
Walsh, George T., 57
Walterscheid, August, 60
Ward, D., 93
Ware, Nimrod, 87
  W. B., 201
Warlick, Joe, 93
Warren, David Barton, 72
Washington, ——, 274
  George, 36, 77, 100
Washington Baptist Church, 3
Washington-on-the-Brazos, 1, 6, 162
Washington County, 63
Washington Hotel, 118–119
Watson, Billy, 103
Waugh, Beverly, 185
Waxahachie, Texas, 63
Weaver, W. Abram, 32
Webb, I. B., 152–153

Mrs. I. B., 152–153
Weber, Armand, 50
  Mrs. E. H., 71
Weeks, Benjamin, 20
  Mary, 20–21
Wehmeyer, Adolph, 240
Weise, Daniel, 314, 315
Weisskoppf, Franz, 236
Welch, W. A., 81
Wells, Dick, 73
  L. N. D., 67, 81
Wendish Heritage Society, 315
Wendl, Aemilion, 50
Werner, ——, 235
Wesley, John, 183
Wesley (Gunter) Bible Chair, 169
Wesley Chapel Methodist
  Church, 159
West, C. A., 167
West Belt Line Road, 67
Western Europe, 253
Western Heights Church of
  Christ, Dallas, 84, 98, 101
Western Orphan Asylum, 244
Westmuenster community, 243
Westphalia, Germany, 59
West Texas Conference, 179, 269, 276
Whaling, H. M., 167
Wharton County, 215
Wheatland, Texas, 98
Whipple, Josiah W., 155, 157, 175
Whitaker, B. F., 3
  Charles H., 3
White, Alex, 272
  Brian, 70
  John, 73
  John B., 95, 96
  Joyce, 70
  K. Owen, 16–17
  L. S., 98
  Robert Leon, 69
  Thomas, 70
  Walter, 70
Whitehurst, A. S., 167
White Rock presbytery, 211
Whittinghill, D. G., 22, 28

371

Wiemar parish, 221
Wiggins, J. H., 206
Wilcoxon, Mrs. Lee, 71
Wilde, Frances, 60
Wiles, C. Preston, 145
Wilkins, B. C., 29
  James H., 73
Willeford, Miss Mary D., 22
Willhoite, Warren, 95
Williams, C. A., 273
  C. L., 167
  Mellie, 274
  Mrs. William L., 32
  Samuel A., 168, 174
  Sid, 22
  William Hall, 129
  William L., 32
  Wilson W., 274
Williamsburg, Pennsylvania, 245
Williamson County, 215, 225,
  292, 294
Willing Workers, 309
Wills, Buck, 78
Wilmeth, C. M., 65, 100
  J. B., 64
Wilson, Albert, 70
  Homer T., 73, 74
  Hugh, 191, 192
  John, 163
  Lamore, 273–274
  Pansy, 70
  Terry W., 167
  William K., 166
  Woodrow, 32
Winchester, Texas, 179
Wind family, 223
Winn, P. A., 153
Winsor Oil Company, 315
Wisconsin, 117
Wise, Judson, 70
Woehl, Jerry, 75
Wohlschlegel, Johannes H., 233
Wolf, Sidney, 259
Wolfe Hall, 133
Wolfe Hall of Saint Mary's Hall,
  131

Woman's Missionary Society,
  165, 188
Woman's Missionary Union
  Auxiliary, 2
Woman's Society of Christian
  Service, 165, 188
Wood, Gen. Frank, 70
  Louise, 70
Woodville, Mississippi, 259
Woodward, D. K., 130
  Sarah, 196
Woolam, John C., 166, 185
World War I, 154, 183, 227, 247,
  251, 256, 266
World War II, 37, 79, 169, 176,
  218, 221, 241, 294, 297
Worley, A. E., 96
Worsham, Judge Archer B., 18
  Milton R., 129
Wren, Sir Christopher, 46
Wright, David R., 11
  Isaac, 157
  Linus, 33
  S. J., 28
  W. H., 66
Wright family, 11
Wuppenthal, Germany, 238
Wurster, William W., 262
*Wurstfest*, 232
Wuthrich, ——, 241

**Y**
Yarnall, John, 211
yellow fever epidemic, 179
Yorktown, Texas, 231
Young, Robert, 155
Youngbloom, C. O., 311
Young People's Society of
  Christian Endeavor, 78
Ysleta, New Mexico, 36
Ysleta, Texas, 36, 44

**Z**
Zaiontz, Ludwig, 290
Zelezik, Joe, 216
Zimmermann, Pastor, 314
Zion Evangelical Lutheran